DEBATING THE FUTURE OF THE PUBLIC SPHERE

Debating the Future of the Public Sphere

Transforming the public and private
domains in free market societies

STEPHEN EDGELL
Department of Sociology
University of Salford

SANDRA WALKLATE
Department of Criminology
University of Keele

GARETH WILLIAMS
Department of Sociology
University of Salford

Avebury

Aldershot · Brookfield USA · Hong Kong · Singapore · Sydney

Published by
Avebury
Ashgate Publishing Limited
Gower House
Croft Road
Aldershot
Hants GU11 3HR
England

Ashgate Publishing Company
Old Post Road
Brookfield
Vermont 05036
USA

British Library Cataloguing in Publication Data
Debating the Future of the Public Sphere:
Transforming the Public and Private
Domains in Free Market Societies
  I. Edgell, Stephen
306.342

ISBN 1-85628-845-5

Library of Congress Cataloging-in-Publication Data
Edgell, Stephen.
    Debating the future of the public sphere: Transforming the public
  and private domains in free market societies / Stephen Edgell,
  Sandra Walklate, Gareth Williams.
        p.   cm.
    Includes bibliographical references (p.   ).
    ISBN 1-85628-845-5 : $55.95 (est.)
      1. Privatization--Congresses. 2. Human services--Congresses.
    3. Free enterprise--Congresses. I. Walklate, Sandra.
    II. Williams, Gareth, MD. III. Title.
    HD3842.E34   1995
    338.9--dc20
                                                                94-38132
                                                                CIP

Reprinted 1996

Typeset by
Pauline Gordon
Dept of Sociology
University of Salford

Printed and bound by Athenæum Press Ltd.,
Gateshead, Tyne & Wear.

Contents

Figures and tables   viii

Editors and contributors   x

Acknowledgments   xv

Preface   xvi

Introduction   1

1 Politics and the public sphere in free market   7
societies

    1. The public sector under seige   9
      Frances Fox Piven

    2. The mass media and the public sphere: the crisis   25
      of information in the "information society"
      Peter Golding

    3. Recent European and American conceptions of   41
      democracy and politics and the public sphere
      Maurice Roche

2 From public service to private provision: 63
redrawing the boundaries

   4. The end of work: public and private livelihood in   65
      post-employment capitalism
      Elliott Currie

   5. Are prisons part of the public sphere? Privatization   79
      and the problem of legitimacy
      Richard Sparks

   6. The sectoral dynamics of policing   99
      Les Johnstone

   7. Public participation in health: empowerment or   113
      control?
      Georgina Webster

   8. The process of excluding "education" from the "public   125
      sphere"?
      Janet McKenzie

   9. Green consumerism: blurring the boundary between public 147
      and private
      Peter Simmons

3 The experience of the public sphere   163

   10. Bodily experience in public space   165
       Richard Sennett

   11. Going to town: routine accommodations and routine   177
       anxieties in respect of public space and public
       facilities in two cities in the north of England
       Karen Evans, Penelope Fraser and Ian Taylor

   12. Men in public domains   199
       Jeff Hearn

13. What happened to the sociology of the street?   221
    Joel Richman

14. Men of steel: gay men and the management of public   235
    harassment
    Carol Brookes Gardner

4 Postscript   255

15. Of matters public and civil   257
    Christopher G. A. Bryant

Bibliography   269

Figures and tables

Table 2.1   Party support of newspapers 1966-1992   33

Table 2.2   Ownership of communication facilities among households   38

Figure 6.1   Sectoral and spatial dimensions of policing   103

Figure 7.1   Strategic model for community participation   118

Figure 8.1   Factors in the elimination of potential interest in education   126

Table 8.1   Proportion mentioning an issue as one of the two most important in influencing their vote in the general election   128

Table 8.2   Knowledge and interest frequencies   129

Table 8.3   Expressed interest in Education   130

Table 8.4   Education consumption and party identification   144

Figure 12.1 Historical timescales in conceptualising   209
            public patriarchy

Table 12.1 Private patriarchy, public patriarchy, and   208
           related concepts

Table 12.2 Comparisons of public and private "zones"   212

Editors and contributors

Stephen Edgell is Professor of Sociology and Head of Department of Sociology at the University. He is author of *Middle Class Couples*, 1980 and *Class*, 1993; and co-author (with Vic Duke) of *A Measure of Thatcherism*, 1991, as well as numerous articles in British and American sociology and other social science journals.

Sandra Walklate is Reader in Sociology at the Department of Criminology, University of Keele. She is author of *Victimology* (1989); co-author of *Theories of Welfare* (1984); *Introducing Policework* (1988); *Critical Criminology* (1993); co-editor of *Victims and Offenders* (1992); plus numerous articles in professional and academic journals.

Gareth Williams is Reader in Sociology at the Department of Sociology, University of Salford. He is co-author of *Private Risks and Public Dangers* (1992); *Locating Health* (1993); *Challenging Medicine* (1993); *Researching People's Health* (1993); plus numerous articles in various sociological and medical journals.

Christopher G. A. Bryant is Professor of Sociology at the Department of Sociology, University of Salford. He is author of *Sociology in Action* (1976); *Positivism in Social Theory and Research* (1985); co-editor of *What Has Sociology Achieved* (1990); *Giddens' Theory of Structualism* (1991); *The Great Transformation? Change and Continuity in East Central*

Europe (1994); plus numerous articles in British, American and European sociology journals.

Frances Fox Piven is Distinguished Professor of Political Science and Sociology at the Gráduate School and University Center of the City University of New York. She is co-author (with Richard Cloward) of *Regulating the Poor* (1971:1993); *The Politics of Turmoil* (1974); *Poor Peoples' Movements* (1977); *The New Class War* (1985); *The Mean Season* (1988) (co-authored with Fred Block and Barbara Ehrenreich); and *Why Americans Don't Vote* (1988). She is also the editor of *Labour Parties in Postindustrial Societies* (1991).

Peter Golding is Professor of Sociology and Head of the Department of Social Sciences, and Co-Director of the Communications Research Centre at Loughborough University. He is an author and editor of numerous journal articles and books, including *The Mass Media*; *Making The News*; *Images of Welfare*; and *Communicating Politics*. In addition he is co-editor of the *European Journal of Communication*, and a Visiting Professor at the Universities of Tampere, Brussels, Fribourg, Oslo and Tartu.

Maurice Roche is a Senior Lecturer in Sociology at the Sociological Studies Department of the University of Sheffield. His research interests include social theory; the sociology and politics of citizenship; the sociology and politics of urban culture; and cultural policy. He is the author of *Rethinking Citizenship*, 1992.

Elliott Currie is Professor of Legal Studies at the Centre for Study of Law and Society at the University of California and Vice-Chair of the Eisenhower Foundation in Washington, D.C. He is author of *Confronting Crime*; and *America's Problems*; and co-author of the Eisenhower Foundation Report, *Youth Investment and Community Reconstruction*.

Richard Sparks is Senior Lecturer in Criminology at the Department of Criminology, Keele University. He is co-editor (with Phillip Brown) of *Beyond Thatcherism* (1989); and (with John Muncie) of *Imprisonment: European Perspectives* (1991); author of *Television and the Drama of Crime* (1992); and co-author (with Will Hay and Tony Bottoms) of *Prison and the Problem of Order*, (forthcoming).

Les Johnstone is Principal Lecturer in Criminology at the School of Human Studies, University of Teeside. His research interests include policing; private security; vigilantism; the politics of law and order; social control and the state; and social theory and he has published various articles on police accountability; police management; privatisation of policing; private security; vigilantism and crime prevention. His most recent book is *The Rebirth of Private Policing* (1992).

Georgina Webster is a partner in a small independant training and consultancy organisation called 'Labyrinth'. Labyrinth specialises in community involvement, organisation development and equal opportunities work within a broad health focus. She contributed to the *Public as Partners Toolbox*, published by the Health Gains Conference 1992 and the report *Responding to Local Voices: A Guide to Training and Organisation Development Approaches*, published by the NHS Management Executive in 1993. This paper is based on work within different localities and cities to build public participation as empowerment into the work of statutory and voluntary organisations.

Janet McKenzie is a Senior Lecturer in Sociology at Anglia Polytechnic University. Her research includes voters attitudes to education as a political issue; and political activity relating to education policy. She is author of *Education as a Political Issue* (1993); and "Perspectives: A Rough Map", in *The Sociology Teaching Handbook*, (Edited by Chris Middleton) (1994).

Peter Simmons is based at the Centre for the Study of Environmental Change, at Lancaster University.

Richard Sennett is Professor of History and Sociology, and University Professor of the Humanities at New York University; and Senior Research Fellow of the School of International and Public Affairs at Columbia University. He is also Chair of the International Committee on Urban Studies; Chair of the International Advisory Committee in Barcelona; Chair of the Advisory Committee on Cities; Member of the Committee For New York; and Co-chair of the Task Force on Race. His research interests include the relation of family structure to urban life; the influence of city life on the transition from adolescence to adulthood; urban studies; the historical sociology of cities; cultural dimensions of political legitimacy; and the relation between urban design and the social life of modern cities. Author of *The Fall of Public Man* (1977); *The Conscience of the Eye* (1990); and *Flesh and Stone* (1994).

Karen Evans is a Research Fellow in the Department of Sociology at the University of Salford. She is currently senior researcher on a project investigating community safety, personal safety and fear of crime in two inner-city areas in Salford. She is has written and published work on the effects of racism on housing policy and, with Bernard Foley from the University of Liverpool, a number of papers on tenant participation and housing co-operatives. Her current interests include issues around sexuality and space and black people's use of public space. She has co-authored a paper investigating marginal use of public space with Penelope Fraser.

Penelope Fraser is a Research Fellow in the Department of Sociology at the University of Salford. Her current research interests include fear of crime and personal/community safety in the urban context; questions of personal safety and fear of crime as they affect the everyday lives of young adolescents in the urban context; the contemporary urban experience and its impact on "public well-being" in public space. She is co-author (with K. Bottomley and A. James) of *An Evaluation of Area Accommodation Strategies: A Study of Home Office Circular 35/1988* (1992); and (with Karen Evans) of "Difference in the City: Locating Marginal Use of Public Space", in *Conflict and Consensus in Social Policy: Racism, Citizenship and the Environment*, (forthcoming).

Ian Taylor is Professor of Sociology in the Department of Sociology at the University of Salford. His current research interests include crime, fear and other adaptations to global economic change in the north of England; firearms, the drug trade and international crime. His publications include, editor of *The Social Effects of Free Market Policies* (1991); and (co-editor with Valda Blundell and John Shepherd) of *Relocating Cultural Studies* (1993).

Jeff Hearn is Reader in Sociolgy and Critical Studies on Men in the Department of Applied Social Studies at the University of Bradford. His research interests include men and masculinities; gender, sexuality and organisations; and men's violence to women; and he is co-editor of *The sexuality of Organisation* (1989); *Men, Masculinities and Social Theory* (1990); and *Men in the Public Eye* (1992).

Joel Richman is Professor Emeritus at the Manchester Metropolitan University. His research interests have included street ethnography; gynaecological and obstetric ideologies; pregnant fathers; forensic psychiatry; ward cultures and treatment; the moral order of psychopaths; and nursing, mergers and managers. His publications include *Traffic Wardens: Ethnography of Street Administration* (1983); *Medicine and Health* (1987); and *Health* (1992).

Carol Brooks Gardner is Associate Professor in Sociology and Women's Studies at Indiana University. Her current research interests include social interaction; gender; disability; and ethnography; and her most recent publication is *Passing By: Gender and Public Harassment* (forthcoming).

Acknowledgments

This volume grew out of an international conference on *The Public Sphere in Free Market Societies* held in Manchester 8-10 January 1993 at Parkers Hotel. We would like to take this opportunity of thanking all our academic and non-academic colleagues in the Department of Sociology at the University of Salford who supported this event, the Vice-Chancellor who gave us his backing, all those who participated in it, the entertaining after dinner speaker Michael Sheehan, and especially the conference administrator Tony Kearon, whose hard work and initiative did much to ensure organizational success. We are also pleased to acknowldege the support of The University of Salford Bookshop (Blackwells) and the Campaign to Promote the University of Salford (CAMPUS).

We are grateful to Richard Sennett and his publishers Faber and Faber Ltd. of London and W. W. Norton Inc. of New York, for permission to reprint an extract from *Flesh and Stone*, published on the 24 October 1994, Faber and Faber Ltd.

A special word of gratitude is owed to all the contributors to this volume, to Eva Elliott and Jones who helped with the proof reading, and to Pauline Gordon who prepared the camera ready manuscript with great skill and good humour.

Preface

The post 1945 expansion of the public sphere in Britain was first halted and then reversed during the 1980s. Under the stress of economic circumstances and a concomitant state fiscal crisis, the idea that market forces were the only way forward enjoyed a renaissance - summed up by the term "there is no alternative". Thus liberated from the fetters of the state, private self-interest would, it was argued, facilitate economic growth and public well being.

At the political level, the advent of Thatcherism in Britain (and Reaganism in America) heralded the implementation of policies informed by the tenets of economic liberalism. Nothing was sacred; hitherto taken-for-granted collective ways of organising and distributing basic necessities such as water, energy, health and pensions, were jettisoned. A new political-economic lexicon emerged in which privatization, marketization and value for money enjoyed a prominent place. This was all achieved in the relatively short space of a decade, in the face of a divided and therefore sporadic opposition. This was led in turn, and largely in vain, by radicalized public sector managers and professionals, militant public sector workers, and notably the coal miners, and various groups of public sector consumers (Edgell and Duke 1991).

The social implications of the recrudescence of nineteenth century ideological verities extolling the virtues of freedom of competition, capital and consumer choice, involved the playing down of the obverse, namely the freedom from want. The resulting social imbalance is reminiscent of

Galbraith's famous 1950s distinction between "private opulence and public squalor" (1962, p.211). The renewed relevance of this contrast can be illustrated dramatically with reference to two news items reported on the same day towards the end of 1993. One referred to the health service ombudsman's report of the "suicide of an elderly mentally-ill woman after she was sent home from hospital because no bed could be found for her" (*Guardian* 3 December 1993, p.5). The other involved the announcement by the Royal Bank of Scotland of an unexpected twenty-fold increase in 1992 of pre-tax profits, which boosted the price of the bank's shares and resulted in one multi-millionaire executive making a "paper profit of nearly £500,000" in one day (*Guardian* 3 December 1993, p.19).

Notwithstanding the every day evidence of public parsimony and private profligacy, the almost total denudation of the public sector would not have transpired, and could not continue, if it had been perceived as an unproblematic success. Conversely, rolling back of the state and other manifestations of the decline of the public sphere, to the reputed benefit of the private, is a matter of considerable concern. As citizens, as well as social scientists, we appreciate that the debate about the future of the public sphere transcends political and academic boundaries. It was with this general idea in mind that we decided to organize an international conference devoted to what is arguably the most profound and urgent issue facing free market societies - the future of the public sphere.

With the active and enthusiastic support of our colleagues at the University of Salford, and in particular those in the Department of Sociology, we called for papers that offered prognosis as well as diagnosis. The response was excellent and contributed to a stimulating and enjoyable event held in Manchester 8-10 January 1993. Our thanks to all concerned.

However, the quality and diversity of the papers presented created an acute selection problem when it came to assembling a coherent book length collection of revised contributions. The net result is a book that inevitably does less than total justice to the many (over sixty) and varied interesting papers based on the latest scholarship and research which featured in all the conference sessions. The following chapters and the way they are organized reflects the dominant themes that emerged from the conference. We have eschewed abstract analysis in favour of grounded accounts that would hopefully inform public debate and public policy.

Stephen Edgell, Sandra Walklate & Gareth Williams

Salford, July 1994

Introduction

In the last decade or so free market societies have been on the ascendent in most western societies. The political consensus over the propriety of publicly owned and controlled utilities, services, and goods has disappeared, and has been replaced by a belief in consumer choice and the free market as the guiding principles of social and economic life. This ideological and cultural transformation has had an impact across a wide range of sectors and "publics". In debates about education, social services, housing, health, prisons, and the police, similar arguments are being heard. These debates seem to be underpinned by a question that is being asked with increasing urgency: what is the future of the public sphere in free market societies?

Ideas about the public sphere, the public interest, the public sector and public services have a long history and a range of contemporary meanings. Whilst some commentators in Britain refer back to what they now perceive as the Golden Age of Bevan and Beveridge, the electoral success of the Conservative Party - the main advocate of the new "free market" ideology - suggests that a sizable proportion of the voting population are no longer convinced by the post-war idea of "the public sector". At the same time many people remain uneasy about the "marketization" of schools, buses, hospitals, and other public services. This uncertainty has given rise to a growing concern with new ways of conceiving of political obligation. Alongside the notions of consumer choice, public debate is increasingly conducted in terms of "rights", "empowerment", and "partnership".

Discussion of these issues is taking shape in a variety of quarters, and there has been an interesting convergence of interest among people working in disciplines that have traditionally been separate. But this is not simply an academic issue. It deals with matters at the centre of public debate about democratic values and processes. Many of the issues being addressed by academics in universities and research institutes are at the heart of the daily activities and decisions of those working in departments of social services and education, in voluntary sector agencies and in pressure groups. They are also international, with many of the same questions being addressed in the US and Europe. The readings which follow touch upon all of these and related issues in a variety of ways.

Part One of this collection draws our attention to some of the political dimensions of the features with which we are concerned. Frances Fox Piven sets the scene for such a political analysis. Comparing and contrasting the US and UK she observes the re-emergence in both countries of the nineteenth century conditions of poverty, homelessness and the force of pathology. These features of the 1990s have been met by a loss of confidence and uncertainty by those on the left which has been exacerbated by the success of the ideological attack on the notion of the welfare state. This ideological attack has promoted a view that the public sector itself is responsible for school dropouts, drug use, crime and the "underclass". She goes on to suggest that the policy responses to these social conditions have the power to create new constituencies. Constituencies which may either be fragmentary or unified but which nevertheless demand new institutional arrangements to meet their demands. This is nowhere more selfevident than in the increasing presence of women in the labour force and is thus suggestive of a certain political optimism in the possibilities emanating from such arrangements.

The processes associated with the broadcasting of information about the kinds of transformations of which Fox Piven speaks is the concern of Peter Golding's contribution. He offers us a critical review of Habermas's concept of the public sphere. He is particularly concerned with the lack of attention paid to the audience within that conceptualisation. He argues that as diversity within the national press has declined and questions have been raised about public service broadcasting, alongside the advance of what he calls the "centripetal state" and the growth of unequal access to communications, the public sphere has to be seen as a domain increasingly inhabited by those embracing Galbraith's "culture of contentment". The exclusionary processes implied by Golding's analysis are countered by Maurice Roche's observations on the problem of "decadence" and the "breakdown" of social ethics in modernity. Utilising Durkheim's concept

2

of anomie and matching that with the language of citizenship, Roche considers the counter anomic tendencies of both feminism and ecology and their implications for the current processes of social change.

Part Two of this collection turns our attention to the debates concerned with the public and private provision of services. Capturing the flavour of diversity within the conference, these contributions address the questions of work, the criminal justice system, health, education, and the "greening" of the consumer. Elliott Currie addresses the issues of the purpose of work in post-industrial societies. He offers an analysis of the changes in the labour market of advanced societies in which he argues that it is not the decline of agricultural work which is responsible for precipitating the crisis of the urban underclass, but a decline in the availability of work across the whole economy; from General Motors, to IBM, to the Bank of America. A trend which is not only occurring in the US but is also apparent in the UK and Japan. Echoing the works of William Morris, he asks some provocative questions about the relationship between work and non work.

The next four papers take a much more detailed and substantive look at how the changing patterns of work are manifesting themselves in particular areas. Richard Sparks, for example, considers the debate relating to privatisation in the prison system. He suggests that debate, focused as it has been on whether or not private prisons are managerially competent or financially moral, has deflected attention from the question of legitimacy. He argues that the "single greatest danger inherent in the privatisation movement is the depoliticization of what has hitherto been known to be an arena of deep public controversy". In a similarly challenging vein, Les Johnstone points to the problems inherent in adopting an oversimplistic view of policing. In examining who engages in the task of policing, what they do and where they do it, it is clear that policing has always been composed of a "mixed economy". Within this mixed economy the public and private spheres of policing are to be understood as strategic arenas in which arguments are deployed and political conflict takes place.

Georgina Webster turns our attention to a different dimension of the public/private debate; that of how to ensure public participation in the delivery of services. This has taken the form of encouragement to "listen to local voices" in the National Health Service, and Webster offers us a mode, based on local experience which endeavours to achieve this from the "bottom up" and the "top down". In education, however, Janet McKenzie reveals that few people take an interest in education as a political issue. Recent government policies have tended to define changes in education as technical, rational and nonpolitical. This combined with a complex gendered equation in understanding the importance of education as a political issue has resulted, according to McKenzie, in only a superficial movement towards consumer power and the squeezing of education from public discourse. Peter Simmons, on the other hand, documents the way in which the power of the consumer in the marketplace as expressed in product related preferences has been marked by a move from **green** consumerism to green **consumerism**.

The third and final part of this collection draws our attention to the spatial dimensions and experience of the public sphere. Richard Sennett was the final plenary speaker at the Conference. He asked the question; what makes a dead public space? In asking this question Sennett was suggesting that we view the city as comprising parts which do not speak to each other and moreover for experiences of such public spaces to change demands a different vision of the city. This theme is explored in a number of ways here.

Karen Evans, Penny Fraser, and Ian Taylor offer an empirical investigation and analysis of the urban experience in two cities in the North of England. This sociology of the urban experience offers a detailed taxonomy of the public's relationship with those cities, where, when and how people use them. The city centre is identified as a predominantly male experience in which a wide range of activities (other than shopping) occur. Joel Richman interestingly develops such concerns by pointing to the significant absence of a sociology of the street and what such an absence renders invisible from the urban gaze as a consequence. Jeff Hearn takes a conceptual development of this notion of invisibility further. For him the concept of the public domain fails to make explicit the need to focus on men and masculinities. He suggests that an analysis which did this would expose the "multiple oppressions and intersections of men's power as men with other powers or lack of powers". It is important he feels to recognise that men's experiences are contradictory and fractured. It is therefore necessary to search for more complex models and understandings of the relationship between the public and the private. Recognition of the contradictory and fractured nature of men's experiences is the implicit concern of Carol Brooks Gardner's contribution. She provides us with detailed accounts of the nature, extent, impact and response to the non violent harassment of gay men in public places; gaybaiting. These accounts offered by gay men, point to the significance of the subtleties associated with everyday public life and how they are experienced by Others.

Chris Bryant closes our collection with an overview of the conference themes. He identifies both the continuities and absences in the debates which took place in Parkers Hotel in Manchester during January 1993. We hope that this selection of papers provides you, the reader, with a more than adequate feel for that debate and the directions in which it is likely to move during the 1990s.

Stephen Edgell
Sandra Walklate
Gareth Williams

Salford
July 1994

Part 1
POLITICS AND THE PUBLIC SPHERE IN FREE MARKET SOCIETIES

1 The public sector under seige

Frances Fox Piven

This paper focuses on the public sector, and particularly on the welfare state programmes, rather than the more sweeping "public sphere". Not so long ago, most people who paid attention to such matters took for granted an expanding and buoyant public sector. Of course, not everyone thought this inexorable growth of government domestic programmes was a good thing. But critics and advocates alike agreed that government played a large role in economy and society, and that its role was likely to expand. Consistently, the grand theories developed about these government activities were theories which argued that whether desirable or not, the programmes of the modern welfare state were an inevitable development.

Theories of state expansion

One such theory posited that the growth of the public sector was a necessary corollary of industrialization and urbanization, which created both the imperatives and the capacities for public intervention. Thus the growth of industry was said to generate needs for infrastructure and for regulation which could not be met by private actors; the parallel growth of cities and the decline of intact village communities and extended families also generated new needs, particularly for the care of the aged or the indigent or the disabled, which could only be met by public authority. And, since the societal transformations which generated new needs also

9

created great wealth which could be tapped by the state, the convergence of needs and resources resulted, albeit by a complex process,[1] in the development of public welfare state programmes.[2]

Another and more recent grand theory treated the growth of the welfare state not as a corollary of industrialism, but as a corollary of patriarchy. From this point of view, many public programmes could be explained by their functions in shoring up the traditional family and enforcing traditional gender roles. Early variations of this perspective treated these patriarchal functions as an aspect of capitalist reproduction, reasoning that the family was the site for the reproduction of labour power. Later work, however, severed patriarchy from capitalism and treated the imperatives of patriarchal reproduction as the primary dynamic in the creation of welfare state programmes.[3]

Perhaps the grandest theory of all emphasized not industrialization as such, but capitalism, and the class actors created by industrial capitalism, as the main explanation for the growth of the public sector. The focus here was on class interests, and the conflicts generated by class interests. On the one side, industrialization meant the growth of the proletariat, whose numbers, organization, and consciousness would expand as industrial capitalism expanded. An increasingly self conscious and organized working class would in turn become the base for labour or socialist political parties. And these parties, together with their trade union partners, would promote government programmes which shielded the working class from market insecurities and employer power. In the happiest variants of this perspective, welfare state programmes would ultimately accomplish the "decommodification", and the empowerment, of labour.[4]

There was also a less happy view of the impact of industrial capitalism which ceded the balance of power to other side of the class war. In this view, the welfare state was less the expression of working class interests than the instrument for the domination of workers. Welfare state programmes arose from the accumulation requirements of big capitalists, who tried to transfer the costs of reproduction to the state. Or they arose from the political legitimation requirements of a capitalist state that used the programmes to quiet workers made surplus by the advance of capitalism. By this reading, the programmes were significant because the tokenistic benefits they provided confused workers, obscuring the true nature of the capitalist system, while also eroding class solidarity by fragmenting workers among different programmes.[5]

Academic arguments between adherents of these various interpretations flourished, books and articles were published, and careers were made and unmade. And these disputes were kept alive by the actual empirical murkiness and ambiguity of the politics of the public sector. After all, it was usually hard to actually see fragmented and fractious capitalists acting as a class, just as it was often hard to see workers acting as a class. Still, despite these theoretical disputes about the correct characterization of the basic social structures which gave rise to the welfare state, there was a strong underlying consensus. Everyone agreed that basic social structures accounted for the programmes, and that the persistence and expansion of the public sector was therefore inevitable, whether as a consequence of the imperatives of industrialism, or patriarchy, or capitalism.

But no more. Indeed, this premise has come to seem completely outdated. Welfare state programmes are everywhere under attack, and the attack has been at least partially successful in most rich industrial countries. It has been particularly successful in the United Kingdom and the United States. In these countries, leaders of both industrial and capitalist development, the expectations of the evolution and expansion of the public sector has been abruptly overturned.

If these events have shaken some of our intellectual assumptions, they nevertheless provide a remarkable arena in which to test other propositions, and particularly to test debates about the role of class based actors in the development, or retrenchment, of welfare state programmes. In other words, the empirical murk has at least momentarily parted, and class interests have emerged with extraordinary clarity in welfare state politics. Consider, for example, the business mobilization against welfare state programmes that occurred in both the UK and the US. To an unprecedented degree, business moved into party politics, throwing its money and energies into Republican party politics in the US, and into Conservative party efforts in the UK. Earlier debates about the class character of the welfare state, about whether it was an achievement of the working class or a strategic instrument of the capitalist class, were in a sense superseded by real political events. Business mobilized to put a halt to welfare state expansion, and even to force the rollback of some important government interventions, particularly business and environmental regulation.

Simultaneously, the working class forces that had usually been defenders of the public sector were weakening. Deindustrialization and restructuring was decimating the ranks of the old industrial working class, its unions were tottering, and the political parties with which labour was allied were on the defensive. The poignant collapse of one labour struggle after another in the past decade or so, of English miners trying to prevent the closing of the pits; of the fabled United Automobile Workers at the

11

American Caterpillar plants; of Hormel meatpackers in Minnesota, dramatized this basic transformation on a world stage.

The balance of class forces was also dramatically altered by the indirect political leverage that business gained as a result of the increasing mobility of investment. The definitive lesson of the political power that could be wielded by mobile capitalists was provided by the experience of France in the early 1980s. After Mitterand's first victory, the French Socialists launched a series of expansive welfare state initiatives, with the consequence that French capitalists packed up their money and crossed the border, while foreign capitalists flooded the inflating French market with imported goods.

For a time during the 1980s, Sweden seemed to teach a different lesson. There, welfare state programmes remained intact and even expanded, unions remained strong, and Swedish Social Democrats were returned to power after a brief reversal. But by the end of the 1980s, the Swedish lesson was reversed, the Social Democrats were turned out of power, and Sweden also began to scale back its welfare state programmes in response to the pressures of capital disinvestment. The lesson seemed plain. No social democracy in one country.

If the class politics of welfare state retrenchment are clearer than ever before, so are the class consequences. The rollback of income security programmes in the UK and the US has been accompanied by sharply increased poverty, poverty often so desperate that central city streets are now dotted with medieval tableaux of ruined people, of homeless beggars. And as poverty rates escalate, so does the historically familiar litany which reverses common sense and points to defects in the culture or character of the poor themselves as the cause of their immiseration.

Most important for my argument, the attack on the welfare state has had dramatic consequences for class power relations. To be sure, the programmes are not usually discussed in these terms. Rather, income security programmes are generally defined simply as providing a "safety net" to protect people against the hazards of market instability or biological exigency. But inevitably, income security programmes also have repercussions on power relations, and specifically on the power relations between those who buy labour, and those who sell their labour. Workers who are less secure, have less power. Workers who are more secure, whether because of the availability of outdoor relief or unemployment insurance, have a little more power in their dealings with employers. This relationship seems to have always been understood, at least by the employing class.

The decline in earnings among lower paid workers, who are more exposed both to labour market instabilities and cutbacks in income security programmes, is consistent with this historic relationship. In the UK, the relative wages of lower paid workers have fallen steadily for fifteen years, with the result that pay inequalities are wider than at any time since 1886.[6] In the US, the wages of all nonsupervisory workers fell, by fifteen percent between 1972 and 1992,[7] and the proportion of full time workers whose wages were insufficient to lift a family of four out of poverty rose from twelve percent in 1979 to eighteen percent in 1990.[8] Meanwhile, the rich got richer, as the income of the top one percent about doubled, and their share of net private wealth rose from thirty one percent in 1981 to thirty seven percent in 1989.[9] The economic historian, Claudia Goldin, summarized the consequences: "Inequality is at its highest since the great levelling of wages and wealth during the New Deal and World War II".[10] And the shift in class power which cutbacks in the welfare state both reflected and caused were also apparent in the US in the gutting of unions, whose share of private sector employment fell from thirty percent in 1970 to twelve percent in 1990.[11]

It will be rightly objected that these changes in class relations were not **just** the result of welfare state cutbacks. A massive economic restructuring was also at work in response to accelerating globalization and technological change. But responses to restructuring vary considerably among nations. In the US and the UK, a weaker welfare state at the outset, and significant erosion of these protections in the past two decades, permitted an adaptation to restructuring that emphasized sever cuts, rising income inequality, the evisceration of unions, and the scaling back of public programmes. The point is that the Anglo-American pattern of welfare state cutbacks permitted an adaptation to postindustrial economic conditions at the expense of workers, especially lower wage workers.

The conservative polemic

These developments were historic in scale. They were also plainly visible. One would think they would have caused a rush to throw aside old ambivalences and defend the welfare state, at least among intellectuals on the Left. And there has of course been a defence of sorts. But the defenders lack confidence. Overall, the Left is uncertain, unable to find its ideological footing in this new terrain of conflict over public provision. This may in part be a legacy of earlier intellectual disputes. More importantly, however, I think the Left has been overwhelmed by a series of new arguments against the welfare state. These arguments in effect reverse the older claims that welfare state programmes are functional for the institutions of the larger society, whether characterized as industrial or patriarchal or capitalist. We are engulfed by an ideological campaign which claims instead that the programmes are dysfunctional for social institutions, that they actually cause the problems which they are designed to reverse.

So, for example, where once we thought that the welfare state was a corollary of industrial growth, now we are told that the welfare state is a drag on economic growth. A large public sector is said to interfere with the operation of markets, in several ways. High levels of taxation erode profits and therefore discourage new investment. Income security programmes in particular burden employers with high nonwage labour costs which discourage employment expansion. At the same time, these programmes create perverse incentives, drawing people out of the labour market by the benefits they provide, with the consequence that poverty actually increases. All of these arguments are made more emphatic of course by the threat of disinvestment. Because public policies affect labour costs and profit levels, internationalism means that each nation's public policies will be pitted against the public policies of other nations in a bidding war for business investment.

I said this was an ideological campaign against welfare state programmes. But like all powerful ideological campaigns, it invokes aspects of lived experience. Capital **is** more mobile than ever before, and some capital does operate on a world wide scale. Profits **are** affected by tax rates, and income security programmes do affect wage rates, and affect the docility of workers as well. But all capital is not mobile, and not equally mobile, and profit rates and wage rates are affected by much else besides tax levels and welfare state programmes. The argument is ideological in the sense that it describes in simple and sweeping terms what are actually qualified and variable relationships. Like the nineteenth century laissez faire argument from which it is descended, this neo laissez faire doctrine treats part truths as the only truths.

Another strand in the ideological assault on public programmes has found adherents on both the Right and the Left. This is the argument that welfare state programmes have perverse effects not on the economy, but on "civil society". Of course, different people mean different things by civil society, but at the core of this critique is the idea that intrusive government bureaucracies displace and weaken community and family. The growth and elaboration of government programmes leads to the atrophy of community practices of caretaking, and the atrophy also of the values of self responsibility and mutuality which those practices fostered.[12] A more vitriolic line argument focuses on the impact of welfare state programmes on the family. Income security programmes in particular are said to contribute to the breakdown of the traditional two parent family, and even erode the capacities of single parent families, whose adult heads become slothful and dependent, losing the ability to be models for their children or to exercise discipline over them.[13]

Taken together, these arguments constitute a sweeping rejection of the welfare state. The public sector not only retards overall economic growth, but instead of ameliorating a variety of social problems, it is in fact responsible for their increase, for rising poverty and the spread of a host of pathologies associated with the "underclass", from school dropouts to drug use to crime.

The charges are unsettling, and demand scrutiny. But they do not stand up. In the US, an entire generation of researchers turned away from explorations of the sources of poverty and social pathology in economic and social structures, to take up instead the agenda of the largely conservative assault. Literally hundreds of studies were done to examine the narrow question of the impact of welfare cash benefits on family and work behaviour, for example. But the conclusions of this body of carefully specified, methodologically sophisticated and expensive body of work did not bear out the charges.[14] A report released by the General Accounting Office in 1987 summed up the studies that had been done since 1975 and concluded that "research does not support the view that welfare encourages two parent family break up", that it "has little impact on the childbearing rates of unmarried women", and that the availability of welfare does not significantly reduce the incentive to work.[15]

A word of caution. I myself think it reasonable to assume that patterns of public provision can and do affect work and marital behaviour. But the effects are obviously complexly determined, and by much besides welfare state programmes. Even to the extent that a simple incentive model is useful, the consequences of public provision are compounded of the relative material and nonmaterial costs and benefits of **both** welfare and work, and of both welfare and two parent family life. What the American research actually shows is that the disincentive effects of welfare receipt on wage work, or on the maintenance of two parent families, are weak when programmes provide low benefits, and couple those low benefits with stigmatizing practices.[16] On the other hand, the disincentive effects of much more generous programmes would be offset by better terms of work, and by programmes that also provided support to two parent families.

The contention that public provision has perverse effects on the economy and family might have been illuminated by a comparative perspective. After all, many European countries have more generous income support programmes, and thus afford an opportunity to empirically evaluate these hotly argued charges. And, while there has certainly been a great deal of research conducted on these issues in the US, it has for the most part been comparative only in the rather limited and parochial sense of comparing state level Aid to Families with Dependent Children programmes to discover whether differences in state benefit levels are associated with differences in relevant outcomes.[17] A more telling comparative survey of national data would quickly reveal that the UK and the US, world leaders in welfare state retrenchment, are certainly not the world leaders in rates of economic growth. They are at the head of the pack, however, in measures of deindustrialization, falling wages, rising poverty levels, and crumbling unions.[18] Perhaps the reason is that strong welfare states inhibit a business strategy of disinvestment, breaking unions, restructuring work, and forcing wages down.

Nor does a comparative survey give support to the thesis that welfare state programmes have corrosive effects on community and family life. True, rates of crime, drug abuse, single parent family formation, and homelessness are on the rise everywhere, as a reasonable observer might expect during a period of wrenching economic transformation. But all of these problems or pathologies are more widespread in the US and in the UK, where welfare state retrenchment has gone furthest, than in countries where the welfare state has remained more or less intact. If a strong public sector really does produce perverse effects, then one must wonder why it is that the streets of New York and London are so troubled by the vagrant poor, and not the streets of Stockholm or Oslo?

Finally, the trends in the various symptoms of social disintegration which are said to be caused by the welfare state actually suggest a reverse causality. In the US, welfare state benefits for the poor and the unemployed have been steadily reduced for nearly two decades. If it were indeed the case that these programmes cause poverty, promote the breakdown of two parent families, and spur rising rates of out of wedlock births, then rolling back these benefits should presumably reverse these ill effects. Of course, the reverse has occurred. As the programmes shrink, indices of poverty and social disorganisation rise, and these rising indices in turn ironically provide the fodder for the continuing ideological assault on the welfare state.

However, neither scholarly evidence nor common sense has seemed to matter very much in the heated campaign against welfare state programmes. On the contrary, the sheer repetition of charges about the perverse effect of the programmes on economic well being, on community cohesion, and on family life, has had shattering effects on public support for welfare state programmes. Not least, it has had shattering effects on Left intellectuals, even on those who in the past defended the welfare state. Indeed, the loss of confidence has been so total that even the organizations of welfare state professionals and employee unions, despite their clear stakes in the programmes, shrink from a forthright defense of the public sector.

Reform solutions?

In this hostile political climate, almost everyone has come to agree that the welfare state is deeply flawed, that the programmes must be rethought and reformed. Not surprisingly, this apparent consensus on the need for reform conceals real differences. People on the Left have always been critical of key programmes for being niggardly, divisive and humiliating in their treatment of people. These flaws reflect stiff political opposition to the programmes, much of it from business interests. But whatever the hopes of the Left, the proposals being advanced as reforms promise to worsen the problems of low benefits and client harassment. In particular, reform proposals focus on the ostensible disincentives to responsible work and family behaviour of current programmes, and on the familiar complaint that centralised welfare state bureaucracies suffocate community capacities. I turn to a discussion of these reform proposals.

At the top of the reform agenda, in both the US and the UK, are welfare to work schemes, sometimes called workfare. Indeed, talk about "ending welfare as we know it" turned out to be Bill Clinton's most popular issue during the Presidential campaign of 1992, and he has continued to keep his welfare proposals bubbling, turning to them especially when he is in trouble on other fronts. The main idea here is to transform cash benefit programmes into job training and placement programmes. There is a liberal variant of the schemes, and a conservative variant. The liberal variant would introduce time limits on the receipt of cash benefits, and in the interim provide education and training to recipients, help them with job search, and offer "bridging" or short term subsidies for childcare and health care, which of course are very important, especially in the US where low wage workers often do not get health benefits. The conservative version, sometimes called "tough love", would not entrust government to enforce work, but rather accomplish the same result by cutting people off benefits.

At first glance, the liberal variant of the welfare to work reforms seem reasonable. After all, life on the dole is hardly to be desired, and the reforms promise funds for training, and some childcare and health care for poor people. Even better, some workfare reform proposals call for increasing the income from work, whether by raising the minimum wage, or through tax credits or other wage supplements for the working poor. Who can be against making life a little better for the poor by providing services, higher incomes, and the chance for a bit of respect?

But talk aside, that is not what is likely to happen. In the US, where welfare to work schemes are more advanced, cost estimates for even pared down reform packages come to many billions of dollars. The prospect of the Congress appropriating such amounts for a small and benighted constituency of poor women is politically unreal. The advertised services are simply advertisements. And as the vaunted promises of services and wage supplements are scaled back, the liberal reforms resemble more and more the conservative "tough love" alternative, the cold turkey solution to "welfare dependency". And quite apart from the human travails this would cause, the proposals take no account of deteriorating labour market conditions. If there are not enough jobs now for those who are searching for work, either in the UK or the US, what will be the consequence of pushing more people into the search for work, except to displace some of those now working, with the consequence that they will end up needing benefits? And if wages for the less skilled have been falling, what will be the effect of forcing still more vulnerable people in the scramble for low wage work, except to press wages and working conditions down even more?

Taken together, these difficulties account for the paltry success of welfare to work programmes that have already been implemented in the US. Much publicised stories of individual successes notwithstanding, policy evaluations show that the results are in fact insignificant,[19] and even those "successes" are typically shortlived, if only because the childcare and healthcare subsidies which temporarily make work a feasible alternative are time limited. No matter, the politics of reform escalates, all to the steady drumbeat of criticism of those who are "dependent" on the dole. It is difficult to escape the conclusion that what is going on is in fact a politics of scapegoating, a societal ritual of degrading those who do not work, thus making more tolerable by contrast the worsening circumstances of those who do.[20] Meanwhile, there are no studies of what happens to the people who are the targets of the numerous sanctions for failure to conform to one or another of the elaborate new regulations entailed by the workfare schemes.[21]

18

The other main reform strategy that seems to have captured the imagination of a good many people in the UK and in the US is directed against the bureaucratic centralization that presumably characterizes the public sector. To remedy this, schemes are advanced to decentralise government programmes, or to "empower" citizen clients through new participatory arrangements, or even to privatise the programmes. The Bush Administration, for example, heralded "empowerment" as the essence of its strategy for reforming public housing, and turned a few showcase projects over to tenants to manage (while the vast majority of projects were stripped of maintenance funds). And analysts with the conservative Heritage Foundation have proposed turning welfare state programmes over to local government and private agencies, not withstanding the long and grim history of local relief, and indeed notwithstanding the fact that the harshest of the American cash programmes, unemployment insurance and welfare for single parent families, are already decentralised to the states.[22]

Nevertheless, the possibilities suggested by initiatives to replace central bureaucracies are captivating, particularly when applied to programmes that provide services rather than cash. The code words, decentralisation, participation, empowerment, are after all terms that historically belong to the Left, and they evoke images of an accessible and variegated welfare state, infinitely responsive to diverse needs, offering virtually a bazaar of brightly coloured public services. Here indeed is the possibility for recapturing for civil society some of the terrain occupied by the state.

But once again, the American experience is sobering. In fact, talk of centralised bureaucracies notwithstanding, many of our most important services are decentralised, or privatised. Our schools are run by localities. Many of our services for children, the mentally handicapped and the aged are also decentralised, and local governments in turn often contract with private agencies, some of them "nonprofit", others proprietary, to provide these services. Many nursing homes and old age homes, for example, are run by profit making organisations.

The accumulated experience with these arrangements surely does not provide support for decentralisation. Rather the history of scandal suggests that decentralisation and privatisation encourages not the care and mutuality of a vigourous civil society, but abuse of the young, the infirm, the aged. The reason is obvious. On the one hand, the clients of these institutions are vulnerable and powerless; on the other, decentralisation and privatisation shield the agencies from public accountability. No wonder each successive scandal produces calls for more effective, state or federal oversight which at least restrain the practices of these agencies.

A left perspective on welfare state reform

These observations about the current spate of welfare state reforms should not be taken to mean that there are no problems. Indeed, I think there are huge flaws in existing programmes, both in the UK and the US. Benefits are far too low, and the more needy the target population, the lower the benefits; council housing or public housing is designed with technocratic arrogance and then allowed to crumble for lack of maintenance; services are inadequate, and fashioned with indifference to the users, and so on. Perhaps most important, elaborate conditions are attached to the provision of cash or inkind aid or services, with the consequence that bureaucrats gain enormous discretion, and citizen clients are stripped of the capacity to know or defend their rights in the programmes.

These distortions in the welfare state reflect a history of political conflict over the programmes, and particularly the opposition of the better off, who have always resisted the supporting of the public sector with their taxes, and by employers, who resist the "decommodification" effects of income support programmes. But over time, the concessions made to conciliate opponents compound the political problems of the programmes, because flawed programmes discourage support by a wider public. Thus income support programmes that treat people badly help to construct the caricature of the pauper or the "independent" poor which then discourages public support. Barren and corroding housing projects become images of the public sector. Revenue structures which shift the burden of costs to the working class spur resentment. And fragmented programmes which divide citizen clients among a dizzying array of different agencies, presumably to match programmes more precisely to varying needs, politically disable people by the confusion they create, as well as by the divisions they construct among constituencies. These mean spirited and divisive features of the programmes are the problem, and over the longer run, our efforts to reform the public sector should be directed to their elimination.

But all of this notwithstanding, the welfare state is still an achievement, and for some of the very reasons that have figured largely in the conservative assault. Earlier analyses which posited a functional consistency between welfare state programmes and industrialism or patriarchy or capitalism have been proven to be at least partly wrong. As the programmes developed and expanded, they provoked conflict, and the conflicts help to reveal just what has been accomplished. Critics who argue the perverse effects of the programmes on the market, the local community, and the family have in a way hit precisely on the essential value of the public sector.

Half a century ago, in the wake of the Great Depression, Karl Polanyi reflected on the nineteenth century ideal of the unregulated free market.[23] He called it a utopian ideal which, if pursued unyieldingly, would destroy humankind, turning society into a jungle. Polanyi thought humankind craved security as much as it craved economic gain. The welfare state is an achievement because, in the face of market processes that relentlessly undermine established patterns of individual and social forms of life, it provides people a measure of security.

The critics who celebrate the market and condemn public programmes are not hostages to consistency. Any argument that is ammunition against the welfare state will do, and so even while the unregulated market is celebrated, so is the traditional community which it always destroys. But this too is a simplification at the service of propaganda. The critics forget the tyrannies of the traditional community. True, the local community might sometimes shield those of its members who were helpless. But it might also scorn and destroy them and in any case, the price extracted for care by the community in conformity and subservience was large. Public programmes, the regulations and benefits proffered by anonymous bureaucracies, can provide some shield, some succour, against the harshness and despotism of the local community.

Or critics glorify the traditional family. It is true that adult children sometimes loved and nurtured those who became old or disabled. They also sometimes became their keepers and even their exploiters. One hardly needs to wonder whether the old would readily give up their state pensions and the lives independent of their children that pensions make possible to return to the bosom of the family. Or consider whether women caring for children, often shielded from abusive spouses (and abusive employers) by the independence they gain from supplemental assistance or child allowances or single parent benefits, would be better off if they were forced to return to the presumably private realm of the patriarchal family.

I do not mean that the public sphere is inherently more benign than other spheres. I mean rather that human needs are better met, and human possibilities better protected, when the tyrannies exercised in one sphere, whether in politics, the market, community or family, can be counterbalanced by the protections people are able to develop in another sphere. In just this way, the rights and protections that ordinary people forged over time through democratic politics sometimes offset the tyrannies to which they are subject in the family and the community. Perhaps most important in an era of mobile capital and plundering capitalists, the legacy of public protections we call the welfare state provides some defense against the excesses of unrestrained capital.

21

Notes

1.	This characterization of the "logic of industrialism" perspective is of course simplified. In most variants, the structural imperatives generated by industrialism and urbanization were not the whole of it. The emergence of new needs, and new resources, were accompanied by cultural and political changes, as well as the development of new state organizational capacities, which accounted for the translation of structural imperatives into government programs. T.H. Marshall (1964), developed the best known account of the bearing of the cultural and political concomittants of capitalist industrialization on the welfare state.

2.	For the classic statement of this perspective, see for example Wilensky and Lebeaux 1965; Cutright 1965 and 1967; and Wilensky 1975.

3.	Various formulations can be found in Eisenstein 1981 and 1983; Fraser 1987 and 1989; Shaver 1987; and Ursel 1988.

4.	For an elaboration of the decommodification argument, see Piven and Cloward 1982, chapter 1, and Esping-Andersen 1985.

5.	For examples of this perspective, see Gough 1979; and O'Connor 1973.

6.	See Balls 1993, p.3

7.	See US Bureau of the Census, March 1992.

8.	See US Bureau of the Census, March 1992.

9.	See Piven and Cloward 1993, pp.362-65, for a summary of the data.

10.	*New York Times*, April 20, 1993, p.1.

11.	See Brody 1992, p.33.

12.	The grand argument is made by Habermas, 1987.

13.	For an extreme version of this argument, see Murray 1984. More recently Murray has argued in the press for the simple elimination of income support for sole parents, allowing that orphanages might have to be expanded to care for their children. See also Kaus 1992.

14.	On the rise of female headship, see Cutright 1974; Ross and Sawhill 1976; Ellwood and Bane 1986; and Smith and Cutright 1985. On illegitimacy, see in addition Ellwood and Summers 1986; and Wilson and Neckerman 1986. And on divorce and seperation, see also Minarik and Goldfarb 1976; and Cutright and Madras 1974.

15.	For a critical review of this research, see Piven and Cloward 1987. The most recent research shows extra ordinarily high levels of work effort by recipients in the US. See Harris 1993.

16.	For a discussion of disincentive effects, see Piven and Cloward 1987, pp. 85-8.

17.	These studies are critically reviewed in Piven and Cloward, 1987. For other reviews, see also Wilson and Neckerman 1986; and Bane and Ellwood 1994.

18.	See for example Smeeding and Rainwater 1992; Brody 1992; Hall 1986; Jessop, Bonnett and Bromley 1990; Lange and Garett 1986; Hicks 1988; see also Esping-Anderson 1990.

19.	For a discussion, see Piven and Cloward 1993, pp. 387-93.

20.	This was one of the explanations for relief policy originally put forward in Piven and Cloward 1971.

21.	For a rare example of such an investigation, of the misery resulting when "employables" were cut from a number of state General Assistance welfare programmes in the US, see the Centre on Social Welfare Policy and Law, February 1994.

22.	For an argument in favour of this proposal, see Butler and Kondratas, 1987.

23.	Polanyi, 1957.

2 The mass media and the public sphere: The crisis of information in the 'information society'

Peter Golding

Dialogues within the social sciences have their own irrationality. Concepts sometimes acquire an allure and attention beyond the specific utility and application intended by their authors. The notion of the public sphere is an interesting example. Constructed by Habermas with close historical attention, and developed by him within the much larger project central to his work of understanding the formation and later deformation of the structure of public life, Habermas' concern with the possibility of free and rational communication as the basis for a healthy democracy has flourished within a rich philosophical debate about communicative competence and the "universal validity basis of speech". Its political and historical resonance has only more recently drawn the attention that its concern with the intelligibility, rightness, and veracity claims in speech acts has attracted in a general theory of communication.[1] Some would even argue that the work in which Habermas introduces the notion of the public sphere "gives nothing less than an archaeology of the ideas and ideologies that inform current practices and policies of the mass media" (Peters 1993, p.542).

This recent interest in the concept has been particularly evident in debates about the changing role of the mass media in public life. There are two reasons for this. First, the development of the press forms a key element in Habermas' account of the evolution of the public sphere, while its twentieth century progress looms large in his pessimistic narrative of the refeudalisation of public life. Second, the translation and dissemination

25

of Habermas' ideas in English, has coincided with the crisis in public service broadcasting, and indeed in the public sector more generally, in the UK in particular, though more widely in western Europe. The notion of a forum for open and rational critical debate of public processes inevitably chimes with a theoretical account of the possibility of such a public sphere. At its simplest, as Dahlgren points out:

> The public sphere is a concept which in the context of today's society points to the issue of how and to what extent the mass media, especially in their journalistic role, can help citizens learn about the world, debate their responses to it, and reach informed decisions about what course of action to adopt.(Dahlgren 1991, p.1).

It is not difficult to see why this natural affinity should seem so obvious. The ideal function of the media, as defined by Dahlgren, is precisely that proclaimed by public service broadcasting in its various charters and proclamations. For example, Charles Curran, a distinguished former Director General of the BBC, sets out the manifesto as follows in his memoirs:

> It is the broadcaster's role, as I see it, to win public interest in public issues...Broadcasters have a responsibility, therefore, to provide a rationally based and balanced service of news which will enable people to make basic judgements about public policy in their capacity as voting citizens of a democracy (Curran 1979, p.115).

In seeking to rediscover and apply the notion of the public sphere to analysis of the media, however, a number of reservations have been entered. First, Habermas' historical account has been attacked for its over-optimistic and idealised view of the role of the media in early capitalism, especially in Britain which provides a key case study for his analysis. Not least the institutions of the public sphere were not merely bourgeois, but male. More extensive feminist criticism addresses the essentially gendered nature of the public sphere itself, whose defence and reconstruction thus become the ambitions of a blinkered patriarchy rather than a comprehensively progressive and emancipatory political programme, blind to the necessary appreciation of difference within the "public" (Fraser 1990). Other writers, however, have recognised that in focussing on the masculine liberal limitations of Habermas' concept, they risk:

a tendency to focus on internal, oppositional identity at the expense of a consideration of the media's role in hindering the establishment of a representative space necessary for democracy in late capitalism (McLaughlin 1993, p.614).

Other fundamental objections have been lodged against Habermas' historiography. The rise of the bourgeois press in Britain undoubtedly both represented and nourished an independent bourgeoisie. However, the achievement of independence of the press from the state, often portrayed as a heroic battle for freedom of ideas, is better understood as a by product of the growing commercial viability and vitality of the industry, especially following the emergence of joint stock companies in the mid nineteenth century. Alongside this development the emergence of a truly widespread forum for popular debate, founded in rational discourse, was as far from the reality of newspaper development as possible. As James Curran points out, "the newspapers celebrated by Habermas were engines of propaganda for the bourgeoisie rather than the embodiment of disinterested rationality" (Curran 1991, p.40).[2] Habermas sees the decline of the radical press as an opportunity for the return of rational discourse. The press as a forum for rational-critical debate is "released from the pressure to take sides ideologically; now it could abandon its polemical stance and concentrate on the profit opportunities for a commercial business" (Habermas 1989, p.184). The radical press of the first half of the century is not so easily swept from the scene, however, and the ideological role of the rapidly expanding middle class press between the ending of the "taxes on knowledge" and the "Northcliffe revolution" is difficult, with hindsight, to characterise as divorced from ideology. On the contrary, that emergent press plays a potent role in the formation and crystallisation of late Victorian bourgeois ideology. Prior to that, just as the bourgeois public sphere more generally was, in its very essence, a repressive instrument resisting emergent working class organisation, so, specifically, the bourgeois press had been a successful inhibitor of the radical press itself.

Habermas' tendency to present a rosy "Golden age" vision of the emergent public sphere is also matched by his inclination, in the view of many critics, to be unduly bleak about the present. Dahlgren argues, for example, that the decline of the nation-state, the segmentation of audiences, the rise of new social movements, and the extending range and availability of new communications technologies, all indicate a more vibrant and progressive communications environment than described by Habermas (though the latter was writing thirty years ago). A similar view is advanced by Thompson, who argues that:

> The development of mass communications has created new opportunities for the production and diffusion of images and messages, opportunities which exist on a scale and are executed in a manner that precludes any serious comparison with the theatrical practices of feudal courts (Thompson 1990, p.115).

Whereas in Habermas' account politics has been transformed by the growth of public relations and stage management, for Thompson this makes politics more visible and thus accountable. Where, for Habermas, the media have been destroyed as fora for a public sphere by commercial imperatives, for Thompson this underestimates the active power of audiences. I shall return to the latter point below.

An interesting variant on this critique is provided by Scannell. In a prescient article written a decade ago, Philip Elliott wrote fearfully of the decline, as he saw it, of the arenas within which the role of the intellectual, as independent critic and commentator, could be played out. The "culture of critical discourse" was being eroded by the "disappearance of the public sphere" as communication and distribution facilities were succumbing to an international regime governed by the imperatives of the late capitalist market (Elliott 1982). Scannell's response to such critiques is to raise the risk of throwing the baby out with the bathwater. To bemoan the limitations of public service broadcasting, for example, is to abandon any possibility of holding onto the ideals it represents. The bleakness inherent in the Habermas view, as in that of Elliott, is "remote from the actual circumstances of ordinary conversation and mundane social interaction, which..... characterise the communicative domain of broadcasting". Rather than seeking, in the fora of the public sphere, the means by which rational argument can arrive at sound conclusions, we should "characterise the impact of broadcasting as enhancing the reasonable, as distinct from the rational, character of daily life in public and private contexts" (Scannell 1989, pp.158-161).

Habermas' account is thus attacked for both its over-rosy portrayal of the emergence and early character of the public sphere, and for its unduly pessimistic characterisation of the present. A second critique is concerned with the form, rather than the historical accuracy, of Habermas' account. In particular there is the problem of argument by metaphor. What, in fact, is the public sphere? Descriptions necessarily resort to spatial or physical terminology. Is it a place - the coffee houses, salons, and meeting places of early urban capitalist society? The struggle to get a handle on a vision of something described as the space within which rational and universalistic political discourse could occur between the private realms of civil society and family, and the realm of the state and court (public authority) is not helped by the essentially non-social notion of a sphere. Literally? Clearly not. Do we mean something analogous to the forum or agora of ancient societies? Again, clearly not. But if we mean a form of relationships, a "publicness" underpinning interpersonal and formal relations, then the notion of a "sphere" is clearly quite inadequate for sociological analysis. Even critics find it difficult to escape this terminology. For example Curran cites classic liberal theory as envisaging the public sphere as the "space between government and society" (op.cit. p.29). But what can this possibly mean, institutionally and behaviourally?

A third critique which has been launched against Habermas' concept within analysis of the media derives from the growing movement within studies of audiences, fuelled theoretically by cultural studies, and empirically by ethnographies of audience behaviour, which stresses the activity of media consumers. Whatever the restricted nature of media provision, audiences are semiotically powerful, able to subvert the meanings and intentions of texts, whose polysemic character permits a diversity of interpretations and reception. Indeed meaning only emerges in the active collision of audience with text. For enthusiastic devotees of this "rediscovery" of the active audience the social determination of meaning destroys the dominating potential of media output, and restores to audiences a true measure of their cultural potency, much underestimated by the determinism of more pessimistic accounts.[3]

Finally Habermas has been criticised for an undue concern with news media, and with an inadequate attention to the variety of genres from which meanings and values can be derived. Again, the implication is that the stage management of politics and the restricted character of news media do not warrant an account of the media in terms of the deformation of the public sphere, since this ignores the plentiful diversity of the meanings and pleasures to be derived from and created in the consumption of other forms of mediated communications. This is not to deny the ideological character of soap operas, comedy, consumer magazines, or film, merely to invite attention to the complexity of the cultural forms and discourses on offer.

Habermas' concept has been taken as prescriptive, both in terms of the forms of public debate, and in terms of the locus of debate. My purpose here is not to engage in any extended way with either Habermas or his critics. Rather I simply wish to note one or two ways in which the more critical, or if you like, pessimistic readings of Habermas' account, may be validly applied to the current state of mass communications practice and policy. In doing this I cite four examples. These are; the threat to public service broadcasting; the decline of a diverse national press; the continuing advance of what I have elsewhere termed the centripetal state (Golding 1986, Golding 1992); and the growth of unequal access to communications.

Whither public service broadcasting?

The model of the BBC, assuming what Lord Reith, the corporation's first Director General called the "brute force of monopoly", and claiming to provide education, entertainment, and information as a public service to high professional standards in the public interest, has informed the statutory basis and occupational ideologies of most national broadcasting systems, both across Europe and further afield. Indeed commercial systems, like the ITV network in this country, have themselves readily assumed the mantle of public service broadcasting (PSB) as enthusiastically, and sometimes more so, than quasipublic bodies such as the BBC.

The emergence of new technologies providing for a major diversification of delivery systems, via cable and satellite especially, together with the rapidly rising cost of maintaining national public broadcasting systems without substantial advertising support, have conspired to threaten the very fabric of the public service broadcasting systems. Where buttressed by governments ideologically inclined to commercialisation and privatization anyway, as in the UK, the move away from the PSB model has been rapid.

Two features of this shift are relevant here. The first is the growing marginalisation of programmes designed to provide for an informed public debate about policy and politics. Rising costs and the need to maintain a foothold in a fragmenting marketplace put at great risk such genres as current affairs and documentary which can provide for these needs. In 1993 leading documentary programmes, including such market leaders as *40 Minutes* and *First Tuesday* were axed from the schedules. It has become increasingly clear that, within ITV, it is intended to move the flagship current affairs programmes from the core of peak time viewing. As Paul Jackson, Director of Programmes for Carlton, which has taken over the London weekday franchise from Thames, suggested in 1992:

Those who argue for current affairs to stay in peak time are just not accepting things as they are...under the new licenses ITV is mandated to be a popular channel that gets an audience, earns revenue and sustains business (*The Guardian*, 1 Sept. 1992).

Cuts in documentaries and educational programmes are already in train, exacerbated by the fall in advertising revenue due to the recession. A report on children's television points to an acute fall in factual content in favour of cartoons and entertainment formats.[4] The obligation to carry at least two half hour current affairs programmes in peak time under earlier Independent Broadcasting Authority (IBA) rulings disappears under the new franchise agreements from 1993.

As casualisation in broadcasting increases many jobs have been lost, including those in factual programmes; in all BBC staffing dropped by 10 per cent between 1986-92. The more obvious threat to the Corporation's future, however, is posed by the rethink on its role engendered by the renewal of the Charter in 1996, and the public debate invited by the recent Green Paper (HMSO, 1992). While less traumatic than many had feared, the Green Paper invited a rethink on "new directions for public service broadcasting". Hints appear that the BBC could be reduced to a rump, producing only programmes that would not be commercially viable, a ghetto of worthy but unwatched public service. As the Green Paper suggests:

> With more services and greater choice available to audiences, the programme obligations placed on or undertaken by the BBC might be relaxed. Alternatively if the BBC has a special role in the range of broadcasting services, the programme obligations could be tightened (ibid. para 4.23).

It is clear then, that, at the very least, the public space represented by a national broadcasting system dedicated to providing extensive, prominent, and diverse cultural resources for an informed citizenry is uncertain to survive current scrutiny. But it is sometimes argued that this diversity can be maintained by the much richer array provided by the press.

A free and diverse press

The last Royal Commission on the Press came to a conclusion which has been manifestly obvious to any observer of British newspapers, when it

31

noted that:

> There is no doubt that over most of this century the labour movement has had less newspaper support than its right wing opponents and that its major beliefs and activities have been unfavourably reported by the majority of the press (Royal Commission on the Press 1977, pp.98-99).

While it is possible to argue that partisanship has declined as newspapers remorselessly struggle to survive in an adverse financial climate, it is difficult to sustain any argument that the press as a whole provides a full range of possible means of expression and opinion.

This is most dramatically illustrated by the 1992 general election.[5] In principle during an election the media bring before the electorate a range of promises and evaluations of policy across the breadth of public affairs. In fact, in all media during the 1992 election coverage of issues was profoundly limited. Much of the coverage dwelt on the media themselves, or centred on the polls, which were second only to economic issues as the most frequently covered topic. As the months of remorse and self evaluation continue to erode their credibility, it is worth recalling that polls featured as the main topic in 12 per cent of broadcast election items and no fewer than 21 per cent of tabloid stories. Campaign coverage was dominated by the economy and the election itself. Some topics, like social security, Europe, energy, local government, and transport all but sank without trace.

As Table 2.1 shows, the circulation advantage of the right wing press has advanced steadily over the years, giving it an edge of nearly 50 per cent on Labour supporting national newspapers. The death of labour papers, and the growth in circulation of the newly partisan Sun, have between them ensured that this figure has risen substantially.

Bias is an unhelpful term in assessing news. It suggests a position of objective neutrality from which someone deliberately imparts a deviation. But where is that position? In the 1992 election there were two quite distinct campaigns. In the avowedly partisan tabloids, though never as scurrilous or vitriolic as some predictions had feared, the headlines and commentary were remorselessly tendentious. Almost from day one we had "Labour's first Dirty trick", and "Labour Votes to Tax Poor" (*Daily Mail*). The *Sun* warned of "Labour Squeeze On Triers". More personal attacks on Mr Kinnock gathered pace in the latter part of the campaign, especially as his leadership qualities were extracted as **the** issue from the Jennifer Bennett saga ("Neil in panic", *The Sun*). A more confident

Table 2.1

Party Support of Newspapers 1966-1992 (by circulation)

Election advice of papers by circulation:

	1966	1970	1974(i)	1974(ii)	1979	1983	1987	1992
Conservative (C)	56	55	68	47	66	75	73	66
Labour (L)	43	44	30	29	28	22	25	25
Liberal (Li)	4	5	5	5	0	0	3	0
Winning Party	L	C	None	L	C	C	C	C

promotion of Mr Major followed ("A Man for All Reasons", *The Sun*).

The expected personal smears and mud-slinging were less in evidence. Indeed the papers seemed grateful for such diversions from the tedium of the election as the Fergie-Andy rift and Jason Donovan's court triumph. However we were treated to a full front page description of Jack Straw's holiday cottage (*The Sun*, "I'm Alright, Jack"), and Michael Meacher's wife's interests in private nursing homes (*Daily Star*, "What Mrs Meacher Does in Private"). More traditional targets were commonplace (*The Sun*, "Lefties Put Boy in care of Lesbian Crook"). Occasionally this seemed a little desperate, as in a *Daily Mail* story exposing the astonishing news that one of Labour's economic advisers lives in a detached house in Longworth, under the headline "Luxury Life of a Guru".

Only late in the campaign did the nastier edge of the "race card" begin to show, with stories following Kenneth Baker's speeches on the Immigration Bill appearing under headlines like "Kinnock Won't Curb Flood of Bogus Refugees" (*Daily Mail*). The *Daily Express* front page two days before the election was covered with "Baker's Migrant Flood Warning", and *The Sun*, among others, editorialised about the "threat of massive immigration" under a Labour government (Golding and Billig, 1992).

Of course the *Daily Mirror* is there to add some balance. But five of the six papers declared for the Conservatives, a circulation advantage of roughly three to one. Does this have an effect? A MORI poll in 1992 found that only about one in six readers of *The Mail* and *The Express* voted Labour (while 18 per cent of the Mirror's readers voted Conservative). Other studies suggest a marked swing among floating voters towards the party supported by their newspaper in the weeks up to the campaign, probably enough to create a swing of about one per cent from Labour to Conservative. No mean figure in a close election.

Beyond the specificities of partisanship, however, lies a larger question of the capacity of the popular press to act as an interlocuter in a dialogue of political discourse with a diverse and represented public. The political economy and corporate mission of the daily press now constrain such ambitions whatever the fluctuating character of the papers as party fanzines. What really counts is the longer term forging of beliefs and values in a culture that may well have become inexorably conservative.

The public relations state

All states seek to promote the best view of their policies and practices. But in recent years the UK media have been under unprecedented pressure to reflect and disseminate government views. The BBC particularly has had a torrid time defending its editorial independence in the face of frequent and intense government hostility. The temporary banning of a programme interviewing a Sinn Fein representative in 1985, the banning of a feature on the Zircon spy satellite and a subsequent Special Branch raid on BBC offices to seize films in 1987, the complete banning of broadcast interviews with Sinn Fein, UDA, and paramilitaries in 1988, major rows over the BBC's reporting of the Libyan bombings, have been but the more dramatic highlights of a continuous battle of attrition to which the mischievous rabble rousing and applause of the popular press, ever eager to undermine the BBC, some would argue from vested interests in new commercial broadcasting opportunities, have been a clamorous chorus. Mr Major's refusal to join the "bash-the-broadcasters" bandwagon during the Gulf War was seen by many understandably bruised and suspicious journalists as just a lull in the underlying campaign of which the manipulation of war reporting was the most significant evidence. Hostilities were readily resumed under the ever ready generalship of Lord Tebbitt during and after the 1992 general election.

At the same time the government has been engaged in a build up of its own publicity and press relations activities on an unprecedented scale. Government expenditure in this area rose from £20 million per annum in 1975 to £200 million by 1988. By 1988 only Unilever and Proctor and Gamble spent more on advertising than the government. A significant enhancement of this process has been created by the substantial sums spent on promoting major programmes of privatization. The sell off of the water industry was supported by campaigns costing £42 million, more than twice that spent on gas privatisation, while it was reported that electricity privatisation was likely to be promoted by an advertising bill of over £100 million (*Observer* 3 September 1989).

In May 1990 the Government Energy Secretary, John Wakeham, was appointed to coordinate government publicity and information, and new proposals to give senior ministers PR "minders" were revealed (*Independent on Sunday* 17 June 1990). Growing political protests about these developments led to the appointment of a public enquiry by the National Audit Office, which showed the very major programmes of expenditure undertaken by, for example the Department of Trade and Industry on its "Enterprise Initiative", but this report, like the subsequent report from the Committee of Public Accounts, was more concerned about value for money and cost effectiveness than about the niceties of political propriety.[6] Subsequent policy development has continued to be buttressed by major public relations enterprise, including the health service reforms and the introduction of the Council Tax, culminating in January 1994 in the announcement by the Secretary of State for Education that he was to spend over £2 million sending a leaflet into every home in the country giving the government's views and advice on morality, citizenship, discipline, and family values.

But public relations has both negative and positive elements. The growing unease felt in many areas of public life about the use of government information as a tool of secrecy, came to a head in the publication by such an august and conservative body as the Royal Statistical Society of a report into official statistics, suggesting
their preparation and form had become too much an instrument of state public relations. The Society declared itself no longer confident that:

> the organisational framework in which [government statisticians] work offers the best protection against undue pressure.... we are clear that the indirect result of the post Rayner reforms have been harmful to quality" (Royal Statistical Society, 1990).

Such horrors as the recurrent redefinition of unemployment, or the disappearance of the series on low incomes, fuel such unease. Research material produced under commission from government departments is only published with the prior consent of the relevant minister. That the elementary accounting of public life can no longer be made available for public and independent scrutiny can but be a major threat to the quality and substance of the public sphere, however defined.

Unequal access to communications

Where communications goods and facilities are available only at a price there will be a finite capacity to have access to them, limited by the disposable spending power of individuals and households. Spending on services generally has grown significantly in the last generation. In 1953-4 spending on services made up 9.5 per cent of household expenditure; by 1986 this proportion had risen to 12.7 per cent, and in 1992 spending on leisure goods and services alone accounted for 15 per cent of household expenditure (33 per cent in the highest income brackets). All expenditure on personal and household services and on leisure goods and services now amounts to over a third of household expenditure. Within this global figure spending within the home has risen as a proportion, linked most significantly to the television set as an increasingly dominant hub of leisure time and expenditure. On average British adults in 1992 spent 27 hours a week watching television broadcasts, and an as yet uncertainly calibrated amount of time using television for related activities, such as viewing videos or playing computer games. As the range of hardware required for such activities grows, however, so too does the demand on private expenditure necessary to participate in them.

As Table 2.2 shows there is a marked difference in the ownership of home computers and videos between different income groups, a gap that is unlikely to diminish substantially due to two factors. First, income differentials themselves have sharply widened in the last decade. During the 1980s wage increases for the highest paid fifth of male workers were 42 per cent higher than for the lowest paid fifth. In addition the gap between households dependent on social security benefits for their income and those in the labour market has also increased. Between 1979-91 the poorest fifth's share of total post-tax income fell from 9.5 per cent to 6.6 per cent, while that of the richest fifth rose from 37 per cent to 44 per cent (*Economic Trends* May 1993). The disposable spending power of different groups in the population is thus significantly polarised. Second, such goods require regular updating and replacement, disadvantaging groups with limited spending power and cumulatively advantaging the better off. Owning video or computer hardware requires expenditure on software, owning a phone means spending money on using it. Thus limited spending power is a deterrent not only to initial purchase but to regular use.

However not all expenditure on communications goods involves expensive acquisition of equipment. Television programmes can be viewed once you have a set to watch them on, as most people do, while many cultural materials are available as public goods; they are paid for from taxation as a common resource - public library books, for example. This is not a static situation, however. A shift in the method of distribution of cultural goods from being public services to private commodities signals a substantial change in the opportunity for different groups in the population to have access to them. If television channels, or individual programmes, are accessible by price, as is envisaged for much of the new television structure heralded by the 1990 Broadcasting Act and the more recent Green Paper, then consumption of television programmes will be significantly governed by the distribution of household incomes. Similar

Table 2.2

Ownership of Communication Facilities
Among Households in Selected Income Groups, 1992

%	TV	Cable TV	Telephone	Video Recorder	Home Computer
Weekly Income (£)					
60-80	97.6	4.0	73.6	30.4	3.4
130-160	99.1	7.1	85.2	57.6	8.8
200-240	97.8	7.2	86.6	70.4	14.7
370-420	99.1	13.1	95.3	85.6	23.3
800+	99.1	13.1	99.8	90.0	43.9

Source: Family Spending: A Report on the 1992 Family Expenditure Survey,
HMSO, London 1993, Table 4, p.6.

considerations would come into play if, for example, public libraries were to make greater use of powers to charge, as was proposed in a government Green Paper in 1988, even though, at the time, such proposals were shelved.

If subject to the discipline of price cultural goods acquire an artificial scarcity which makes them akin to other goods of considerably greater scarcity. Yet the notion of a public sphere presupposes that all members of the public, presumably coterminous with citizenship, have access to the communication resources which allow them to participate in the dialogues and discourses implicit in the very notion. The substitution of consumption gradients linked to market forces for citizenship based on communication rights is inherently a denial of membership of a public realm.

Conclusion

In this chapter I have illustrated the attraction of Habermas' concept of the public sphere for students of the role of the mass media in public life. While Habermas' historiography and analysis are open to widespread criticism, not least from himself in more recent writings, it is clear the concept continues to resonate with some of the key policy concerns of contemporary debate. I have suggested that there are more grounds for Habermas' pessimistic reading of the contemporary era than for his construction of the past, at least in this country, and that there are good reasons to be sceptical of those with undue enthusiasm for the likely social impact of new communication and distribution technologies. In particular the deepening threat to public service broadcasting, the severe partisanship of the national press, the public relations character of the centripetal state, and the widening inequalities of the communication marketplace, all support a view which diagnoses the public sphere as a domain inhabited by those comfortably ensconced within J.K. Galbrath's "culture of contentment", (1992)[7] while excluding significant and populous sections of the community.

It would be defeatist to conclude, however, that all is lost. These are contested social terrains in which other, possibly greener shoots can be detected. One can only take encouragement from the observation of Sir John Stokes, one of Lady Thatcher's staunchest supporters, who told the backbench 1922 Committee shortly before the 1992 general election was called, "People never talk about politics in the pubs. But now they are starting to. I regard that as a sinister sign". But it is a sign, if nothing else, of something we may loosely define as the public sphere.

Notes

1. See Keane 1984 ch. 5, and Villa 1992.

2. See also Garnham 1986.

3. See for example, Fiske 1987. For a critique see Golding 1990, or Schiller 1989 ch.7. For a valuable overview see Curran 1990.

4. See Broadcasting Standards Council 1992.

5. See Golding et al. 1992, and Billig et al. 1993.

6. National Audit Office 1989; Committee of Public Accounts 1990, HMSO, London.

7. Galbraith, J.K. (1992), *The Culture of Contentment*, Houghton Muflin, Boston.

3 Recent European and American conceptions of democracy and politics and the public sphere

Maurice Roche

This chapter is concerned with the popularity, within much of contemporary politics and ideology, of the idea of citizenship, and in particular the notion of citizens' obligations. These ideas and ideals are of central importance to the theme of this collection of studies, namely the problem of understanding the changing nature of "the public sphere", (and related notions of "the public interest" etc.), in modern societies. My discussion is intended to be an exploratory one, opening up issues and possible directions for further analysis rather than aiming to present detailed conclusions. In this spirit the chapter aims to offer a provisional account and interpretation of citizenship and obligations theories and rhetorics in movements such as neoconservatism, environmentalism, and feminism, particularly the latter. I suggest that these theories and rhetorics can be usefully understood in terms of a sociological and normative theory of the anomic characteristics of social life in modernity, characteristics which tend to undermine the legitimacy, and even the intelligibility, of human obligations. As part of this account I suggest that new approaches in social theory are needed to adequately come to grips with the nature and scale of anomie problems in late twentieth century society, and I outline some elements of one possible new approach in terms of a "rational humanist" social theory of human obligations.[1]

Introduction

In *Rethinking Citizenship* (Roche 1992), I analysed some of the main ideological and structural changes in contemporary Western societies which are currently challenging us to reconsider and reconstruct our dominant conceptions of citizenship. I focused particularly on the social dimension of citizenship and on contemporary debates about social rights and obligations in a period of crisis and criticism in relation to the welfare state. Our dominant conception and discourse of social citizenship is largely rights centred and is connected with the emergence of various forms of the welfare state.

The welfare state, together with the dominant conception of social citizenship, is widely understood to have emerged in response to both the objective social problems (e.g. poverty and class inequality) generated by industrial capitalism and also the expression of the pressing need to address those problems by social and political movements. In this sense the "long revolution" of the "evolution of citizenship" (Marshall 1963) and the "growth of rights" (Turner 1986) is usefully understood as being motivated not only by egalitarian ideals and utopias, but also by more defensive and pragmatic concerns to counter industrial capitalism's tendency to generate divisive social problems, particularly involving social (i.e. cultural, economic, political) inequality. In general it can be said that citizenship theory and practice in modernity, particularly its distinctive politics and discourse of citizen rights, developed through a range of "egalitarian" and, importantly, "counter inegalitarian" social and political ideologies and movements. In contrast with this it is notable that the contemporary politics of social citizenship, whether on the Right, Left or Centre, is, in various different ways, distinctively obligations centred.

The dominant paradigm of social citizenship with its emphasis on social rights had its high tide in the early postwar decades in which welfare state services were being built and developed. Since that time the politics of rights has been further expanded and enriched by the development of ideologies and institutions concerned with "human rights" of various kinds (e.g. the United Nations, and the European Court of Human Rights.[2] Parallel to this modern development of a "rights discourse" a "duties discourse", a rhetoric of obligations, has also developed in contemporary political and ideological debate. Both the Right and the new social movements have made equal, if distinct and different, contributions to this duties discourse.

Duties have stimulated a considerable amount of political conflict in the post war West (e.g. the anti-conscription/anti-Vietnam war movement, "tax payers" revolts' against welfare state spending, and the British anti-poll tax movement). But it is notable that they have been relatively little analysed in the social and political theory of citizenship.[3] This neglect is all the worse in that late twentieth century popular politics seems to be accumulating "duty discourses" and obligation rhetorics, particularly in such areas as internationalism, environmentalism and the anti-nuclear weapons movement. That is, there is a certain popular recognition in the West that, respectively, rich nations have duties to poor ones, all nations and individuals have duties to nature and the environment, and also that they have profound duties to future generations regarding both the conservation and transmission of humankind's environmental and socio-historical "heritage".

Besides this radical wing of the new duty discourse in contemporary politics in the 1980s in the USA, Britain and elsewhere, Right wing politics developed the duty discourse of personal responsibility and of the social obligations of citizenship. The ideological challenge of this wing is most clearly and articulately expressed in the development of American Neoconservative social thinking which has dominated social policy debates during the Reagan and Bush Presidencies and which remains an influence in the Clinton Presidency (Roche 1992 Part II, 1994a, 1994b).

The rise of a duties discourse is connected, according to my analysis, with a range of changes in the social structural configurations around contemporary capitalism, notably in culture (post-modernism), economics (post-industrialism) and politics (post-nationalism). These structural changes have generated new forms of the old social problems (e.g. new forms of poverty) together with historically unprecedented problems (e.g. mass over-consumption, structural under-employment, and global ecological crises, etc.).[4]

In the light of this analysis, in this chapter I will argue along the following lines. Firstly, problems of social inequality (i.e. political, civil, and economic inequalities) are perennial and ongoing political concerns in the development of industrial capitalist societies and have fuelled their characteristic movements for political, civil, and social rights, and generally the growth of modern forms of citizenship. However the contemporary (late twentieth century) politics of citizenship is connected with the rise on the one hand of the New Right and neoconservatism, and on the other with new social movements such as feminism and environmentalism. This politics is concerned with promoting new and/or revived conceptions of citizen's responsibilities, obligations and duties in addition to (and in some cases instead of) the promotion of rights.

Secondly, the new social problems which contemporary movements are concerned with have been generated by structural change in the modern capitalist order. These new problems can be conceived as contemporary versions of the classical sociological problem of "anomie". Modern anomie problems help to explain and interpret the distinctive character of contemporary ideologies' concerns for citizenship, and particularly for citizens' responsibilities and obligations. Whatever the characteristics may be of "egalitarian" (or "counter-inegalitarian") ideologies, rhetorics and forms of politics, they can be interpreted usefully and importantly as "counter-anomic" in motivation and purpose.

To develop this argument it is first necessary to review the problems addressed by some contemporary social and political ideologies, (i.e. neoconservatism, ecology and feminism) together with their concerns for the ideas of citizenship and obligation (section I). We can then outline the modern problem of anomie, reinterpret and renew the theory in terms of universalistic conceptions of social humanity, rights and responsibilities appropriate to late twentieth century social conditions (section II), and relate this conception to the social and political ideologies discussed in section I (Conclusion).

I. Citizenship, obligations and political ideologies

Background

The motifs of citizenship and of a need to promote new or renewed social obligations of citizenship are widely present in the contemporary political landscape. On the Right wing, for instance, nationalism, and thus national citizenship, has begun to have a central ideological significance in contemporary Europe.[5] This is true even within the EU (which is nonetheless embarked upon the construction of transnational institutions and thus new spheres and conceptions of post-national citizenship, Roche 1992, ch.8, 1994b). But it is particularly true in the post-Communist East where militant and dogmatic versions of nationalism have reawakened or have been invented in recent years. While on Europe's borders there is the resurgent Islamic theocratic fundamentalism of Iran and others.

These types of essentially Right wing/authoritarian ideologies conceive of citizenship as membership of the national (and in many of these cases, religious) state and as carrying a very heavy burden of loyalties and obligations with it. Extreme nationalism promotes ideals and myths of ethnic purity and national homogeneity within the nation state's territories. It decries the contemporary Western political ideals of democratic

44

pluralism and multiculturalism (which, in terms considered earlier, can be seen as positively anomic ideologies and institutions). Theocratic fundamentalism decries most forms of culture and social life other than itself as at least morally questionable and as at worst "decadent". From this Right wing point of view Western society as such is inherently anomic and problematic.

On the contemporary Left, with the demise of Communist utopianism, with socialism's and social democracy's crisis of intellectual and popular credibility, and with much talk about the need for rethinking, citizenship has become a focal concern,[6] albeit mainly in the form of a renewal of the traditional rights oriented rather than obligations oriented citizenship. It remains the case however that even within these ideologies the days of the "duty free" rights agenda seem to have gone and there is considerable implicit recognition of notions of rights, duties, reciprocity and of the moral and political importance of responsibility and obligation. In this context various Centre Left positions such as American Communitarianism (Etzioni 1992, Bell 1993, also Wolfe 1989) and British Ethical Socialism (Halsey and Dennis 1988), have been proposed. Like the Right wing ideologies noted above, these positions also operate with versions of citizenship which explicitly stress obligations. But they do so in terms of civil society and personal moral responsibility rather than loyalty to the state. In addition, they identify and criticise a range of conditions and tendencies in modern society which they explicitly identify as anomic and thus problematic, and in this they share some of the same concerns as contemporary neoconservatism (below Conclusion, and Roche 1992 Part II). To illustrate some of these points we can briefly consider two of the "new social movements", i.e. ecology and feminism, on the Left or radical side of the spectrum.

New social movements, citizenship and obligations

It may at first glance appear to be something of misrepresentation of feminism and ecology to present them as being political ideologies and discourses centrally concerned with promoting concepts of obligation and duty. They are surely quintessential modern rights claiming discourses. They are surely about the extension of moral and citizenship based rights into the relatively uncharted territories of i) the "personal", the "private" and the "body" in the case of the women's movement, and ii) animals, plants, land, air, sea - in a word "nature" - in the case of the ecological movement. This is no doubt true, up to a point. But there is also in these movements undoubtedly a stronger, more explicit and more sophisticated

45

understanding than is to be found in one sided rights movements of the fact that rights imply duties. What is more, ecology and feminism understand better than many rights movements do that the duties that rights imply are not all state duties. They understand that these duties are also, importantly, claims against other members of civil society and/or claims against ourselves. We must now consider these movements in a little more detail, beginning with some brief observations about ecology and then giving slightly more attention to feminism.

Ecology and citizenship: If anything, the ecological movement, even more clearly than feminism, is concerned with the politics and morality of obligation and duty. Of course it champions rights, and it does so in two distinct registers at that. In the first register ecology champions the rights of the non humans (animals, environments, nature etc.) on behalf of the non human, rights with are claimed against humans. Nature's rights thus imply (and with ecology's help, impose), duties for humans. Ecology thus addresses itself to the often agonizing debates and struggles within and between modern human states and societies, and indeed within each individual, between on the one hand human needs, desires and rights, and on the other hand, duties we impose on ourselves by our recognition, such as it is, of the rights of the nonhuman. A discourse implying, or indeed often asserting, "rights of nature" and thus, correlatively "the obligations of humanity", is a common characteristic of environmentalist philosophy and ideology. It is often expressed in terms of the need for humans to have an attitude of "reverence" for the Earth (e.g. Porritt 1984, p.10) and to live "in harmony" with nature. Sagoff, for instance, expresses this in the language of contract, and speaks of "the covenant we have made with nature" (Sagoff 1988, p.141).

It is certainly possible to dispute whether the rights and duties recognised in this form of ecological analysis are "genuine", given that they have very different features from conventional moral and citizenship based rights and duties recognised between people. For instance, "nature" is not a conscious moral agency or a citizen, and only such entities can be said to understand and possess rights, to choose to claim them, to know when they are satisfied etc. Humans can in principle make no rights claims against nature, nor can we discuss with nature the adequacy of the discharge of our duties to it etc. However such criticisms as these are somewhat less undermining of ecology's moral discourse when its second register is considered.

In its second register ecology champions nature and the environment on behalf of posterity. This perspective is commonly expressed in terms of the concept of humans' duty of "stewardship" regarding nature (e.g. Skolimowski 1981, p.54).[7] Thus generations of humans as yet unborn are assumed to have rights to an environment at least as resource rich and as undegraded and undamaged as the one the present generation inherited. This consideration imposes important conservation obligations on contemporary nation states. This view in favour of "intergenerational equity" and the need to conserve at least "the global commons" has been powerfully articulated in various United Nations reports since the 1980s, most notably in The Brundtland Report, *Our Common Future*, (Brundtland et al. 1987). The "rights of future generations" are deemed to impose duties of environmental "stewardship" on all individuals, communities, organisations and nations (e.g. Brundtland 1987, Steward, in Andrews 1991). Sagoff argues for instance:

> Our obligation to provide future individuals with an environment consistent with ideals we know to be good is an obligation not necessarily to those individuals but those ideals themselves. It is an obligation to civilisation to continue civilisation (Sagoff 1988, p.63).

Like nature, future generations cannot reciprocate the performance of duties. It is thus not unreasonable to argue that in this way (and of course in many other non ecological ways) an intergenerational moral relationship or community exists in human affairs. This implies that all explicitly or implicitly purely intragenerational conceptions of social justice and of the proper distribution of ecological and other forms of welfare must incorporate an intergenerational element which imposes a set of unreciprocated duties on the present generation to provide ecological welfare to future generations.

Whether or not the sphere of civil society and of our social citizenship can be said to include animals, as ecologists, or at least many "animal rights" supporters might wish to propose, is obviously arguable. However, in its second register ecology challenges the dominant paradigm of social citizenship in a number of ways. Firstly, it asserts the importance of human duties, indeed it asserts their primacy in some respects over human rights. Secondly, it requires us to rethink what we mean by welfare so as to include environmental factors and values. Thirdly, it expands the sphere of our relevant civil society beyond the nation state level to the global level and to other ecological relevant levels from the global to the local; also it expands it beyond the present generation and requires us to consider the intergenerational dimension of our sociality and of our moral and citizenship duties.[8]

Feminism and citizenship: The women's movement has had a sometimes ambiguous relationship with the theory and practice of democracy and citizenship. In the early suffragette period the movement represented a clear and qualitative extension of democracy, citizenship and citizen's rights. In its post war revival in the 1960s and 1970s, and particularly in its various "revolutionary" and "radical" forms, feminists sometimes adopted a cynical stance to the allegedly "patriarchal" character of democracy (and associated political forms such as "the liberal state" and "the welfare state"), analogous to Marxism's cynicism about "bourgeois" democracy (and the liberalism, statism, and welfarism associated with this in the post war period). Also, analogous to non democratic practices of Communist parties, the "sisterhood" had difficulties in accommodating democratic practices involving rights to free speech, criticism and diversity within its politics (Rowbotham 1986).[9]

The analogy here derives from different sources, however. For Communism politics was about the achievement of the good society through authoritarian means if necessary (the "dictatorship of the proletariat", "the leading role of the Party","democratic centralism", etc.), and while private property was undoubtedly political, "the private sphere" and "the personal" *per se* were not. Feminism's problems, both in theory and in practice, with democracy, citizenship and associated "public sphere" based conceptions of politics, derived from precisely opposite sources. They derived largely from feminism's commitment to the concept that "the personal is political", and thus from its attempts to incorporate "the private sphere" (particularly the sphere of the family) in its political theory, and to accommodate "the personal" (particularly "sisterly" trust and solidarity) in the practice of Movement politics.

However, that being said, evidently much of the politics of the women's movement, not least as a movement of "liberation", involves the promotion of claims for "women's rights" and freedoms. Such rights and freedoms are only intelligible in theory and sustainable in practice in terms of an acceptance of some kind of democratic constitution and polity, and some version or another of a politics of citizenship. This has been recognised in various ways in feminist political theory.[10] Indeed Dietz argues that:

> Feminist political practice..(needs to)...become an inspiration for a new citizenship...(f)eminists must become self-conscious political thinkers - defenders of democracy.. (Dietz 1992, p.78).

In addition to being interpretable as a special kind of citizens' rights movement, feminism must also be understood as a movement concerned importantly with a number of types of obligations and duties. These are state duties, male obligations and women's own obligations, and we can take each of these in turn. Firstly, many of the most substantive rights claims are in fact claims which can only be seriously addressed by using the power and authority of a democratic state. For instance claims for the satisfaction of basic welfare needs and claims to freedom from male violence. Women's movement politics also typically involves claiming assistance and support from the state in order to take an equal part with men in civil society, i.e. claims for the state to support equal citizenship.[11]

Secondly, an important part of the thrust of women's rights claims is intended to be felt directly by men rather than by the state. Feminism challenges men in modern society to recognise the existence of patriarchal order and of the manifold ways in which they both dominate women's lives and benefit from so doing. Advancing the cause of women's rights challenges men to change themselves and to change their ways of relating to women in order to honour those rights. In effect, feminism challenges men to accept a duty to act against the patriarchal order in which women are second class citizens and to act for equality, a society of equal citizenship.

One of the key spheres in which the issue of women's rights and men's obligations evidently needs to be pressed, and is being pressed, is "the (allegedly) private sphere", the sphere of the family, although the same sort of problems are at issue in the spheres of employment, education, leisure/public space etc. As far as the family goes, the promotion of women's rights first of all requires a major and difficult reordering of the unequal social citizenship involved in the typical pattern of the social division of labour, with female specialisation in housework, child care and other carework and male specialisation in employment (e.g. Oakley 1974, Pahl 1984). Men in modern societies are challenged by the claims of women's rights to acknowledge equal social citizenship in the division of labour and to do something about it. One step in a progressive direction here is undoubtedly for men to accept a greater share of the duties and burdens of housework, child care and other carework. Another is for men to treat the main division of labour between domestic/care work and employment as at least a joint decision with their partner, jointly reviewed and jointly changeable. This latter step is obviously bigger and more difficult for individual men than the former because of the influence of prevailing labour market conditions and their structural biases in favour of men. However, these biases look likely to ease significantly during the

1990s, albeit under the influence of economic (capitalist) rather than ideological (feminist) factors.

The personal politics involved in attempts to redistribute work duties in this way presupposes at least relatively civilised and civil (and to mention affectionate) relationships between male and female partners and any children they may be responsible for. One of the achievements of the feminist movement has been to reveal the significant degree to which, such civil norms and values have historically been dishonoured and are currently dishonoured in families. The minimal duties of respect and civility which are required in public society are equally required in order for the private realm of the family to exist in a healthy and just way. But the elementary civil duty not to violate and abuse others appears to be unrecognised or dishonoured by the significant minority of men in modern societies which is responsible for domestic violence and abuse against women and children. The women's movement, by pressing women's rights to respect and civility in intimate relationships, reasserts and seeks to impose clear and basic moral duties on men. These duties underpin male claims to being members of a community with laws and a peaceful political process. In this sense feminism challenges men to remember the moral conditions of their citizenship. It challenges the state to use its authority coercively to remind men about these conditions if they happen to forget or ignore them.[12]

Thirdly and finally, there is the issue of women's obligations. Whatever reordering of the division of labour between men and women within the family might ultimately be achieved, it remains the case that many women may well continue to devote much of their time and effort to child rearing. Even if a widespread "new social contract" for the division of parenting and other familial carework (e.g. for the elderly) is ever achieved on the basis of equality and negotiation, for some feminists at least, women are more likely than men to commit themselves to the role of family-maker/parent; the role of "motherhood" is as important as "sisterhood". That is, there is the argument for women's "difference" from, as well as equality with, men. From this perspective freely chosen "motherhood", with all of its parental obligations of care for children etc, is as important for the progress of the women's movement as is a form of "sisterhood" which involves women in committing themselves largely, or even exclusively, to public spheres such as employment and formal politics.[13]

Obligation is clearly a difficult subject for feminism. Indeed from some points of view feminism could, in principle, be understood as a critique of the very idea of social obligation, and to a certain extent the movement, in practice, as a "women's liberation" movement, did so understand itself. That is, the patriarchy and male domination the movement struggles against could well be defined precisely in terms of the obligations males, and male defined tradition, have long imposed, and continue to impose, upon women, particularly family obligations (Finch 1989). However even feminist political theorists who argue for "the priority of freedom" in the struggle against patriarchy, and its priority over all other considerations, such as obligation, nonetheless acknowledge the importance of the concept of obligation for feminism. Thus Pateman argues:

> Feminists have no need to jettison the concept of obligation or, indeed, freedom,... (Self-assumed) (o)bligation is...a means through which individuals can exercise, maintain, and sometimes...enhance their freedom... (Pateman 1992, p.182).

Hirschmann goes further than this to argue for a new feminist ontology and epistemology concerned as much with "nonconsensual", "non-negotiable", aspects of human relations (such as infant care, where infants are not capable of consenting to or negotiating about the care relationship), involving "nonconsensual obligations", as with those aspects amenable to a process of negotiation, consent formation and the kind of self assumption of obligations Pateman is concerned with. Thus Hirschmann argues that:

> Taking obligation as a starting point is very different from taking it as an end point. ....(As) a starting point, from the perspective of women's experience, nonconsensual aspects of human relationships are vital to our humanity. ...(F)eminism requires that men, as well as women, recognize and fulfil these given obligations. Only then can both men and women take part in greater and more genuine choice (Hirschmann 1992, p.187).

In summary, it is arguable that feminism is a social and political ideology and movement which is importantly concerned with the promotion of citizenship, and in particular with the promotion of citizens' obligations as well as citizens' rights. The main obligations we have briefly considered are; the state's duties to service women's civil rights (e.g. security, equality of opportunity etc.) and social rights (e.g. welfare) claims; male obligations in various spheres, but particularly in the family; and women's own obligations, whether understood in "self-assumed" or "nonconsensual" terms.

51

II Anomie theory: modernity and rational humanism

In this section we can consider briefly some of the features of modernity which may help to interpret and explain the currency of the language of citizenship and rhetorics of obligation in contemporary political ideologies and movements. The language of citizenship is a "common denominator" language, which lends itself to the assertion and affirmation of common (national, community) identity and membership. The language of obligation used in association with it underscores these assertions and affirmations. From a sociological point of view, we can make the observation that these sorts of ideological and discursive repertoires are most likely to be brought into play, and to be used in politics in social and historical periods and conditions in which traditional conceptions of social identity, criteria of social membership, and norms and moral obligations have become threatened, are uncertain and unclear, and are in various ways disorganised and deregulated.

Such periods and conditions have been classically analysed in sociology in terms of the problem of modern society's potential for "anomie". However the classical conception of anomie, developed in and applied to late nineteenth century Western societies, is lacking in important respects and needs to be reconstructed if it is to be of use in understanding social and political problems in late twentieth century Western societies. Such a reconstruction is difficult to envisage because it pulls against the grain of conventional sociological theorising in two respects.

Firstly the reconstruction of the theory of anomie needs to be relevant to a post national era in which a transnational level of society (a "global" capitalist economy, "global culture" etc.) is emerging. As against the conventional wisdom in sociology of societal difference, intrasocietal determinism, and societal relativism this requires a more universalistic kind of sociological conceptualisation providing for the possibility of strong intersocietal comparisons.

Secondly the reconstruction of the theory of anomie needs to provide a normative, or explicitly normatively relevant, conceptualisation of the problem of anomie. This runs against much of sociology's conventional disciplinary identity as a non normative, "positive social science", intellectually disconnected from and agnostic about debates in social philosophy and political theory around competing normative conceptions of "justice", "morality" etc. To do this, in turn, requires that sociology open itself to normatively relevant theories of "human nature" of the kind which provide for explicitly normative conceptions of "human needs", "human rights", and "human obligations".

52

It is not possible to do justice to this complex agenda facing contemporary social theory in the context of this particular chapter. Nonetheless, in the spirit of exploration with which we embarked on this attempt to interpret and explain the currency of the language of citizenship and obligation in contemporary politics and ideology, a provisional sketch of some of the key aspects of the theory of anomie, and of its reconstruction in terms of a theory of "rational humanism", can be offered at this point.

A classical sociological view: Durkheim's concept of anomie

The classical sociological conception of anomie is that offered by Durkheim (1964, 1970).[14] Given limitations of space, I will focus on this conception without reference to other subsequent influential theories of anomie (e.g. Merton 1968, ch.6,7). In Durkheim's original conception of the problem, anomie refers to a state of moral deregulation in societies in general and also in personalities. Moral deregulation is associated with a loss of limits on human wants, drives and behaviour. For Durkheim the cause of anomie lies in the development of the modern social system and in personalities' responses to this. In particular Durkheim noted problems of social integration, social solidarity and anomie in modern society attendant upon the ideology of individualism, the complex form of the general societal "division of labour" and the capitalist/market based economy distinctive of modernity.

Although he was optimistic about modern society's overall problem solving capacity, Durkheim saw the capitalist economy in particular as structurally prone to anomie because capitalists and firms usually demand and often get minimal legal and moral regulation of markets. However, capitalists' capacity to regulate their own affairs patently did not include, in Durkheim's period (nor does it in our post Keynesian and post national era) the power to control the socially and economically damaging effects of the business cycle. Anomie is particularly evident in the labour market and the employment of labour by market based/capitalist organisations. Business cycles impose an objective finiteness on booms and on slumps which is not recognised (or if recognised tends to be ignored), in people's subjective perceptions of their economic contexts and in their personal planning in economic and other terms. Personal expectations and habits formed in booms are not functional for or adaptable to those needed in recessionary conditions and periods, and vice versa. The recurrent objective movement in modern economies from growth to recession, from boom to slump, thus exerts a recurrently destabilising influence on modern society and is a generative factor for anomie. It is consistent with Durkheim's view, although he does not himself cite it, to illustrate the anomic tendencies of the labour market in capitalist economies by referring to the negative psycho-social effects of cyclical and structural unemployment, effects which have been established in many subsequent social scientific studies (e.g. Jahoda 1984, also Roche 1990).

In general, in Durkheim's analysis anomie is strongly connected with social change, particularly with rapid social change involving crisis ridden transformations. Disorganisational and reorganisational social dynamics are typically experienced by people as at least confusing and stressful disturbances of the social environment which situates and helps identify them. For Durkheim the social environment is (among other things, but perhaps above all else), a constitutive and regulatory environment. In his view all individuals need such an environment to be fully human, that is to be socially competent, to be able to control their desires and limit their wants, and thus able to live as autonomous beings. Rapid social change poses problems of adaptation to individuals who may or may not be capable of reorienting themselves and finding the regulatory support they need in the changed social environment. Individuals' failure to adapt, and/or the failure of regulatory environments to emerge for them to adapt to, can result in various sorts of attitudes and behaviours Durkheim evaluated in negative terms, including experiences of alienation and dehumanisation in work, family breakdown, loss of meaning and self control in life in general, and self destructive behaviour including suicide.

Although Durkheim evidently regarded anomie as a major problem in modern society, he also seemed optimistic that it could be managed and countered through the organisational and regulatory potential of such things as mass primary and secondary education, corporatism and professionalisation in the sphere of employment and the economy, and socialist ideals in the sphere of politics. In this optimism he could perhaps be said to have anticipated some of the features of the "organised" (or "Fordist") form of capitalism which ensued in the early twentieth century and which in turn was completed by the growth of the welfare state in most Western capitalist societies by the mid/late twentieth century.

However, as against this sociological scenario, the last quarter of the twentieth century has seen a major renewal of capitalist dynamics and structural social change beyond the era of "organised" capitalism (Lash and Urry 1987) and the welfare state (Pierson 1991, also Roche 1992 Part III, 1994b). In this situation problems of anomie, namely problems of disorganisation and deregulation in people's societal environment, involving experiences of disorientation, nihilism and self destructiveness, have been renewed and have also appeared in new forms. Whether in terms of the classical or renewed conception of anomie, social phenomena distinctive of late twentieth century Western society such as consumerism (the mass cultivation of attitudes of envy and greed, insatiability and addiction towards objects and possessions) and the ecological crisis, are usefully seen as anomic (unlimited, self destructive etc.)

For the new forms of anomie to be adequately theorised we need to develop, in addition to a coherent conception of the changing configuration of contemporary Western society, a new ontologically based and normative social theoretical perspective which I refer to as "rational humanism".[15]

Rethinking anomie theory: a rational humanist perspective

The "rational humanist" perspective I propose here is unfashionable in sociological terms, and also in terms of Anglo-American analytic philosophy. In the sketch of the perspective which follows, reference is made to unfashionable conceptions of such things as "human nature", "human needs" (and thus derivatively "human rights"), and "human obligations and responsibilities".[16] The perspective thus aims to provide a realistic and reasonable basis for normative theory which seeks not only to describe and understand but also to evaluate social actions and varieties of social environments in terms of their actual or potential contribution to the sustaining and flourishing of human life and rationality.

Conventional and fashionable sociological world views, where they are not simply societally determinist, tend to be relativistic (culturally and historically) and "constructionist" about key intellectual (and in philosophical terms, ontological) framework concepts such as notions of Self, Humanity, Reason and Nature. They can also be either presumptuous about the "evident" normative implications of their analyses of these sorts of notions or, in more "scientistic" (i.e. "value free" and "metaphysics free") mode, can aspire to an indifference about the normative dimension and the related ontological dimension.

As against the conventional and the fashionable, what I believe is needed in social theory and in the social sciences in general, and in the understanding of citizenship in particular, is a sociological (or better, a sociologically informed) world view which treats these sorts of philosophical framework concepts in a more universalistic and realistic manner and, connected with this, which also contains an explicit and normatively relevant ontology. Intellectual resources for developing this rational humanist perspective beyond the bare sketch of it given here are available in philosophy in the Enlightenment tradition, (particularly Kant's world view and moral philosophy, Roche 1992, ch.9) and in the Phenomenological tradition, (particularly in existential phenomenology and in analyses of the lifeworld, Roche 1973, passim). Other intellectual resources are available in modern social and political theory, for instance Human Needs theory (e.g Plant et al. 1980, Doyal and Gough 1984, 1991) and Human Rights theory (e.g. Turner 1993).

The core of this world view is a universalistic ontological or species conception of human beings as autonomous entities (or more accurately as entities with a potential and need for autonomy, active agency, and identity). Human beings are constituted by distinctive, and distinctively interconnected, animalic embodiment, rational, and social characteristics, and their activity is fuelled by and largely concerned with the satisfaction of needs and wants associated with these characteristics. This view has some parallels with positions which claim that human's species based "vulnerability" is a basis for "human rights", (although the latter position makes less out of the human capacity for rationality than is being claimed here, e.g. Turner 1993).

Humans' animalic embodiment characteristics include their distinctive body type and capacities, brain size and capacities, long dependent infancy, development stages and life cycle, health potential and illness vulnerability etc. Their rational characteristics include their capacity to be selfconscious, to reason abstractly and creatively, to decide between alternative courses of action, to control emotions and drives, etc. Their social characteristics include needs and capacities, actions and interactions concerned with socialisation (in infancy, childhood and recurrently); identity (socially established uniqueness and reidentifiability etc); sociability (public/peer recognition and intimate/ peer emotional/sexual bonding); communication (language development and use, nonlinguistic communication competence etc); work (structured activity within or between organisations involving the production of material, information or service production to satisfy various needs (physical survival, physical health and flourishing, mental health and life quality, etc).

Humans' ontological or species characteristics of autonomy potential, embodiment, reason potential and sociality help to establish criteria for morality and politics, and criteria also for anomie. Rational humanist morality does not call unrealistically, as many moral positions including Christianity and socialism traditionally have done, for a stance of selfless and/or disinterested altruism. It allows rational self interest to be fully part of the moral and political decision making environment. Indeed it construes individuals' own basic need oriented projects as morally obligated (rather than being conceived of, in the first instance, as

56

constituting rights claims against others).

In the spirit of Enlightenment rational humanism, and of one of its great expressions, namely Kant's moral philosophy (albeit in pragmatic/ prudential, existentially realistic and ontologically grounded terms alien to that philosophy), we can say that people have obligations to themselves (Kant 1965, 1964). For instance people can be said to have basic "natural human obligations" (in addition to, and arguably prior to, whatever "human rights" they may be said to possess) to do whatever they can to survive/protect their own lives, to care for their health, and to control the influence of emotions and drive states on their thinking and behaviour. Acknowledging selfcare and selfcontrol obligations is not only a principled matter which honours the general and basic obligation we may be said to have to the humanity (the human life, autonomy and reason) we possess, but, in more pragmatic and utilitarian vein, it can also be socially beneficial in reducing the burdens of care and control we may otherwise place on others when our human needs are read as providing us with rights claims against others.

Admittedly where human beings with undeveloped autonomy (infants and children) or impaired autonomy (e.g. the physically or mentally ill) are concerned, a different moral stance is necessary. In these particular sorts of human conditions, the co primacy of the needs and rights of others, and thus our obligations to the humanity they possess, needs to be recognised. And these sorts of obligations, particularly in the familial relations of parents to young children, and of adult children to aged parents, can be recognised, whatever the cultural differences between family systems, as "natural human obligations" which provide at least children and aged parents with a particularly strong, realistic and practical claim to possession of "natural human rights". However, even here our obligation to service the rights of others cannot be said to be unconditional; any such obligation needs to be weighted against the obligations of selfcare and selfcontrol if its servicing is not to be self defeating. An overworked and overstressed parent, prone to "burn out" and loss of emotional selfcontrol is operating according to an unrealistically altruistic and self sacrificial ideal of good parenting. They are likely to be less capable of sustaining good quality long term care to their children, and may even be damaging and abusive to them, as compared with parents who do not feel guilty (and indeed are justified from a rational humanist point of view) in making time, space and resource to also attend to their own personal and life needs.

Anomie, then, can be conceived in terms of a rational humanism perspective as a characteristic of actions and systems which are unlimited and unregulated by the needs and obligations of human life and rationality, which tend to undermine rationality and degrade human life whether in the actors or in those affected by their actions, and which are dehumanising and self destructive in human species terms. Contemporary political ideologies and their versions of citizenship, indeed the whole fashionability of the idea of citizenship as such, to a significant extent can be seen as responses to the renewal of anomie problems in modernity. We will take this theme of "negative" anomie a little further in relation to neoconservatism, ecology and feminism in a moment.

However it is worth noting that anomie is not by any means an unambiguous phenomenon and that it is possible to see it is a "positive" phenomenon as well as a "negative" one. That is the anomie motif and process figures in many features of modern society that are widely valued and seen as among modernity's strengths rather than among its flaws. For instance there are the values and pleasures of elite artistic creativity and common human playfulness (e.g. Huizinga 1971); "value free" science and the infinite pursuit of knowledge (e.g. Weber 1967); individual freedom and "negative" freedom (i.e. freedom from constraint and limit); the free society as essentially "open" (i.e. as relentlessly anti traditional and self critical, e.g. Popper, 1966), the good society as essentially (and disorientingly) complex (i.e. politically, culturally, and even ethically pluralist, e.g. Mouffe 1991, also Roche 1994c) and so on. These highly valued aspects of modernity can usefully be referred to as examples of what might be called "positive anomie". However in the Conclusion, in applying the concept of anomie to contemporary political ideologies and social movements, the focus of will be restricted to the "negative" aspects of anomie with which we have been mainly concerned in this discussion.

Conclusion: Anomie, counter anomie and citizenship politics

The discussion in this chapter has suggested that (negative) anomie problems are some of the main kinds of social problem which fuel and motivate many aspects of contemporary political movements and ideologies whether on the Right or Left of modern politics. On the Right, for instance, American neoconservative politics, social policy and conceptions of citizenship since the mid 1980s have been preoccupied with anomie problems. This is evident in many of the main societal and social policy analyses and diagnoses provided by the main neoconservative writers (Roche 1992, Part II, 1994a). Anomie problems are central to their discussions of the general societal crisis they see facing the advanced industrial societies, particularly America. Anomie is also central to their accounts, diagnoses, prognoses and policy recommendations concerning contemporary poverty and the "underclass".

In each of these spheres of discussion and debate neoconservative analysis tends to focus on problems of "decadence" and the "breakdown" of social ethics in modernity. These problems include firstly moral problems connected with the anti traditional culture of individual freedom and "permissiveness" which has been fashionable since the 1960s. Secondly these problems include changes in family structures and institutions, changes in patterns of cohabitation and child rearing which neoconservatives see as involving a "breakdown of family values", particularly a breakdown in the binding and obligatory character of marriage relationships and parental relationships (Roche 1992, ch.5).

Finally neoconservatives are concerned about problems stemming from structural changes in labour markets, and in the nature and role of employment and work more generally in contemporary society, changes which they choose to see as involving a "breakdown of the work ethic" (Roche 1992, ch.6). According to this analysis for people in modern societies there is a breakdown in the obligatory character of employment searching, employment holding and hard work in employment. All of this connects, of course, to other aspects of the more traditional conservative position relating to conservatives' perennial concerns for "law and order" (and hence for the obligations involved in obeying the law, preventing and compensating crime, finding, judging and punishing criminals, etc), and for the nation's survival, identity and integrity (and hence for the obligations involved in patriotism, military service and defence spending).

The general implications for neoconservatives' social and political thinking of these forms of moral "decadence" or deregulation, these forms, then, of anomie, is that a politics of citizenship needs to be promoted which emphasises the social obligations of citizenship. Politics needs at the very least to be counter anomic, ethics and moral regulation need to be restored, and a politics (a rhetoric and practice) of citizen obligation is seen as the best way to make progress on these fronts. These neoconservative themes are very evident features of British Conservatism and also of American "new" Democrat party ideologies in the early 1990s.

However it is possible that a similar sort of analysis could be said to hold, on the Left or Centre/Left of politics, about the attitudes and perspectives of the New Social Movements. Their conceptions of citizenship (such as they are) could be said to be fuelled and motivated by problems of anomie as much or even more than those of social inequality. In order to make the case for this argument it is necessary, as I have suggested in this chapter, to reconstruct the sociological theory of anomie, and also to shift from a conventional sociological perspective towards a new perspective which I have called "rational humanism". In these terms it is possible to judge the problems addressed by the key "new social movements" of ecology and feminism as problems of anomie and the movements as "counter anomic".

The personal, corporate or systemic problems these movements address are anomic in that they involve failures on the part of individuals and groups, corporations and governments to recognise or honour traditional humanistic obligations; these are failures to act, as we say, "responsibly". The ecological movement is concerned about the degradation and destruction of environments and of animal/lifeforms; of future generation and contemporary generation human habitats, life quality and life resources; in terms of a rational humanist perspective ecology's problems are anomie problems. Feminism is concerned with the problems posed by the scale of traditional and contemporary male failure (through hate or fear of women, whether by choice or through social incompetence) to recognise, negotiate over and contribute to the work of rearing and socialising children. In terms of a rational humanist perspective feminist problems are anomie problems.

Feminism and ecology can be interpreted as being counter anomic in their political discourse and in the general thrust of their political project. The new social movements implicitly and explicitly make use of the language of citizenship (Roche 1994b). As we have seen in this chapter, this discourse serves the movements' efforts to propagate and popularise radical new understandings of the nature and demands of human obligations and responsibilities in spheres ranging from the interpersonal to the ecospheric and intergenerational. I have argued that these movements can be usefully understood as importantly counter anomic in motivation and purpose. This perspective provides observers and supporters of the new politics with some criteria, in particular rational humanist criteria, by which to judge them. That is to say, contemporary political ideologies and new social movements can be judged by their effectiveness in diagnosing, intervening in and controlling the causes and effects, the scale and incidence, of the anomic processes and problems which animate them.

Notes

1.   I would like to thank an anonymous reader of the journal *Theory and Society* for some helpful suggestions on feminist theory in relation to part of the argument in section I of this chapter.

2.   See also Paul 1984, and Turner 1993.

3.   For exceptions see Janowitz 1980/81, and Walzer 1985.

4.   For more detail see Roche 1992, Part III, 1994b.

5.   See for example, Brubaker 1992, and Roche 1994d.

6.   See for example, Andrews 1991, and Mouffe 1991.

7.   See also Atfield 1983, ch. 3, p. 10 and Steward, in Andrews 1991.

8.   On these ecological and intergenerational issues see also Roche 1992, ch.9, 1988b, 1989.

9.   For an alternative version, arguing for the democratic character of feminism's practice see Dietz 1992.

10.   See also Elshtain 1981, and Phillips 1991.

11.   See for example, Lister 1990a, 1990b; also Phillips, Benton and Ellis, in Andrews 1991.

12.   On these issues see also Roche 1988a, 1992, ch.5.

13.   See for example, Hirschmann 1989, 1992a, 1992b, and Elshtain 1993.

14.   See also Lukes 1981, chapters 7, 9, and 13, and Hilbert 1986.

15.   For alternative renewals of the anomie concept and applications to the analysis of contemporary social problems see Orru 1987, Mestrovic and Brown 1985, Dahrendorf 1988, and Habermas 1987.

16.   For fuller discussions of these conceptions see Roche 1973, 1987, 1990, and 1992.

Part 2
FROM PUBLIC SERVICE TO PRIVATE PROVISION: REDRAWING THE BOUNDARIES

4 The end of work: Public and private livelihood in post-employment capitalism

Elliott Currie

Let me begin by confessing to a bit of strategic exaggeration. Really: the **"end"** of work? "Post-employment capitalism?" Obviously, that's stretching things considerably. Work is of course still very much with us: most of us, for better or worse, still have to work, and most of us **will** have to work for the forseeable future. But it's an exaggeration that I use advisedly, because I think it points to a very important truth. There are enormous, indeed epochal, changes afoot in what we rather abstractly and bloodlessly call the "labor markets" of the advanced societies. Those changes are underway across the entire post industrial world. And they promise to alter in fundamental ways the character of work as we know it.

Those changes present us with a situation of great opportunity, and great peril. That sounds like a cliche, but in this case is very real. These shifts in the character and distribution of work **could** open up new possibilities for creating a more civilized society of genuine abundance; they could also drive us into ever greater social insecurity, deprivation, and conflict.

The most important of those emerging changes in the shape of work is simple: there is going to be less of it. Or, more precisely, less of what I will call "livelihoods", meaning not just any sort of "job", but good work. Work that accomplishes something useful, provides a reasonable standard of living, and offers the worker some sense of participation and contribution - of economic "citizenship". It is in that sense that we are indeed moving toward "post employment" capitalism.

There is an analogy here with the idea of "post industrial" society. When we talked about entering a "post industrial" era we did not mean that there would be no more industry or that manufacturing would disappear, but rather that a profound shift was underway in how people made their living and in what sorts of things were produced in modern societies. Likewise here: I am not suggesting that work will really "end", in the sense of disappearing altogether, but rather that what was once a generally predictable link between economic growth and livelihood is becoming steadily weaker and more tenuous.

Put in a more visceral way, when I was growing up, it never crossed my mind that if I stayed clean, went to school, and "applied myself", I would not have a decent job that would support a reasonably secure and dignified life. Today that prospect is increasingly faced by more and more people, not just in the United States or the United Kingdom but throughout the world. Not just the uneducated or the "undeserving" or the "underclass", but many of the respectable and the prepared as well. In the 21st century, at the rate we are going, the **majority** of people in the post industrial societies will face that prospect. And that enormous change will have taken place not only during my lifetime but during my adulthood.

This shift, to be sure, is not altogether new. It began many decades ago in agriculture: in the US, the rapid decline of agricultural work was largely responsible for precipitating the deepening problem of the urban "underclass". What is new is that the shift is now taking place across every sector of the modern economy, and around the entire globe. Every sector, not just manufacturing but also "services", not just "traditional" industry but new, "high tech" industry; among so called "knowledge" workers as well as the unskilled and semiskilled. We talk a lot about "deindustrialization", but what we are now witnessing goes far beyond the decline of traditional blue collar industry. It is a condition of endemic labour surplus in virtually every sector of the global economy.

I think this is truly momentous for the future of global society. It will be the context for something that looks like the historic socialist dream of liberation from useless toil, or it will be the context for growing immiseration and volatility on a scale we have never seen before. Which way it goes will depend, in keeping with the theme of this conference, on the achievement of a new and radically different balance between public and private. In this case, between public and private determination of the structure and purposes of the labour market.

I am aware that these are large assertions. So let me offer some evidence. It is not hard to come by. When I first began thinking about this issue some months ago, I started with the modest idea of keeping a small file of clippings from newspapers and magazines about problems of joblessness and layoffs in various countries. Very quickly my small file began to overflow, and by now has become a small mountain of clippings which threatens to inundate my entire office. And that small mountain grows noticeably higher each week, chronicling a truly extraordinary decline of livelihood in the post industrial countries.

Consider just these recent examples of what are euphemistically called "workforce reductions", culled almost at random for the United States over the past year or so:

> General Motors, 80,000 jobs lost.
> IBM, 25,000 next year, over 125,000 total since 1986.
> Pratt & Whitney jet engines, 4800.
> Monsanto Chemical, 3200, 10% of their work force.
> Boeing Aircraft, 9000.
> Dupont Chemical, 8700.
> Apple Computer, 1800.
> Wordstar Software, 26% of the work force.
> Digital Equipment, 18,500.
> Dayton-Hudson Stores, over 1000.
> Northwest Airlines, 3200.
> United Air Lines, 2800. Announced as I boarded a United flight to come to this conference.

What is troubling about this list is not just the sheer numbers, but the **variety**. General Motors, where we are talking about the ultimate loss of tens of thousands of jobs, is no surprise. It is an example of old style, traditional, blue collar manufacturing (and a poorly managed one to boot), and the decline of big firms in those industries, while certainly devastating, is hardly news. But then there is IBM, not only a "high tech" corporation but for many years the dominant high tech corporation in the world; and also a company that, in sharp contrast to most American firms, had maintained a no layoff policy for decades. And IBM is only one of literally dozens of high tech companies sharply cutting their work force in the last several months. California's Silicon Valley, near where I live, which was supposed to be an inexhaustible well of good jobs for highly skilled, educated workers and the harbinger of the "knowledge economy", is beginning to look like an economic disaster area, as the list of companies engaging in "workforce reductions" grows as long as my arm: Apple Computer, Digital Equipment, and many others.

And then there is the service and financial sector which, of course, was supposed to be, and for a while was, the source of the new jobs that would replace the lost livelihoods of industrial America. But here on my list are also Bank of America, ITT Hartford Insurance, and many, many more.

Note too, that we are not simply talking about **failed** companies. Companies that got the deserved reputation of being "dinosaurs" in their respective industries, that could not adapt well to market changes and went under because of poor management. That description surely fits GM to a large extent, and IBM until recently. But what about Boeing Aircraft, the company that continues to dominate the world commercial aircraft industry and that indeed, for a time, was almost entirely responsible for any good news in America's balance of trade figures?

Nor is this lengthening list merely a reflection of America's peculiarly precipitous decline relative to more efficient economies. In some cases, again, that is surely **part** of our problem. But my list includes companies throughout the industrial world. In Britain the list is dismayingly similar, both in its abundance and in its variety:

British Telecom, 25,000 jobs cut.
British Aerospace, 7000.
British Petroleum, 20,000 total, 9000 over the next three years.
Barclay's Bank, 18,000 over five years.
National Westminster, 15,000.
BBC, 1,250.
Lucas Industries, another successful competitor in several of its markets, 4,000.
Rolls Royce, 950.

On the Continent the same pattern increasingly prevails. Daimler Benz, the biggest industrial corporation in Germany, 27,500 jobs to be cut. Siemens, the electronics giant, 3000 plus jobs to go in its semiconductor division. And, in a sure sign that the 1980s are really over, Perrier, bottlers of overpriced mineral water, will cut 750 jobs, over 14% of its work force.

Even in Japan, we are now seeing, for the first time in recent history, the beginnings of a labour surplus, and that surplus has had troubling ripple effects throughout Japanese society. Workforce reductions (with Nissan Motors, for example, planning to cut 4000 jobs) has prompted pressure on women to stay out of the labour force; and even pressure on the famed system of "lifetime employment".

Again, the scariest part of this trend is not the news about the collapse of old industrial dinosaurs. It is the news about job losses in some of the most successful companies around the world, including those on the cutting edge of much vaunted new technologies. Companies that have done everything right strategically and which as a result are prospering mightily, raking in growing profits and an expanding market share.

We have a particularly illuminating and particularly disturbing, recent example of this in the US, which powerfully illustrates the depth and significance of the trend toward what I am calling "post employment" capitalism. It is the case of the Compaq Computer corporation. Compaq is one of our biggest computer companies, among the first to build the so called "clones" of IBMs machines. The company developed a strong reputation for high quality products during the 1980s. In the past few years, like IBM itself, it came under huge pressure from newer clone makers that were producing at very low cost. Market share started to slide precipitously. Profits took a tumble.

Compaq responded boldly by coming out with new lines of low cost, high quality computers that successfully undercut the clone makers in price. Result? Compaq's fortunes happily reversed. The new machines are extremely successful. They quickly knocked a few of their weaker competitors out of business. Yet, the rub. In the same news article describing the company's remarkable turnaround is the announcement that Compaq plans to lay off around one thousand workers. A roughly ten per cent reduction in their work force!

Now, that is new. Especially because what is going on here is not confined to this company alone, or to one sector of the economy. Or to my country. Take the banks, for example. In the US, while banks have been laying off thousands and thousands of employees this year, and sharply reducing hours and benefits for thousands more, they have also just enjoyed their most profitable year in recent memory. American banks are making money hand over fist, and are simultaneously laying off thousands of workers.

This phenomenon, of widespread job cuts amidst success, helps explain why we in the US are now undergoing what has come to be called a "jobless recovery". Since the third quarter of 1992, the US economy, as measured by Gross Domestic Product, has generally at a quite frisky clip (reaching eight percent by some estimates), at the end of 1993. Yet unemployment overall has remained stubbornly high, and job reductions by major US companies rose to well over 2,000 a day in late 1992 and early 1993. The pace of post slump job growth in this "recovery" has been slower than in any upswing in recent memory.[1]

Now, if we could put these worldwide job losses down simply to the

69

global "recession", explaining them away as a temporary, cyclical aberration, that would be one thing. We could then argue that if we just got growth going again, we would get the jobs back. We would expect a little pain in the meantime, but after all, pain comes with the territory in "market" economies, and we all know a certain amount of insecurity is the price we pay for freedom with a capital **F**. But when strong, successful, expanding companies in the private sector as well as weak ones continue to shed employment, even in the midst of brisk economic growth, then something much deeper and far more ominous is happening.

Up to now, the trend towards "jobless growth", and the vast spectre of joblessness generally in the industrial societies, has been oddly downplayed in our public discourse. Everybody knows it exists, you can hardly avoid it if you read the newspapers. But no one seems ready to really consider its implications. In that sense, the global epidemic of joblessness is a bit like the proverbial 900 pound gorilla who comes to the dinner party. Nobody can exactly ignore its presence, but nobody really wants to **confront** it head on either.

How do we explain these trends? What exactly is going on here? I think what is going on is enormously complex. But stripped to its essentials, the most important underlying cause of the epidemic of joblessness and the ominous trend towards "jobless growth" is a massive and almost certainly **permanent** crisis of overcapacity in the private economy, overcapacity in virtually every sector of the private economy. That trend is exacerbated by other developments in specific sectors, notably by the late blooming but now very rapid introduction of labour saving technology in industries like banking and finance. But it is the overcapacity, I think, that is most fundamental, and that will prove to be the Achilles heel of the "market miracle" that was supposed to usher in a new era of global prosperity and social peace around the world.

Put simply (no doubt too simply), markets for most goods and services in the advanced societies are not growing nearly fast enough to match growth in the worldwide capacity to produce them. Especially as more and more countries around the world develop their **own** capacity to produce goods and services that were once produced by only a few of the most advanced. And it seems clear that in many cases those markets cannot grow fast enough to match the capacity to fill them. There are structural and ecological limits to how many cars you can sell, how many banks or airlines can service relatively stable populations, how many desktop computers or boxes of computer software for that matter, you can convince people they need. Or how much steel. In 1992, steel companies in the European Community were producing collectively about 140 million tons of steel, but had the capacity to produce around 190 million. That does not count the US and Brazilian and Korean producers nipping at their heels. This despite recent significant increases in demand for steel for construction in Eastern Europe. And despite years of brutal "restructuring" that has already taken place in that industry, which has laid waste to whole cities in both Britain and America.

Again, this is surely **partly** a cyclical phenomenon that could improve, to an extent, with the end of the global recession (if there is an end to the global recession). But the over arching problem remains: that there is a limit to how many steel companies (or airline companies or computer companies) can successfully coexist in the global economy. Thus the need for all of them, if they wish to stay competitive, to "downsize". To cut costs by figuring out how to produce more efficiently with fewer workers and, more generally, to shrink to fit the realities of markets growing far more slowly than capacity.

That is the overriding logic behind most of the mass job cuts in most economic sectors in the US. With the exception of some industries like banking, it is not so much, nowadays, that huge numbers of jobs are being lost because of the introduction of new labour saving technology. In manufacturing that looked like the wave of the future some years ago, but seems to have generally "peaked" today. What is more often going on is simpler. On the one hand, a shrinking process, as more and more companies wake up to the hard realities of endemic overcapacity and glutted markets; on the other, the desperate need to cut costs to the bone in order to be one of the survivors in that relatively stagnant market. A market that is accordingly characterized by the most brutal competition in memory. That is what, for example, happened at Compaq Computer. What Compaq's management said they were doing was what some called "pre-emptive cost cutting": they were already well ahead of the pack, but they dumped 1000 workers in order to ensure that they **stayed** there.

I could spin out examples on and on. But the basic point is this. It is now the inherent logic of the global market economy to "shed" employment. It sheds employment now principally because of an intrinsic tendency towards endemic overcapacity. A tendency which, in a classic irony of market logic, can only worsen as companies become more efficient at doing what they are in business to do.

To be sure, we can envision some ways out of this conundrum. For example, we can envision a respite from endemic overcapacity because of potentially expanding markets in the former Soviet Union and Eastern Europe, or in the Third World. However, for a variety of reasons, I do not believe even this expansion can alter the long run trend, although

71

properly managed development in those areas could certainly slow it down. In the long run, there is, there can be, **no private sector solution** to the crisis of overcapacity. Nor therefore a private sector solution to the inevitable social crises which that trend is already bringing and which will worsen in the future. Namely, mass exclusion from meaningful work; the resulting declining income and social well being; rising poverty among increasing numbers denied access to livelihood, and a widening gulf between them and those who are able to cling to the remaining stable and well rewarded jobs; social pathology and social conflict on an unprecedented scale.

Now I have to admit, the idea that the private market cannot solve the looming crisis of joblessness is not exactly universally accepted. On the contrary, in the US at least, there is an astonishing myopia about the ability of "market forces" to resolve that crisis. Albeit maybe later rather than sooner, and perhaps requiring the help of some strategic government intervention, but nevertheless the solution is somewhere down the road. There is among our politicians and pundits a sort of ideologically driven optimism on this issue that I find almost schizophrenic in its detachment from the evidence. An optimism that reflects the degree to which, in America, our political culture and economic discourse is suffused by a nearly religious faith in market solutions to all problems.

There are two main approaches to the job crisis dominant nowadays in the US, and in **other** countries too. With desperate brevity and at the risk of losing some of the real world complexity of the political debate, let me call them the "free market" and the "neoliberal"[2] models; or conservative and interventionist models.

The conservative or neoclassical refrain on these matters is familiar and holds few surprises, the market knows best. Indeed, the more extreme proponents of this view would argue that there can be no prolonged mass joblessness as long as we leave the market alone to adjust the price of labour to the demand. As long as we "clear" the markets for labour, as they say, by such devices as getting rid of pesky union rules and minimum wages and social and health benefits, and so on, that artificially raise the cost of labour and restrict its "flexibility". Do enough of that, and pretty soon everybody will be back at work.

Well, there are lots of technical reasons why that assumption will not work, but in the interests of time let me skip over those and just look at the real world for a moment to see the utter failure of this argument. The most revealing negative example is the United States itself. We are, after all, the country that has put the free market model of employment policy into practice most consistently among the industrial nations, a fact which our corporate leaders and our business press rarely fail to celebrate. We have the weakest unions and the fewest job protections. We have the most meagre benefits, and the most "flexible" workforce, i.e., the one most vulnerable to dislocation and reshuffling by their employers at will. (Whenever I see that word "flexible" used to describe the workforce I am seized by a vision of workers being bent into pretzel shapes by their employers, probably a fairly accurate image.) We have also recently had relatively low and falling wages compared to most of our economic competitors.

We put the market model into practice, in other words, more fully than anyone else in the developed world. Yet we maintain a stunning official unemployment rate of nearly 8 per cent at this writing, and a real rate of "nonemployment"[3] probably closer to 14 per cent. Among the highest in the advanced economies. To the extent that we have achieved significant job growth, we have done so at the expense of wages and benefits, creating what is increasingly described as a "low wage, high turnover" economy (Marshall and Tucker 1993), characterized by escalating numbers of the working poor.

In short, we have tried the market strategy from the beginning, and in the twelve years under Reagan and Bush we radically intensified it. But our labour market is a disaster area, and the steady weakening of prospects for decent jobs and dignified wages ripples outward to exacerbate problems from homelessness to violence to drug abuse.

What about the neoliberal alternative? Well, it is an improvement. The neoliberal model recognizes the theoretical and social failure of the free market approach and lays out a strategy which is indeed better, but which in my view, does not challenge or much alter the overarching trend toward endemic joblessness.

Simply put, the assumption driving this model is that much of the job problem, and indeed many of the troubles of a generally floundering economy, derives essentially from a mismatch between workers' skills and the needs of the growing "knowledge" economy. We have far too many relatively uneducated and unskilled people who are increasingly being marginalized. Because, while they were useful in the days when unskilled or semiskilled labour powered our industrial machine, they cannot compete in an economy more and more dominated by jobs requiring high skills, by what Robert Reich (1992), Clinton's new Labour Secretary and the most thoughtful theorist in this vein, calls "symbolic analysis".

The remedy then is essentially an educational one. You improve the schools generally so that our students no longer rank toward the bottom in international comparisons. You develop apprenticeship programs and

73

otherwise improve what we call the "school to work transition". You get private companies to invest more in training and retraining workers.

All of this, I hasten to say, is to the good. These strategies, if done well, are both useful and necessary and will indeed improve the quality of life, the efficiency and competitiveness of the economy, and the quality of work, as far as they go. But, for reasons that should by now be clear, they do not go far enough. As my list indicates all too clearly, the reality is that we are shedding employment around the world in the so called "knowledge economy", the realm of the "symbolic analyst", just as fast and sometimes faster, than we are losing jobs for less skilled labour. Remember Compaq Computer. In 1992 Compaq's share of the US market for personal computers increased by nearly fifty per cent. And the number of engineers it employed **fell** by twenty per cent.

The global economy is simply not reliably generating the virtually unlimited numbers of "symbolic" jobs that are at least implicity (in Reich explicitly) assumed in the neoliberal model, but tending to diminish them or, at the very least, not to produce enough of them to counter the galloping losses in other sectors. So there is "jobless growth" in the "information economy" too. This helps explain why many of my students graduating from the prestigious flagship of California's public university system can not find a job to save their lives. Or why eleven per cent of recent British graduates describe themselves as "desperate for a job". Or why a whopping twenty eight per cent of recent Australian graduates are "looking for work".

Turning that situation around via the private economy, through market mechanisms, can only happen if there is either a rapid expansion of markets for existing goods and services in the "knowledge" economy or a sudden emergence of new technologies that could underpin the rise of truly vast new markets. Could either of those happen? Sure, in theory. But I am sceptical. Just as with steel, there are limits to the number of computer software or cellular communication companies, for example, that can coexist even in a generally expanding market. Software, for example, is still an expanding market, and we in the US already dominate it. But it is not adding significant employment, and indeed as the industry gets deeper and deeper into its current, extremely brutal "shakeout", there will probably be less.

All of this gets very technical and somewhat speculative. But I think the bottom line, in a nutshell, is that the scale of new markets, or of new employment generating technologies, would need to be truly enormous to offset the inherent market driven tendencies to overcapacity and hence to endemic joblessness. Thus there is no "knowledge society" or "information economy" solution to the problem of jobless growth. None, at least, within the confines of a fundamentally private labour market. Again, the neoliberal approach is both more rational and more humane than the conservative one. We would indeed, if it were strongly put into practice (as it **may** be by the Clinton administration), see a better match of human capacities to economic needs. For those who got the better training and the better jobs, there would be better wages and an improved quality of life. And we would compete better in the global economy. But all of this within the generally shrinking structure of livelihood in both the national and global economies.

Neither the conservative nor the neoliberal solutions then, can get us out of the looming crisis of post employment capitalism. There is a country not far from here that stands, in fact, as an ominous rebuke to both models. It is called Ireland. Ireland **should** fit the free market model, because it is a relatively low wage country.[4] And it ought to bear out the neoliberal model too, because it also has an unusually well educated workforce, with higher rates of college completion than most industrial countries. And indeed, on one level, the models work as they are supposed to. Ireland attracts a lot of foreign investment, according to *Fortune* magazine, 1000 new companies in the first half of 1992 alone. There is only one problem: none of this has much dented the country's twenty per cent official unemployment rate, the highest in Western Europe. What you have in Ireland, in short, is a great "business climate", and a great workforce full of highly educated "knowledge workers", better than one in five of whom is out of work.

What, then, would be a solution? Is there one? Yes, if, and **only** if, we shift the balance, in the determination of the shape of the labour market, away from the private sector to the public. There is much room for new thinking here, and I will not now try to suggest anything like a detailed blueprint. But it seems to me that there are basically two necessary elements of such a shift.

One is the development of stronger and more aggressive public mechanisms to ensure that the work that remains in the private economy at the end of the process of global "downsizing" is more equitably shared. That implies legislation mandating shorter, perhaps far shorter, work hours; shorter days, shorter weeks, shorter work years, coupled with national level commitments guaranteeing access to work for all. The benefits are many and obvious. We would harness the trend toward declining work to the progressive goal of reducing onerous labour, rather than allowing it to drive us into the regressive slide toward mass joblessness, the proliferation of useless low wage work, and the spread of

75

social impoverishment. We would free workers to devote more time to other aspects of their lives, reduce stress and mitigate the conflict between work and family life. All this allows us both to work less and to enable all to participate in work's benefits; it maximizes inclusion while minimizing degrading and useless toil. But it requires, again, public mechanisms to bring it about. You can bet that private firms will not do it on their own.

The second public sphere mechanism to reverse the crisis of joblessness, and to turn the trend toward greater productivity in a progressive rather than regressive direction, is a very significant expansion of the public and nonprofit sectors of the economy. The principle is as simple and urgent as it is unfashionable. As we develop the capacity to produce far more in the private economy than could ever possibly be consumed, we need to tap that excess capacity and siphon it off to strengthen and expand those public institutions that meet essential human needs. In a country like the United States, where an already meagre public sector has been savaged almost beyond recognition in recent years under the impact of the far Right, that shift is of course especially urgent and the needs especially compelling. We could employ vast numbers of people who are now excluded from real economic citizenship to rebuild our rotting infrastructure, staff our crumbling urban and rural schools, rebuild our collapsed public health care system, build and maintain affordable housing, provide child care, and much, much more. But even in countries with a greater historical commitment to the public sector and a less savage recent assault on public institutions there is much to be gained by a shift from idled, or mindless, private sector labour to employing a far greater proportion of the work force in public tasks, enhancing the social and physical infrastructure, tending the environment, and more.

Perhaps ironically, the decline of work in the private economy, the "end" of the sort of work that is shaped by market rather than human imperatives, frees us, for the first time, to think about the "end" of work in another sense. The other sense that I wanted my title to suggest: the **purpose** of work. If human energies are more and more freed **from** toil for profit in the private economy, they are freed **to** be directed toward goals that we can set publicly and democratically. We get to think about what work is **for** beyond simple economic survival, beyond just getting up in the morning and going to your "job" because that is what people have always done, and beyond the silly accumulation of more and more consumer goods, in a way that would have been impossible before the "post employment" era. That is the great opportunity before us, if we are able to force it into being.

I say "force it" advisedly. Moving in this direction will be a very tough road indeed. Today the fashionable thrust is of course in the opposite direction. From Leningrad to Lima, from Liverpool to Los Angeles, the popular ideology says we ought to be **abolishing** the public sector, not increasing it. Public sector employment is understood in the conventional wisdom as being the villain, not the saviour; the problem, not the solution. "Everyone" knows we have to get rid of "inefficient" public enterprises and shrink "bloated" public payrolls. (The private sector is never described as "bloated," even when it demonstrably is.) There will be fierce and concerted effort to derail any movement to resolve the crisis of joblessness by expanding public work or by expanding the public sphere's influence over hitherto sacrosanct private matters like the hours of labour.

For us, what I think that means is that we must begin, sooner rather than later, to build global democratic organizations strong enough to match forces with the captains of the global marketplace. That is going to be a tough job, an immensely tough job, and one that offers huge challenges for a revitalized Democratic left. But I do not see any alternative way to begin to deal with the spectre of endemic worldwide joblessness or the social chaos and needless deprivation it must inevitably bring.

Almost exactly 109 years ago, in January 1884, William Morris, the great English socialist, gave a speech in Manchester, in which he already confronted these issues in a way that I think is startlingly apropos for us today. The speech was his classic discourse on *Useful Work versus Useless Toil*. In it Morris describes, back in 1884, how advancing technology had reached a point where most of what we really **need** in life can be produced by relatively few people. That development, Morris says, **should** have made all our lives richer and easier. But it has not. Morris stated back then:

> Surely we ought, one and all of us, to be wealthy, to be well furnished with the good things which our victory over nature has won for us. [But instead] The fruits of our victory over nature have been stolen from us (Morton 1973, pp. 86-108).

Stolen because the organization of work was still driven by private profit rather than the goal of civilization and liberation of human energies. Instead of working life getting better, vast numbers of people were employed at "useless" toil, making junk that no one needed and working themselves to death doing so, while others grew poorer and poorer, and sicker and sicker, because they had no work at all. But, Morris said, were we to take the truly useful work that was actually required to provide for our real needs and share it, we would soon discover that "the share of

77

work which each would have to do would be but small...we shall have labour power to spare". It will, he said, "be easy to live".

It will be easy to live. What a simple, but also absolutely revolutionary thought. And he went on. Once we begin working "for livelihood", rather than working to "supply the demand of the profit market", we would not only stop living lives which, he said, were now "scared and anxious as the life of a hunted beast", but in a more positive sense, we would also "have time to look round and consider what we really do want".

Another simple but thoroughly visionary idea, spoken before the dawn of the 20th century. But not a bad goal for the 21st.

Notes

1. Economic Report of the President 1994, Chapter 3.

2. I am using "neoliberal" in its American sense, which very roughly describes the economic strategy of the Clinton administration; a modicum of government intervention overlaid on a basic commitment to market principles.

3. Nonemployment meaning those officially unemployed and those who have dropped out of the labour force and are no longer looking for work.

4. An Irish worker averages roughly $11 US dollars an hour in total compensation, versus over $15 for the US, $19 for Britain, $22 for Germany.

5 Are prisons part of the public sphere? Privatization and the problem of legitimacy

Richard Sparks

The problem: the public faces of a 'private' institution

Controversies over the definition of the public interest in criminal justice are nowhere more intense than in the problem of imprisonment. At least since Sykes (1958) defined the central paradox of the prison as lying in its status as an autocracy within a democratic polity (though that awareness can be dated back to de Tocqueville), commentators on penal politics have been preoccupied with issues of secrecy, accountability and justification in the use of the prison sanction.[1] In Sykes's view prison administrators hold "a grant of power without equal" (Sykes 1958, p.42) in liberal democracies. Consequently any elaboration of the problems of imprisonment and the prospects for penal change must take place in the shadow of the awareness that the prison is in a rather fundamental and irrevocable sense an "authoritarian community" (ibid. p.133).

By contrast Habermas's classic definition of the "public sphere" envisages a space of unconstrained communication (Habermas 1989, p.36). Whatever else prisons may be, and however much one seeks to construct programmes for changing or democratizing their mode of operation, they do not look much like **that**. In these obvious ways there would appear to be some rather drastic problems in situating prisons within any democratically constituted public arena. By tradition, and perhaps by necessary implication, they are sequestered, apart and in these senses "private" places. Moreover, as David Garland has pointed out, such

79

inherent tendencies may if anything have been accentuated in recent times given the development of specialist cadres of administrators and their associated quasi-technical managerial vocabularies:

> The social tasks involved in punishment have been delegated to specialized agencies on the margins of social life, with the effect that they have to some extent become hidden...What was once an open, ritualized dialogue between the offender and the community is now a much more oblique communication carried out in institutions which give little expression to the public voice. Our practices of punishment have ceased to be social in the full sense and have become increasingly technical and professional. (Garland 1990, pp.186-7)

This appears to me to be both true and rather far reaching in its implications. One of these (on which I intend to concentrate) is that we tend systematically to neglect or forget the public dimensions of imprisonment. Simply put, the fact that the practice of imprisonment takes place in the hands of professional specialists behind closed doors serves to obscure the equally important sense in which it is the conclusion of an inherently public series of transactions between the offending citizen and the state. It seems to me that these ways in which the public face of imprisonment is concealed, and its professional/managerial aspect correspondingly emphasized, have been used to lend weight to arguments favouring the privatization or "contracting out" of prison management. That is, where the whole of the issue has been predefined as one of efficient and cost effective administration (as I will go on to show has been the case) it can plausibly be said to be a matter of little consequence whether the administrators themselves are directly employed by the state or not, in some strong versions of the case [2] it can even be maintained that it is preferable that they should not be.

The resulting administrative focus threatens to exclude normative political considerations altogether, indeed to such an extent that some otherwise perceptive commentators on privatization express bafflement that they should be raised at all.[3] I want to maintain a contrary (in fact a diametrically opposite) view, namely that there are conclusive arguments against prison privatization. But these do not lie, as has conventionally been argued hitherto, principally either in the alleged inferiority or lesser competence of private management or in the imputed immorality of making money out of prisons, though neither of these can be discounted (Ryan and Ward 1989). Rather, I want to address the privatization debate

80

on what I take to be a more fundamental level by querying the primacy which privatization enthusiasts accord to administrative and consequentialist concerns. For the dominance of such arguments leads us to take for granted what needs to be shown, namely the conditions governing the legitimacy of the prison sanction as such. And this, I will conclude, returns us irretrievably to the obscured but nonetheless intrinsic "public" character of imprisonment.

In some recent discussion (though not that to which the British Government attends) the problem of legitimacy has returned to haunt penal politics (Sparks 1994). This has two distinct aspects. The first concerns the observed tendency of western penal systems to expand during precisely the same period that has seen the received justifications for their existence subjected to the most sustained conceptual and empirical challenges. This is the context for what Garland calls the "crisis of penological modernism" (1990, p.7). The resulting "legitimacy deficit" (Beetham 1991, p.20) begs the question "Under what conditions is the imposition of a prison sentence normatively defensible?"; a question which the privatization arguments tend to displace as being none of their concern, because it relates to decisions which are deliberated elsewhere. Such a view rests on a sharp separation between the application and the administration of justice and it is for the proponents of privatization to show that such a separation holds in principle rather than as a matter of habit and assertion. Similarly the burden also rests on them to demonstrate that they have a conception of penal purposes which answers the courts' intentions in imposing a sentence.

The second aspect of the problem of legitimacy relates to the internal order of prisons and their deployment of power. The deprivation of liberty (and the attendant "pains of imprisonment") and the imposition of other compulsions (by force in the last instance) on unwilling subjects necessarily stand in strong need of justification. The history of riot and rebellion in prisons[4] suggests, to put it at its mildest, that prisoners do not always respond compliantly to such compulsion. Advocates of privatization tend to argue, when they acknowledge the issue at all, that in providing improved conditions for prisoners they will have minimized the provocations that give rise to such protests. But this is too slight an answer to the underlying question "On what grounds can the internal order of the prison claim justified authority?". As Beetham puts the issue in another context, no exercise of state power can escape problems of legitimation:

Moreover, the form of power which is distinctive to [the political domain] - organised physical coercion - is one that stands supremely

81

in need of legitimation, yet uniquely is able to breach all legitimacy. The legitimation of the state's power is thus both specially urgent and fateful in its consequences. (Beetham 1991, p.40)

The powers involved in imprisonment are a particularly vexed case in point of the relations between state and subject and one whose outcomes can be very bloody.[5] It is arguable that this represents a qualitative difference between the privatization of prisons and most other privatizations, and it remains to be shown whether those who advocate the private management of prisons have answered the point adequately.

I therefore suggest, contrary to the tone and momentum of the current "debate", that it is only by addressing certain basic issues of theoretical principle (to which I return below) that we can attain any clear understanding of the relation between the prison sanction and the public political sphere. It is in this spirit that I now turn to review the arguments for and against private sector involvement in prison management.

The present context: the suddenness of privatization

Any account of the current state of play in British penal debates must be conscious of the rapidity with which the contracting out of prison management has emerged as a favoured official stance. In a sense, therefore, much recent commentary, even a document as influential as the Woolf inquiry into the 1990 disturbances (Woolf 1991), is already obsolete. It is so to the extent that it continues to conceive of the problems of the prison systems of the UK (and their related diagnoses and policy proposals) as essentially those of a unitary state-administered system. It is nigh on impossible to achieve the kind of patient scholarly appraisal which the seriousness of recent penal problems in Britain is widely regarded as necessitating in a period when the very terms of the debate are in a state of such rapid flux. In embracing privatization as suddenly and whole heartedly as now appears to be the case the Government has "moved the goalposts" in the same sense that the San Andreas fault "moves" San Francisco. Such radicalism has plainly wrongfooted many of the penal system's traditional critics, leaving them apparently addressing yesterday's issues and responding to the privatization initiative either with a flat *a priori* repudiation or with an *ad hoc* shopping list of peripheral quibbles (a tension with which bodies such as the Howard League for Penal Reform currently find themselves saddled). This leaves the privatization lobby (of which the Home Office itself must now be reckoned a member) in a

82

tactically strong position, for this is where the radicalism appears to lie, and some of the most acute critics of privatization openly confess the potential embarrassment of being backed into the corner of seeming to defend the ramshackle and unaccountable edifice of the *status quo* (Ryan and Ward 1990, p.47).

A brief chronology of the key moments in the move towards privatization indicates its building momentum. As late as 1987 it was possible for the then Home Secretary, Douglas Hurd, speaking in the House of Commons, to deny, in good faith as far as we know, that there was any prospect of the delegation of prison management to private agencies on the horizon.[6] Yet 1987 also saw the beginnings of serious intellectual advocacy of privatization in Britain, first by the Adam Smith Institute (Young, 1987) and second in a report by some members of the House of Commons Home Affairs Select Committee following a visit to private facilities in the US (House of Commons, 1987). At this point most commentators sympathetic to privatization, such as Sir Edward Gardiner [7] were at pains to explain that they were calling only for "experimental" initiatives and only in the context of the remand system (Fulton 1989, Gardiner 1989). Their hopes for a sympathetic hearing by the Home office were to this extent realized in the publication in 1988 of the Green Paper *Private Sector Involvement in the Remand System* (Home Office 1988).

During the next couple of years these positions (experimental initiatives confined to the remand, escorting and ancillary functions) were quietly consolidated. The underlying argument that there were fundamental distinctions in principle between the provision of services for unconvicted and convicted prisoners convinced many (perhaps including many of those who gave evidence to Lord Justice Woolf to the effect that the practice of holding remand and sentenced prisoners together was inherently detrimental to the interests of the former). In 1990 the Government announced its intention to experiment with contracted out management of the proposed new remand centre at the Wolds on Humberside. The key developmental moment occurred during the passage of the government's Criminal Justice Bill (subsequently the *Criminal Justice Act* 1991), which contained the enabling power for contracting out of remand and escort services. At the report stage of the legislation a clause was added (s.84(3)) empowering the Home Secretary to delete the references to remands from the original provision. This brilliant expedient had the effect that in principle any prison, or indeed the whole of the prison system, could be turned over to private management through application of the affirmative resolution procedure.[8] It may be of little consequence to argue that this provided a slender legislative basis for so large a change of policy, or to point out that it entailed an obvious stratgem for minimizing debate. Evidently it suggested that the Government had adopted a *parti pris* in favour of contracting out and designed to allow it maximum discretion to do so at will.

During 1992 the Wolds remand centre opened, "experimentally", and a research team from the University of Hull was commissioned to evaluate its operation. But well before the researchers had reported, tenders for other prisons, holding sentenced as well as remand prisoners, had been invited. These included the new facility at Blakenhurst, near Redditch and, symbolically, the newly refurbished Strangeways. Home Office ministers began to speak merrily of a "mixed economy" of penal provision. The Prison Service was to be accorded a more autonomous "Agency Status" (in line with Woolf's views), in advance of which all senior managers were to have their positions "market tested". At the turn of the year the Director General Mr Pilling (in post for less than two years) found himself replaced by Mr Derek Lewis, a television executive with no previous prison experience appointed at twice his predecessor's salary (*The Guardian* 22 December 1992, p.3). In keeping with the general governmental aversion to serious public discussion of these issues the latter announcement came during the news famine of Christmas week (on the same day that George Bush chose to give a free pardon to Caspar Weinberger). Thus the then Home Secretary Kenneth Clarke's "defence" of his decisions (*The Independent* 22 December 1992, p.17) was in effect the presentation of a *fait accompli*.

In his article Mr Clarke denied that there was any legitimate grounds for controversy over these decisions, they were those of a hard headed pragmatic meliorist:

> The service I require on behalf of the taxpayer, the public and the prisoner, is effective custody, enlightened regimes and a genuine reformative content delivered efficiently at a reasonable cost. I have no **ideological prejudice** about whether those standards are delivered by public sector or private sector employees. There is no public interest or policy reason why the prison service should not have to demonstrate that it can compete with the private sector in delivering decent conditions and a quality regime, day in day out, at a price which demonstrates good value for money.
>
> (*The Independent*, loc. cit. emphasis mine)

Of course this modest proposal is really a spectacular coup. Logically, a denial of "ideological prejudice" as flat and declaratory as this is a denial that any directly employed public sector is in principle necessary at all, and there is nothing here that would inhibit the contracting out of the system *in toto*. Meanwhile, the characterization of any contrary argument as a "prejudice" forecloses all discussion; so long as they deliver on their contracts, private prisons and progressive penal change are here identified as one and the same thing. The argument has become entirely consequentialist (no matter that seriously to demand that prisons demonstrate "value for money" would be a much more subversive propsal than Mr Clarke intends). There are no intellectual, constitutional or juridical issues at stake. They do not matter. They are "prejudices".

Intellectual advocacy of privatization: Logan and the dominance of consequentialism

In that the Home Office position is so intellectually totalitarian it is necessary to look elsewhere for a more principled account of the arguments in favour of privatization. Not all those who advocate the contracting out of prison management are so chary about acknowledging that there is a moral and ideological dispute at stake. Thus Charles Logan (the most eloquent and disinterested of the American proponents) asserts quite clearly:

> The privatization of corrections, or punishment, is an especially significant part of the broader privatization movement. By challenging the government's monopoly over one of its ostensible "core" functions, this idea directly threatens the assumption that certain activities are essentially and necessarily governmental. (Logan 1990, p.4)

On this basis Logan presents a shrewd and beguiling case. He never denies that private prisons generate and encounter moral and practical problems, only that these are not directly to do with their private or "contractual" character:

> It is primarily because they are prisons, not because they are contractual, that private operations face challenges of authority, legitimacy, procedural justice, accountability, liability, cost, security, safety, corruptibility and so on. Because they raise no problems that are both unique and insurmountable, private prisons should be allowed to compete (and cooperate) with government

85

agencies so that we can discover how best to run prisons that are safe, secure, humane, efficient and just. (Logan 1990, p.5)

This is a far more developed and convincing version of the argument. Provided we accept i) a certain definition of the responsibilities of the state (broadly that it is there to see to it that certain tasks are carried out) and ii) that imprisonment is such a "function", then the delivery of that task by certain delegated agents becomes unproblematic. So it is that in the American context the argument has won over some noted political liberals such as Governor Mario Cuomo. Perhaps indeed there is no specifically **liberal** counter argument.

In essence the liberal-consequentialist view has three main strands:

1. *Purchasers and providers*: It is an axiom of classical economics that wherever possible the purchasers and providers of services should be distinct. Where the state divests itself of the role of provider it ceases to find itself in the embarrassment of having to both justify and inspect its own performance and frees itself from the claims of the "vested interests" of its own employees. It becomes instead a rational consumer in an undistorted market, purposively seeking out the best services at the cheapest price.

2. *The stimulus of competition*: It follows, on this view, that efficiency is inherently advanced by the resulting competition. Instead of allocating its budget to itself the state has in its gift a valuable contract for which others must compete, on terms which the state is free to specify. This breaks down the inertia and restrictive practices of managers and unions. The state shops around, thereby stimulating innovation. Contracts are time-limited. On termination tendering is repeated, and contracts are again allocated to whomever makes the best bid at the time.

3. *Accountability and the destruction of the public sector monolith*: In the view of privatization proponents the above processes necessarily enhance the public accountability of the system in question. It is no longer defensive. The state loses the propensity to conceal or gloss over its own failures. Instead it ruthlessly polices its contractors for signs of inefficiency or abuse. Rather than find himself in the dock on the basis of occasional civil litigation by individual prisoners the Home Secretary becomes in effect their ally and advocate, free to prosecute the contracting company for any breach of contract or

86

legality. Moreover, contractual arrangements are inherently explicit and actionable where governmental administrative procedures are commonly permissive and discretionary. Oversight and monitoring are thereby facilitated and accountability increased.

Taken together these views present an attractive case. Clearly they have convinced Mr Clarke when he argues that:

> To me this is the final answer to the moral question. It cannot be more moral to lock up prisoners for long hours a day with little chance to associate, limited opportunity for visits and little access to work, education or PE than to see them unlocked all day with access to a full programme of useful activities, simply because the poor programme is provided by staff directly employed by the state and the better programme by staff employed by a contractor of the state. (*The Independent* 22 December 1992)

This then in Mr Clarke's view is the whole of the argument, the prison which provides the better material conditions just **is** the better prison. It is assumed that the private sector is inherently better able to provide such conditions, indeed the terms on which their contracts are awarded will ensure that they do so. In the unlikely event that they do not then the mechanisms of competition will weed them out. Thus the "final answer" to the moral argument is an entirely consequentialist answer. It is notable though that Clarke leaves the accountability strand of the argument, beloved of the more ideologically principled privatizers such as Logan (and the argument best calculated to weaken the defences of penal liberals), out of the account. That is, even on a purely consequentialist account not all the consequences appear to be equally important. The "final answer" has already been arrived at on the basis of costs and quantitative regime conditions alone, without reference to questions of public accountability or the enhancement of prisoners' individual and collective rights.

I propose to argue against these positions on the risky procedure of accepting most of their propositions. Let us suppose that there is no inherent reason to think that private contractors will be less efficient, less competent or less prudent in their operations than their state counterparts (leaving on one side unresolved questions about experience, selection, vetting, ethnic minority recruitment, training and organisational complexity).[9] Let us indeed imagine a prison system which is materially improved in exactly the ways that Mr Clarke anticipates.

87

I suggest that there would still be outstanding arguments against the contracting out of prisons which are powerful enough to be seen as conclusive. That is, the pro-privatization case may be correct in points of detail but still not touch the main concerns in the arguments about the nature of state punishment and the justifications for imprisonment. If I am correct it misconceives what is really at stake politically, ideologically and economically in the operation of penal systems.

Three objections to privatization

Before returning in conclusion to the underlying issues of principle which attend the legitimation of any penal system let me outline three specific sets of objections to privatization intiatives as they have so far transpired.

Sentencing practices and prison populations:

a) Is privatization wedded to growth in the prison population? Privatization moves have to date only occurred in earnest in the Western industrial states in those jurisdictions which have experienced the most prolonged and severe problems of high prison populations and high overcrowding, namely, the US, Canada and Great Britain. These are also, not accidentally, the countries where free market political experiments have been furthest advanced. That is, the necessary prior context for the privatization argument to take hold is one which combines a certain dominant view of the role of the state (of the kind which Logan advocates)[10] with a sensed state of emergency or "crisis" in the penal system. Within the US, formerly the world leader in private prisons but about to be rapidly displaced by the UK, the majority of private facilities are concentrated in certain predominantly southern states; Tennessee, Texas, Florida, New Mexico, Kentucky, which have combined particularly severe penal problems with especially acute fiscal difficulties. If privatization only gains momentum and plausibility under the pressure of such contingencies does this compromise its general claims to offer a preferable model for the future of prison systems as such?

Thus privatization offers itself as a policy solution in those situations where prison populations are regarded as escaping willed political control. The private prisons lobby is able to advertise itself as a) easing the fiscal burden on overstretched justice systems and b) providing additional prison capacity rapidly and flexibly. As Lilly and Knepper (1992a, and see below) have shown, serious corporate money will only flow into those

88

systems where feasibility studies suggest a consistent long term return on investments. If one takes the analogy of private provision in health care, the strength of the case rests on an assumption of demand for a certain "good" which is in principle indefinitely large and which in any case outstrips the state's capacity to provide.

Significantly, a favoured term of privatization advocates to indicate their usefulness to the public system and public purse is "supplement" (Fulton 1989, Logan 1990), they address themselves to a perceived shortfall in the state's capacity to fulfill a need, premised on a positivistic equation between an assumed rising crime rate and consequent demand for expanded penal capacity. This defies two important criminological principles, namely a) that prison populations and crime rates are at least semi-autonomous (Young 1988, Muncie and Sparks 1991, Mathiesen 1991), and b) that "supplementarity" is a primary mechanism whereby penal systems expand (Cohen 1985, Nelken 1989) their range and penetration. This contrasts sharply with the lack of interest in privatization in those countries which have more deliberately and successfully chosen to limit penal expansion (Downes 1988, McConville 1990). For these reasons privatization makes sense only where one means to accept a prison estate at or above its present size. Or as the promotional literatures for the private prison contractors more eloquently have it: "As a nation we have an unprecedented need to acquire new prisons and jails" (E.F. Hutton); "The Fastest Way to Put Offenders Behind Bars" (Kellman Industries); "Gelco Space Solves Overcrowding" (Gelco Space).[11]

b) Is privatization wedded to "warehousing"? More speculatively, one might argue that there is an elective affinity between the provision of privately managed prisons and particular philosophies of sentencing. The sentencing principle most commonly espoused to date by private interests in the USA in their advertising is that of incapacitation. Lilly and Knepper (1992b, p.49) document the production of spurious cost-benefit analyses purporting to show the economic effectiveness of extended detention.[12] More generally the separation of punitive from managerial tasks implicit in the privatization argument leads to a focus on the provision of adequate space in which humanely to contain: "We help separate the outside world from the inside world" (Electronic Control Security Inc). To this extent privatization tends to reinforce the more general drift, identified most eloquently by Garland (1990, p.186) towards normalized containment or "warehousing" (alternatively termed by Peters (1986) the "batchprocessing of aggregate phenomena") as a primary feature of the new penality. Indeed at least one US correctional company has constructed a prison quite literally in a converted warehouse so as to facilitate its reconversion to other uses in the event of unprofitability (Weiss 1989, p.31). Others such as Space Master Enterprises use rapidly assembled modular and prefabricated system building methods (Lilly and Knepper 1992b, p.46). In this sense privatization is arguably intrinsically tied to what a number of radical critics have identified as a key function of contemporary penality, namely the containment of "surplus" or dangerous populations (Box and Hale 1985, Mathiesen 1990).

Thus it is on the face of it ironic that the privatization movement in the UK receives its legislative *imprimatur* within the *Criminal Justice Act* 1991. In theory the sentencing provisions of the Act are aimed at limiting prison use, in part by reducing the range of justifications which courts may use in determining sentence. The Act professes to encourage sentencers to use prison as a scarce resource. Yet the smuggling in of the privatization clauses subverts this intention, threatening to allow the prison population to resume its upward trajectory. (If one were a deconstructionist one might suggest that the legislation is in this sense self-sublating.)

The economics of private prisons and the problem of accountability:

a) Is there a "corrections-commercial complex"? Lilly and Knepper (1992b) use the term "corrections-commercial complex" by analogy with Eisenhower's prescient warning of the influence of the "military-industrial complex". Indeed, they point out, the similarity between the political economy of defence and of imprisonment is more than passing in that a number of the key corporate players in the private prisons industry are literally defence contractors looking to diversify in the aftermath of the end of the Cold War (1992a, p.184). The two positions are strikingly comparable. In each territory there is only one domestic customer (the state, or in the US the individual states and the federal government) plus the obvious export markets (other states). The state contracts for what it regards as a vital function. It thus develops close relations of mutual dependency with its contractors and these of necessity are continuing.[13] The companies are politically and economically significant, and they lobby adeptly. Companies of such importance can reasonably expect the state to provide them with reasonably stable market conditions (just as they explore the most propitious overseas markets, for example the emergent capitalist economies of the Pacific Rim and Eastern Europe). Consequently Lilly and Knepper ridicule the notion of perfect competition regularly espoused by privatization advocates as being absurdly unconnected with

90

real conditions. The corrections market is in fact characterized by a single purchaser, a small number of highly capitalized transnational providers and a body of end of the line consumers uniquely unable to exercise purchasing choices (the prisoners). Far from Logan's optimistic vision of a state free to hire and fire contractors at will in the event of unsatisfactory performance or a reduction in demand, the more likely outcome is one of high level dependency on a small number of near monopoly providers.

b) Is this a "sub-governmental system"? What results in such market conditions is a routine exchange of expertise and personnel between government agencies and corporate contractors. In Lilly and Knepper's view this exchange can be characterized as constituting a "sub-governmental system" (1992b, p.45). Governmental and private experts interact regularly and in private, and identify the outcomes of the mutual deliberations as constituting the public interest. Contractors are privy to long-range governmental planning; governments are obligated to protect their contractors' commercial privilege. Non-statutory professional associations such as the American Correctional Association provide influential forums for both policy discussion and social exchange, and a number of commentators have noted the care taken by private sector opinion formers to achieve leading roles within the ACA (Ryan and Ward 1989, Lilly and Knepper 1992b). In sum, Lilly and Knepper argue;

> Reliance on ACA standards by government agencies and private contractors promotes a close working relationship between the ACA, government agencies and private companies. Essentially this means that the policy adhered to is made by a private organization rather than government officials (Lilly and Knepper 1992b, p.50).

This all raises some very basic issues of accountability and political control (not to mention ethical propriety and financial management). Formally of course private contractors are legally accountable to the legislative authorities in each country they operate, but the logic of subgovernments is to minimize the impact of time consuming and expensive legal formality on their operations and avoid adverse publicity. In this sense formal accountability may be a slender straw on which to place one's faith in the face of the globalization of corrections industries (Lilly and Knepper 1992a, p.183, Christie 1993). What is at stake is not principally a tactical response to prison overcrowding or regime conditions but potentially a much larger, indeed epochal, shift in the political economy of punishment.

91

Compulsion, order and control:

a) Can the state delegate coercive powers? The simple, descriptive answer
to this question would now appear to be yes it can and does. As we have
seen the logic of the privatization case rests on a distinction between the
allocation of punishment and the oversight of its administration (the state's
responsibilities) and the practical provision of services (the private sector's
role). Thus Hutto (Vice-president of Corrections Corporation of America)
contends "the administration of justice is the exclusive prerogative of the
state but not of state employees" (quoted in Weiss 1989, p.34). On this
view, talk of public service ethics of prison management, objections to
profit-taking and so on are entirely sentimental and irrelevant (Weiss 1989,
p.41), notwithstanding how strongly these may matter to the self-definition
and morale of the public employees themselves (Saunders-Wilson 1986).

But evidently matters are not so simple. It is difficult to deny that the
privatization of prison management differs from other privatizations in key
respects. The provision of water, power, refuse services and so on are
elementary social necessities, but as such they can be unambiguously
defined as being in consumers' interests and in principle (however
practically limited our choices) we contract for them voluntarily. Even in
other areas of private security provision where powers are delegated (as
in shopping malls) citizens enter premises voluntarily and for limited
periods. In prisons matters are quite otherwise. Prisoners enter prisons by
compulsion and during their confinement the responsibilities which
authorities undertake for their well being are very extensive. As such they
involve practical and symbolic issues of authority (Weiss 1989, p.39). It
is a matter of political and constitutional controversy to determine in what
ways such authority is grounded; just as it is a matter of empirical
uncertainty to ask in what ways it is acknowledged or contested. This is
obviously at issue in respect of formal disciplinary proceedings, sentence
planning, parole hearings and so on. But additionally, no one with the
least familiarity with prisons imagines that such formalities exhaust the
range of deployments of power involved in their daily operation (Sykes
1958, Carlen 1983, McDermott and King 1988). Most observers moreover
agree that such informal aspects of the institutional culture of particular
prisons are at least as important in determining their habitability as any
formal, quantifiable features of their regimes (King 1991, Sparks and
Bottoms 1994). Yet the whole of the privatization argument in Britain to
date has resided in the specification of formal regime contracts, and
neither the government nor the private sector has been much minded to
discuss those features of the distribution of power in prison which escape

such contractual definition.

Indeed one might go further and argue that the whole tenor of the debate has been so constructed as systematically to minimize attention to any of the ways in which prisons involve inherent deprivations, are intentionally punitive or are necessarily sites of conflict and contestation. Instead that debate speaks a sanitized language of service delivery and cost effectiveness. It may therefore be that one of the benefits which governments seek in pursuing privatization initiatives is the depoliticization of penal issues, by being seen to take action to address the issue of overcrowding, by ensuring a consistent provision of new facilities at (purportedly) reduced cost and by confining the scope of penal debates to a narrow range of technical and managerial topics. In distancing itself from the direct responsibilities of management and provision, the state is to some extent spared the negative political charge that penal issues commonly tend to carry. Meanwhile, by developing alternative methods of resourcing it is similarly freed from one source of political pressure to reduce the prison population.

b) What are the issues of legality and liability? There are a number of immediately practical ways in which issues of accountability become more complicated under a delegated arrangement. When the government argues that contracting out increases accountability, what they appear in the first instance to mean is the contractor's accountability to the government itself, rather than the external accountability of the system to Parliament or interested publics. So, for example, it has been argued that the range of issues on which ministers can be compelled to answer questions in Parliament or elsewhere is likely to be reduced; such questions are referred instead to the Chief Executive of the relevant Agency (Kauffman 1992). In turn, operational matters are likely to be referred to the individual contractors who, to date, have jealously regarded certain kinds of information as commercially privileged and declined to discuss in particular the financial details of their contracts (*File on Four*, BBC Radio 4, 2 March 1993).

There arises potentially a problem of "dispersed liability" (McConville 1990, Weiss 1989). Weiss shows that the complexity of private prisons creates a vast new legal *terra incognita* and that government agencies have specifically sought to argue in court that they are not liable in cases of complaint brought by detainees held by private contractors. The issue appears to turn on the court's judgement of whether the detention and its conditions continue to constitute "state action" (Weiss 1989, p.6). In the US the courts have on occasion been prepared to assert this principle.

How this will work in the UK where the courts have historically shown themselves much more reticent about intervening in prison life remains to be seen. But there are a number of issues to do with, for example, the segregation or transfer of "difficult" prisoners, or where the duty of care resides in cases of suicide, in which problems of dispersed liability seem very probable.

As Weiss further points out the costs involved in setting up regulatory arrangements that were really adequate to the issues involved might in any case significantly offset the savings which the government seeks, especially given:

> how much the conservative political agenda has already blurred the ideological and ecological boundaries separating the public from the private realms. Is it likely that prison monitoring bodies would be more effective than other government regulatory agencies, such as those that oversee the nuclear power industry, occupational safety conditions, or the airline industry? Would penal regulation be free from the conflicts of interest, intense lobbying, and the bias of industry trained agency personnel that characterize the state's regulation of other private industries? (Weiss 1989, p.40)

In Britain, whose penal system has historically had very poorly developed lines of accountability, such considerations should give serious pause for thought before further pursuing the path of privatization.

Private prisons and the problem of legitimacy

The institution of imprisonment is surrounded by extreme problems of normative justification. Far from being resolved by privatization these stand much more in danger of being suppressed or displaced. The commodification of imprisonment normalizes its existence and entrenches its social presence at least at its present level. In sundering the connection between the allocation and the administration of punishment privatization does not serve the development of sophisticated and publicly accountable judicial reasoning. Rather, it favours the extension of existing tendencies towards containment and preventive detention as rationales for sentencing. Even in a situation marked by improved formal accountability (which as I have indicated there are in any case grounds for doubting), the privatization of the penal realm edges it away from the centre of any actual or imaginable public conversation about the imposition of just sanctions. It reduces the necessary sense of creative anxiety or unease which ought to attend the practice of criminal justice. Such anxiety would characterize any society which took its own traditions of justice in earnest, which acknowledged the conditional and fragile legitimacy of their present institutional realizations, or which had any imaginative sense of futurity about how present institutional forms could be revised or transcended. The "institutional reflexivity" which Giddens (1990) assumes to be characteristic of modernity only has any progressive implication where conditions for articulate public deliberation are intentionally protected and fostered.

For these reasons the single greatest danger inherent in the privatization movement is the depoliticization of what had hitherto been known to be an arena of deep public controversy. It is therefore necessary that any progressive project in penal politics now begins from a strong and unabashed reassertion of the public nature of punishment. This is not in any sense to argue defensively in support of the status quo. To the contrary, it rests on the view that **contesting** the legitimacy of present practices requires the prior acknowledgement of their political character. It is to this extent astonishing that the central assertion of the privatization lobby, namely that the imposition and administration of punishment are separable "functions", should have gone so tamely unrebutted. The public speech act "I sentence you..." grounds its claim to legitimacy precisely in the unbroken connection it asserts between the state agent who pronounces it and the public institutions which enact it. Moreover, as Lacey (1988) indicates, the articulation of rational justifications and their enactment by legitimately constituted authority may be **all** that differentiate the imposition of a defensible sanction from the *prima facie* wrongful exercise of naked state power. By the same token, the powers exercised by prison governors and prison officers can only be grounded in similar sources of authority. The definition of prison personnel as public employees ought to be seen as simultaneously rendering them answerable to close and continual public scrutiny and, equally, as entitled to public support for progressive and innovative action, just as their self definition as public servants is central to questions of morale and motivation (see Wilson 1992).

In the last instance whoever says "prison" says "force". To grant this is to accept that imprisonment is never better than a necessary evil. Its necessity must always therefore be demonstrated. Moreover, the compulsions, negotiations and compromises which sustain the internal order of the prison inherently involve morally troubling decisions and practices. Logan is thus in one sense correct in arguing that the problems

95

of imprisonment are intrinsic, but his argument is self defeating. It is because they are intrinsic that they only retain such legitimacy as they enjoy by virtue of their public character. In a rather visionary and overheated article, Pease and Taylor (1989, p.192) argue improbably that the rehabilitative aims of imprisonment will be served by the financial rewards and penalties which governments can impose on private contractors. Failing that, they acknowledge, "We will have opened our gates to a particularly unpleasant Trojan Horse". That horse is now within the gates.

Postscript, 1994

During 1993 the momentum towards contracting out as a favoured strand of penal policy substantially increased. Throughout the year the prison population resumed its upward path. This followed a brief but significant pause in 1991-2 as sentencers assimilated the reductionist intentions of the 1991 Criminal Justice Act. Yet, in the wake of some judicial protest and no small amount of hostile press coverage, the 1993 Criminal Justice Act overturned those sections of the 1991 Act most explicitly directed towards parsimony in sentencing (Ashworth 1993). Meanwhile in the face of continuing political difficulties and poor opinion polls (not least in the sphere of "law and order" itself) ministers distanced themselves more and more from the unduly liberal implications of their own flagship legislation. By the end of the year the average daily prison population had registered a startling 16 per cent increase (NACRO 1994).

At the beginning of September the incoming Home Secretary, Michael Howard, confidently declared the success of the Wolds experiment, principally on the grounds of its reduced costs, and signalled that tenders would be offered for a further ten prisons (BBC *PM Programme*, 2 September 1993). A few weeks later, addressing the most aggressively "law and order" oriented Conservative Party Conference in a decade, Mr Howard announced plans for another six new prisons (all privately constructed and managed) on top of those already in the pipeline. "Prison Works" declared Mr Howard, apparently on the basis of a rather freely mixed cocktail of deterrent, incapacitative and retributive grounds (*The Guardian* 7 October 1993, p.1).

The year thus witnessed one of the most drastic coolings of the penal climate in living memory. Not only was the provision of more prison space prioritized (notwithstanding that the rate of increase in question would actually necessitate the opening of one new prison every month) but the internal regimes of all prisons were also to be reviewed. "Butlins" declared Mr Howard, redundantly but to the great satisfaction of his audience, would "not be bidding for the contract". This followed press reports[14] during the summer months to the effect that the Home Secretary was minded to introduce more "austere" prison regimes, apparently on the grounds that "prisoners enjoy a standard of material comfort which tax payers find it hard to understand".

Penologists might have had little difficulty in anticipating all of this. Both Marxist (Rusche and Kirchheimer 1939) and mainstream liberal commentators (Radzinowicz and Hood 1990) largely concur in an historical account of changes in penal regimes that sees the standards of material provision decline during periods of economic recession and/or political anxiety or reaction. The submerged but never extinct dilemma of penal reform (Mannheim 1939), the "principle of less eligibility", again surfaces in explicit penal discourse.

For present purposes what is most clearly apparent from these developments is that the implicit progressivist teleology of Kenneth Clarke's earlier statements (flatly equating privatization with penal improvement) can hardly survive such a deterioration in the surrounding political environment. The idea that the terms on which contracts are offered must inevitably make private prisons preferable from the prisoner's point of view seems more and more open to reasonable doubt. Rather the vaunted responsiveness of the private sector signifies if anything the reverse, namely that prison regimes can be made to react barometrically to the external penal climate (in part by virtue of not being mitigated by the vocational culture, the "restrictive practices", of a cadre of administrators and staff steeped in a meliorist public service ethic). The prospect that penal services might be provided by a private sector not "incentivized" towards relentless improvement but instead constrained by a rhetoric of austerity exposes a range of impending troubles for the legitimacy of the private corrections industry which have until now been largely suppressed.

Notes

1.   For example, Jacobs 1983, and Maguire et al. 1985.

2.   See for example, Logan 1990.

3.   See McConville 1990.

4. See Adams 1992, Cavadino and Dignan 1992, Sim 1992, and Woolf 1991.

5. See New York State Special Commission on Attica, 1972.

6. Quoted in Shaw 1989, p. 47.

7. A member of the Home Affairs Committee and subsequently Chair of Contract Prisons PLC.

8. CJA 1991, s. 84(5), see Wasik and Taylor 1991, p. 148.

9. See Wilson 1992.

10. See also Gamble 1988, and Jessop et al. 1988.

11. All cited in Lilly and Knepper 1992b, p. 51. See also Christie 1993, and Shichor 1993.

12. Cf. the more critical analysis by Greenberg 1991.

13. See also Shichor 1993.

14. For example, *The Observer* 22 August 1993, p. 1.

6 The sectoral dynamics of policing

Les Johnstone

This chapter examines the changing relationship between the public and private sectors of policing, drawing particular attention to the significance of "hybrid" forms of provision - those which are neither unambiguously public nor unambiguously private. The existence of such hybrid forms, together with the renewal and expansion of private sector policing raises two sorts of questions. First, there is the "who? what? and where?" of policing: Who polices? What is policing? Where does it occur? Second, how do changes in the sectoral balance of policing affect traditional conceptions of the public (state) and private (market) divide? For the purposes of examining these questions, the chapter is divided into three sections. Section One considers the 'who? what? and where?' of policing. Section Two addresses the issue of "hybrid" policing. Finally, Section Three examines some of the theoretical implications of the matters discussed.

The who? what? and where? of policing

(a) Who polices?: To have asked the question "Who polices?" twenty years ago would have produced blank incomprehension amongst British police and public alike. At that time it was assumed - however mistakenly - that public police forces enjoyed an exclusive monopoly over those, supposedly, unambiguous social functions which we call "policing":

namely, crime prevention, law enforcement and the maintenance of public order. Yet, even a cursory examination of history would tell us to treat such a view with caution. For one thing, "policing", far from being unambiguous, has always consisted of a dynamic and variable mixture of social functions. For another its provision has always involved a multiplicity of agencies: a complex division of labour between public, private and hybrid elements. Here, it should be remembered that public (i.e. local state) provision of policing dates back only to 1829 in Britain. Prior to that, policing was provided through a mixture of communal, informal and private initiatives (parish constables, "thief-takers", informers, vigilantes, "prosecution associations" and the like). Moreover, there was no simple historical displacement of private forms by the new public provision. In that sense, although vigilantism and private policing have apparently re-emerged in recent years, they have never, in truth, been entirely absent.

Historical examination would suggest, then, that the sectoral division of labour (the balance between public, private and "hybrid" elements of policing) has always been a dynamic one. At present, in the UK, that sectoral balance is, once more, being renegotiated - though more by market forces and consumer demand than by rational political calculation. This process of renegotiation is occuring in three identifiable ways. First, there is privatization of functions hitherto undertaken by public police forces. Recently, for example, several groups of residents have contracted private security companies to patrol streets and housing estates in the North of England (*Police Review* 7 February 1992).[1] Another significant event occured when the Port of London Authority Constabulary, a body established by Act of Parliament in 1802, became the first statutory police force to be privatized.

A second development has been the re-emergence of "citizen self-policing", a phenomenon whose range encompasses everything from the relatively innocuous street patrol to the summary justice imposed by the "vigilance committee". Though vigilante activity is found in its most extreme forms in Northern Ireland's "punishment squads"(Conway 1993), there is evidence of its increase on mainland Britain as well.[2]

Finally, there is the "hybrid" (Johnston 1992) or "grey" (Hoogenboom 1991) area of policing, those forms undertaken by bodies occupying an ambiguous position with respect to the public-private divide. In Britain, such organizations are many and varied (Miller and Luke 1977). Some are organized police forces of significant size, whose personnel have full constabulary powers (e.g. the Ministry of Defence Police). Some are organized forces with more limited powers (e.g. parks police). Some are public bodies which engage in selling police services to private customers (e.g. the Post Office Investigations Department).

(b) What is policing?: Prior to the eighteenth century, if the word "police" was used at all, it invariably referred to the the broad social functions of "policing": "the general regulation or government, the morals or economy of a city or country" (Palmer 1988, p.69). "Policing" thus referred to a socio-political function (rather than merely a formal-legal one) exercised throughout political **and** civil society (rather than merely within the confines of the state). It was only in the mid-eighteenth century that the word "police" began to be used, in its continental sense, to refer to the specific functions of crime control and order maintenance. It was in that context that Peel's "new police" emerged in 1829.

This emergence had two effects. First, it led to the perception that policing was about a narrow range of, largely repressive, functions. Second, it led to the conflation of "police" (a concept relating to a specific personnel) with "policing" (a concept referring to given social functions). In fact, both of these assumptions were mistaken. Long after the "new police" emerged its officers were concerned, not merely with narrowly repressive functions, but with matters relating to the general "regulation" of populations (Donzelot 1979). In effect, police officers had responsibility for a wide range of regulatory functions within municipalities: inspection of lodging houses, weights and measures, rate collection, surveying roads and bridges, supervision of market trading, supervision of the Poor Law and the policing of contagious and sexually transmitted diseases, to name but a few. Policing, in short, was as much about "social", "moral" and "administrative" regulation as about crime control. Nor should one assume that the position is significantly different today. When Colquhoun's *Treatise on the Police of the Metropolis* (1796) asserted that the aim of policing was "to give the minds of the People a right bias" (cited in Philips 1980, p.177) it was establishing principles very similar to those found amongst today's proponents of "community policing" (Alderson, 1979).

Recognition of the diversity of policing tasks has led some commentators to move outside the customarily narrow confines of debate about the police role ("force versus service", "pro-active versus reactive", "fire-brigade versus community oriented"). One solution is simply to define policing as "dealing with all sorts of problems" whilst in possession of a capacity for the legitimate exercise of force (Bittner 1980). The strength of this position is obvious. Not only is it sufficiently all- embracing to incorporate the wide range of activities carried out by police in the past; it can also encompass present activities and those which might be carried out in the future.

The problem is, however, that the formalism contained in Bittner's definition - that a necessary precondition for "doing policing" is the possession of a capacity to exercise legitimate coercion - implicitly restricts policing to the activities of state personnel: those holding the coercive powers delegated to them by the state. The effect of this formalism is to draw a rigid barrier between those activities carried out by the police and comparable (policing) activities carried out by private agents and other bodies. Now, clearly, there are important differences (social, political and ethical) between activities carried out with the legal authority of the state and those carried out without such authority: especially where coercion is involved. But from a conceptual point of view, Bittner's demarcation produces evident contradictions. For example, it is obvious that the public police coerce with the state's authority. Yet, it is equally evident from research on police corruption (Punch 1985) and police vigilantism (Bowden 1978, Rosenbaum and Sedeburg 1976) that they also coerce without the state's authority. To exclude such "extra curricular" acts from the domain of "policing" would seem absurd. Yet, the very act of including them would infer that similar coercive acts carried out by private security guards, lacking state authority, should also be included. And there would be even less reason to exclude those circumstances where private agents exercise limited coercive powers after being granted the authority to do so by the state.

What I have said so far would suggest that policing can be defined neither in terms of the possession of some essential legal capacity, nor in terms of the fulfillment of certain specific functions: functions which can be carried out by public or private agents - or by some combination of both. In so far as these (multifarious) functions can be grouped under any single heading, the heading has to be a broad one. One attempt to tackle this issue is found in Shearing's (1992) proposal to equate policing with "security" or "the preservation of peace". Here, policing is said to consist of preserving some established order from threat: in effect, ensuring that "nothing happens" to subvert that order. Accordingly, for Shearing, policing constitutes a set of practices through which some guarantee of security is given to subjects. Though this approach has much to commend it, it is clear that police have undertaken and continue to undertake activities which are marginal to "security" (e.g. Poor Law regulation and traffic control). An alternative solution, is to incorporate "policing" into the sociology of "social control", though, arguably, the concept of "social regulation" is a preferable one (Johnston 1992). The important point is that whichever of these approaches is adopted, it is possible to incorporate the practices of private, public and hybrid bodies into a common theoretical framework.

(c) Where does policing take place?: Once policing is conceived as a dynamic complex of activities undertaken by private, public and "hybrid" agents, two questions arise. How is the division of labour between those agents parcelled out? Where are those activities undertaken?

I have suggested elsewhere (Johnston 1992) that these issues can best be addressed if policing is seen to consist of two cross-cutting continua: one sectoral, the other spatial.

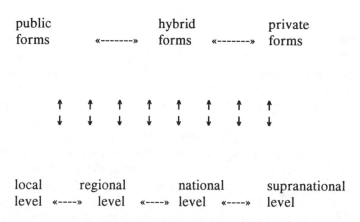

SECTORAL FORMS OF POLICING

public forms		hybrid forms		private forms
	«-------»		«-------»	

local   regional   national   supranational
level «----» level «----» level «----» level

SPATIAL LEVELS OF POLICING

Figure 6.1 Sectoral and spatial dimensions of policing

According to this model, "policing" constitutes different sectoral forms (from public to private) located at different spatial levels (from local to supranational). Crucially, however - as indicated by the horizontal and vertical arrows in Figure 6.1 - those forms and levels overlap and interpenetrate. Policing, rather than having a singular form (e.g. the public form) which is located at a unitary level (e.g. the locality) is a product of dynamic interactions across sectoral and spatial planes. In that sense, any analysis of policing practices, in a given context, will require examination

103

of the particular configuration of forms and levels exhibited by the set of practices under consideration. In effect, the various configurations which comprise determinate modes of "policing" may be conceived of as vertical "slices", or "cross-sections" of those interactions contained in Figure 6.1.

The categories outlined in Figure 6.1 confirm two things. First, that policing is a dynamic rather than a static concept. Second, that in future the most interesting questions about policing are likely to concern, not the categories themselves, but the connections between them. How will increased interaction between public police and private security affect issues such as police legitimacy, social justice and rights of privacy (Cunningham and Taylor 1985, Hoogenboom 1989, Marx 1987)? How will the increased internationalization of private security affect policing and criminal justice policy at different spatial levels (Lilley 1992)?

It is also apparent that once policing is conceived as occupying determinate sectoral and spatial locations, the issue of "where" it takes place becomes more complex. In popular imagery - and in a sociology of police work which has done little more than mirror that imagery - policing is perceived as a "street-level", "crime related" (and sometimes, "service-oriented") activity. This is a sociology dominated by narrow conceptions of "public space" (the streets) and unconcerned by the extent to which social and economic changes have made the concept of public - as distinct from private - space, itself ambiguous. The most dramatic illustration of this ambiguity relates to the growth of "mass private property" - that privately owned public space which provides, increasingly, a focus for social interaction. Here, the archetypal form is the shopping mall where policing is undertaken by "persons who are exercising not only public law enforcement powers but also powers derived from the rights of private property ownership" (Stenning and Shearing 1980, p.240). In this context, the objectives of those engaged in policing will not be determined by public standards. It is the prevention of "loss", rather than the prevention of crime which will be paramount. And it will be "informal", rather than public justice which is invoked in order to achieve that end.

"Hybrid policing"

The adoption of a dynamic model of policing enables one to focus on some of the interactions which take place across sectoral boundaries. One way of illustrating some of the issues which arise from that interaction is to direct attention to those "hybrid" forms of policing which, themselves, encapsulate sectoral ambiguity and contradiction.

At present there are something like 130,000 police officers attached to the forty three "Home Office" police forces in England and Wales. Much has been made of the fact that private security personnel probably outnumber public police by a factor of 2:1. But few have commented on the large numbers of personnel employed by "hybrid" bodies. "Hybrid bodies", as defined here, consist of policing organizations whose status is somehow ambiguous vis-a-vis the public/private divide. This ambiguity can take several different forms. At its most basic, the organization might simply transfer across sectors.[3] More significant, however, is the fact that the very "publicness" or "privateness" of an organization might, itself, be at issue. It is this latter aspect on which I shall focus by examining two examples: one at the municipal level, the other at the national level. In each case these organizations, though clearly in some senses "public", represent particular, rather than general interests. For this reason they are commonly, though erroneously, referred to as "private police forces" by commentators (e.g. Bowden 1978). Though mistaken, that view is understandable since it points to the tension which can arise between these organizations and "Home Office" police forces over the representation of public interests.

(a) Municiple policing: Though the centralizing tendencies of the British state have reduced municipal influence over public police forces, it is important to realize that the legislative basis for municipal police provision remains intact. Two pieces of legislation, the Public Health (Amendment) Act of 1907 and the Ministry of Housing and Local Government Provisional Order Confirmation (Greater London Parks and Open Spaces) Act of 1967 empower local authorities to swear in employees as constables for the purposes of securing local bye laws. Some local authorities (including Birkenhead, Birmingham, Brighton, City of London, Epping Forest, Gloucester, Liverpool and Wirral) have also used specific local acts to establish constabularies for policing parks and open spaces.

The development of municipal provision has been especially marked in London where three forces (at Brent, Wandsworth and Holland Park) have already been established and where seven other boroughs are considering following their example. The largest of the three, at Wandsworth, consists of thirty five officers who undertake mobile and foot patrol in parks, play areas and other urban spaces. The most recently established, at Holland Park, began in 1991 following public concern about anti-social behaviour, crime and vandalism in public parks. The force has an establishment of twelve officers and, like the Wandsworth Constabulary receives some

105

training from the Metropolitan Police Service (MPS).

The emergence of these bodies can be seen as an attempt by local authorities to provide local solutions under local control to public concerns about crime and disorder. The MPS response, however, has been mixed. Though there is recognition that municipal provision relieves Metropolitan officers of some of their burden, there is evident sensitivity about the legal, constitutional and operational implications of this new development in the local division of policing labour. Thus, though the MPS has been involved in training - both Wandsworth and Holland Park officers deliver prisoners to MPS custody facilities, so require basic procedural knowledge - there is concern about its implications. On the one hand, it is recognized that training might prevent a parks constable from exceeding his or her powers. On the other hand, it is feared that should such a situation arise with a trained officer, the MPS might be held accountable.

A more serious controversy has arisen, however, with respect to the legal powers of municipal officers. In 1989, one (non-London) local authority sought Home Office advice on the powers of parks constables under the Police and Criminal Evidence Act. At this time the Home Office view was that such constables enjoyed full police powers within the jurisdictional confines of the park. That view has now changed, largely one assumes due to MPS concern about the expansion of municipal provision in London. Between 1990 and 1991 the MPS Solicitor's Branch issued (somewhat weighty) "advice" on the powers of parks constables (New Scotland Yard, 1990-91). The key component of this advice - that parks constables are not real constables - though adopted as official Home Office and MPS policy is, to say the least, contestable. Indeed, despite this advice, Wandsworth Parks Constabulary still declares that its officers enjoy "all the powers of arrest and search given to the Metropolitan Police whilst on patrol in the parks, commons and open spaces" (Wandsworth Parks Constabulary, n.d.).

What might seem at first sight to be a rather parochial issue, in fact, has wider connotations. Ultimately, the issue of municipal policing, like that of private policing itself, is about the question of which bodies should have control over the regulation of public space. Some years ago a senior police officer suggested that Britain might develop a "two-tier" policing system. The first tier would consist of sworn officers with full powers. The second would consist of uniformed, but unsworn "street wardens" whose job would be to deal with everyday nuisances (Davies 1989). This model has already been developed in other jurisdictions (e.g. San Fransisco and Victoria New South Wales). Though Davies's suggestion was treated with hostility by the British police, her motive for suggesting it was significant.

A two-tier system under police control, she suggested, was preferable to the expansion of private and municipal policing schemes which would "erode the position of the police" (Davies 1989, p.2277). In essence, Davies's proposal encapsulates an issue which is sure to become central to the policing agenda in years to come: which publics are to be represented by whom and by what means?

(b) National policing: Currently, there is much concern about the threatened nationalization of British policing. Few people, however, take account of the fact that Britain already has a number of national police forces. Two of these are worthy of consideration. The Ministry of Defence Police (MDP) was established in 1971 from the former service constabularies. It consists of some 5,000 civilian police officers, which makes it the fifth largest civil police force in the UK. It is responsible for the protection of Crown Propety, the prevention and detection of crime on defence establishments and the physical protection of those establishments. The UK Atomic Energy Authority Constabulary (AEAC) was established in 1954 and consists of some 600 civil police constables who provide similar services for the various UKAEA sites, as well as those run by British Nuclear Fuels (BNFL).

Significantly, both of these forces have been subject to Acts of Parliament[4] though, oddly, that legislation did not provoke any public debate. This is surprising for two reasons. First, though both MDP and AEAC serve specific users, they are - like Home Department forces - civil police bodies engaged, at times, in the (armed) policing of public space. Second, not only are they organized nationally, the legislation of 1976 and 1987 granted them virtually unlimited national operational jurisdiction.

The operational issue is worth considering in more detail since it illustrates some important issues. For the sake of simplicity, let us focus on the MDP, since much of what can be said of it applies equally to the AEAC. The MDP is a civil police force whose field of operation covers both civil and military jurisdictions. It also polices (open) public space and public space which, because of its closed-access, is effectively "private". Any attempt to understand the MDP thus requires some analysis of this complex of cross-cutting (public-private-civil-military) relations. The following examples illustrate some of this complexity:

1   *crime in garrison towns*: policing in garrison towns, such as Aldershot or Plymouth involves Home Department police, MDP and the Military Police. One effect of this is to make the quantification of crime difficult. Though Military Police do not deal with civilan

offenders, the MDP can deal with service personnel where a civil offence has been committed. In practice, however, crimes committed by service personnel tend to be dealt with "in-house" through the military authorities (Holt 1986) and, in consequence remain unreported. Here, then, a process of "informal justice" operates, similar to that found in the policing of (commercial) "private" space by private security.

2   *access to public space*: there is often controversy about the use of public space in and around military establishments. Since the 1930s many military bases have aquired bye-laws making trespass a criminal offence and enabling Crown Servants to remove trespassers with a view to court action (MOD 1986). In fact, the MDP, rather than the military, tends to be used for enforcing this legislation, thereby confirming its role as a "buffer" between civilians and the military (Pead 1986). Enforcement of this role confirms that public space in these circumstances is overlaid by several different forms of "private" restriction (through establishment rules, local bye-laws, and the exercise of police discretion).

3   *firearms*: during times of national tension armed MDP officers will be found on London streets guarding Mnistry of Defence premises. This raises a number of questions. What is the Metropolitan Police view? Given that MDP officers receive firearms training from military instructors, are their rules of engagement compatible with those of other civil police forces and with the principle of 'minimum use of force'?

4   *special escort*: policing and security in and around military bases involves a complex of agencies: local civil police; the MDP; service police forces; the military; contract security; civilian guard forces. A similarly complex pattern of provision is evident when one considers the sensitive issue of movement of nuclear material. Such material is escorted by the AEAC, by the MDP's Special Escort Group and by RAF Special Convoys. That pattern is further complicated by the role of Home Office police forces. Here the constitutional principle of "civil primacy" has to be considered. Once a convoy leaves a military base it is the responsibility of the chief constable through whose area it travels. According to this principle, the local chief constable has operational primacy over both MDP (or AEAC) and the military. The extent to which this

principle prevails is open to doubt. In 1987 there was an accident involving a military convoy in Wiltshire. The Wiltshire Police arrived on the scene within a few minutes, but armed marines from the convoy proceeded to stop, detain and interrogate members of the public. In effect local police were unable to exert primacy in this situation and were unaware of the rules under which military personnel were operating. (Hansard 27 January 1987, col. 290). Here, in effect, the principle that in normal circumstances civil police have authority over public space was subverted by the military.

This brief discussion of some examples of "hybrid" policing confirms that the regulation of public space is undertaken by a mixture of agencies whose "publicness" varies in character. This variation can produce tension: for example, between local/national and civil/military interests. Here it is apparent that there is considerable dispute about the rights of different agencies to represent different "publics". Let us now return to the wider issue of the policing division of labour and, by so doing, consider some of the theoretical implications of current patterns of change in the public-private balance.

Theoretical considerations

In the past social theory has tended to take the distinction between public and private spheres for granted, ignoring the extent of their overlap. Admittedly, on occasions some attempt has been made to conceptualize that overlap. In the last decade, for example, both neo-Gramscian and corporatist theorists have tried to deal with the complexities posed by historical variations in the public-private balance.[5] More recently, writers concerned with changing historical patterns of policing and social control have focussed on similar problems. In conclusion let us consider some of the issues raised by this work.

Policing, it has been argued, has experienced "a quiet revolution" (Stenning and Shearing 1980). Up until twenty or thirty years ago it was (or was at least perceived to be) an exclusively public function. In fact, this assumption was part of a more general tendency to equate "governance", "authority" and "order" with "the state": a tendency which had emerged in the previous century. In that respect, although there was dispute about policing in the 1960s and 1970s - for example, functionalists saw it as integrative, whilst Marxists saw it as oppressive - nobody

109

disputed "who policed".

However, the rapid expansion of the private security sector - which began during the 1960s in North America and a decade later in Europe - has changed things in two ways. First, it is now apparent that the most challenging questions for analysis concern not the sectors themselves, but the interactions between them. It is already clear that in the USA there is routine exchange of personnel and information between public and private policing sectors. Nearer home, there have been several reported cases of joint public order operations involving civil police forces, "hybrid" police forces and private security companies. Examples of this sort raise serious issues of accountability, legality and ethics.

Second, it is clear that these sectoral changes in the policing division of labour demand theoretical assessment. Few would now dispute Shearing's (1992) contention that such assessment requires the deployment of a pluralistic framework - one which recognizes the diversity of agents engaged in policing - though there is still dispute about the nature which that framework should take. At present, it is possible to identify four versions of pluralism: the first two seeing the process as benign; the last two regarding it as pathological.

(a) The complementarity model: Proponents of this view (e.g. Cunningham and Taylor 1985) see private security as the public police's "junior partner" in the fight to reduce crime and maintain social order. Since the police cannot meet escalating public demand for their services, the private sector rushes in to "fill the vaccuum". According to this view, the public and private sectors maintain their distinction but complement each other. The "junior" status of the private sector ensures, however, that the sovereignty of the state is retained. In so far as this position can be related to any social theory, it bears some resemblance to the "functionalist-integrative" view of the police function.

(b) The integrated model: The clearest exposition of this view is contained in a publication of the Solicitor General of Canada (Normandeau and Leighton 1990). Here, the complementarity model is pushed a stage further, the authors suggesting that all agencies which contribute towards the maintenance of order in communities should be encouraged to develop strategic partnerships. This view implies, as Shearing (1992) suggests, that the community and the state are integrated into a single unified system. In effect, as there are, apparently, no contradictions between the parties to this arrangement "the private becomes the public and the public the private" (Shearing 1992, p.419).

110

(c) The "one big police force": Whereas the previous two models look upon the integration of private and public elements with favour, the next model sees the process as pathological. Flavel, for example, bemoans the fact that the development of systematic links between public and private police expresses "an increasingly coherent security ideology" (Flavel 1973, p.15). Like those who adopt the integrated model, proponents of this view tend to assume that a fusion has occured between the public and private sectors of social control. Unlike integrationsists however, the process is seen as far from benign: indeed the more successful the integration becomes, the more pathological are its effects deemed to be for civil liberties.

(d) Corporate pluralism: This last position is subscribed to by Shearing and Stenning (1983). A recent formulation describes it as one where corporations cooperate with each other and with the state as "relatively autonomous guarantors of peace". According to this view, "privatization has prompted a fundamental shift in responsibility for policing, from state to corporate hands, that is challenging state power and redefining state-corporate relations" (Shearing 1992, p.422). The key aspect of this position is that it rejects the notion of political and legal spheres as vertically organized with the state at the apex. Indeed, the conception of power deployed in this model is very much a "decentred" one in the Foucaultian sense. This differentiates the position from the previous one which, despite its recognition of the fusion of public and private sectors, still regards them as fusing into a single hegemonic "lump", the custodian of which is the "one big police force". Like the previous position, however, proponents of "corporate pluralism" regard the process with suspicion: one where corporate access to information is likely to eliminate privacy and hasten in a "Brave New World" of all-pervasive social control. Indeed, the more pessimistic interpretations of this view ultimately abandon the "decentred" model of power for one where corporate domination prevails: "one in which economy infuses governance more completely than even the most instrumental Marxist theories have proposed" (Shearing 1992, p.427).

With the exception of the first, all of the positions outlined here recognize that it is increasingly difficult to differentiate between what is "inside" and what is "outside" the state. This might suggest that the concepts of public and private are becoming increasingly redundant in rigorous social analysis. Significantly, however, they continue to be deployed in political discourse to further desired ends. In that sense, it is more fruitful to see the public and private spheres less as distinct "places" with inherent characteristics, than as strategic arenas where arguments are deployed and where political conflicts are played out.

In Britain there is no better illustration of this than in the debate on "active citizenship". Here, after all, is a discourse whose objective is to redesign the parameters of public and private responsibility. Interestingly, its deployment in the field of policing and crime prevention policy has had unintended consequences. Whilst the Government was happy to encourage "responsible citizens" to join neighbourhood watch schemes in the late 1980s, it remained adamant that they should not "take to the streets". The message conveyed - that watching the street through net curtains was "responsible" whilst patrolling it with one's neighbours was not - sought to ensure that vigilance would remain confined to the private (domestic) sphere. The recent spate of reported vigilante incidents - easy to sanction as merely vigorous forms of active citizenship by those engaging in them - has, however, caused the Government to change tack. In December 1993 Michael Howard, the Home Secretary, declared his support for the involvement of neighbourhood watch groups in street patrol, subject to the drafting of a code of practice governing their activities (Routledge 1993). Yet this decision only confirms the unstable character of "active citizenship" as a discourse: on the one hand, it reasserts the primacy of "responsible" citizenship over "irresponsible" forms; on the other, it further erodes the state's already crumbling sovereignty over policing.

Notes

1.   See also Beatt 1992, Purnell 1993.

2.   For the many reported cases see Johnston 1994.

3.   A good example is the policing of railways. Originally, this was undertaken by a number of private forces. Then, in 1947, a single national police force was established which, we are assured, will continue to function after any future privatization.

4.   The AEAC in 1976, the MDP in 1987.

5.   See Showstack Sassoon 1980, and Schmitter 1985

7 Public participation in health: Empowerment or control?

Georgina Webster

Current Government initiatives emphasise the role of the "consumer" in public services. This is superimposed upon a tradition of wide scale though largely ad hoc public participation, and different social movements pushing for change and empowerment. This paper will focus on an intervention to build a Health Action Area in an inner city part of Birmingham, initially led from the "top" but through the use of community development and organisation development methods, leading to ownership from the "bottom". It will explore the notion of an empowerment-control continuum in public participation, looking particularly and practically at the theories, methods and contradictions involved.

Public participation

The recent health and local authority movement to "listen to local voices",[1] given added momentum by the contractor/provider split for services, needs to be placed within the history of attempts to build public participation in this country. This history affects the skills and knowledge available to take participation forward, the degree of commitment versus despair or cynicism present within the public and other key players, and reveals some of the contradictions that need tackling.

The history of public participation in this country is a dynamic one, involving initiatives from outside of particular communities and initiatives

113

that have developed from within them.[2] Outside initiatives have come from the state, central and local, from voluntary organisations and from benevolent or philanthropic individuals and organisations. Initiatives developed from within have crucially included those developed by social movements and self help groups.

Community work to enable public participation arose as an activity during Victorian times and many of the attitudes embodied in it then have persisted to modern times. They developed out of the work of charitable organisations such as the Charity Organisation Society and university settlements. The latter were essentially buildings located in working class urban areas where middle class and wealthy students were encouraged to live among the poor and help them to develop through good example. An equally powerful influence on practice in this country was the community development approach used by the colonisers in the British Colonies which is epitomised in the contemporary phrase, "Give a man a fish and you feed him for a day: teach a man how to fish and you feed him for life."

Both of these approaches are essentially about "parachuting in" skills and knowledge, rather than building on and developing from experience. In contrast, the other side of the dynamic of community development was a focus on self defined and community defined action and change. It was represented by the emergence of strong autonomous working class organisations, particularly the rapidly developing trade union and early Labour movements, and womens groups and struggles. The Womens Co-operative Guild, for instance, campaigned strongly for the independence of married women and for benefits and better health facilities for working mothers.

This two sided approach to public participation persisted throughout the century with an interweaving of different models along this "control/empowerment" continuum. Social movements were sometimes successful in affecting the shape of government led initiatives and sometimes campaigns were instrumental in establishing the existence of these initiatives. Equally, government initiatives sometimes acted as enablers for community organisation and sometimes affected or attempted to control the shape this organisation took. The nineteen sixties is a particularly active decade in this connection.

This period was a time of discussion about the "poverty trap", the increase in "juvenile crime", the existence of "racial disharmony" highlighted in Enoch Powell's famous "Rivers of Blood" speech. Policy makers responded by talking about "disadvantaged areas" and developed a number of similar initiatives, all at the end of the 1960s. These included the establishment of local Community Relations Councils employing

Community Development Officers as part of the 1968 Race Relations Act; the creation of new generic Social Services Departments, which employed community workers as a strategy of preventative social work, as a recommendation of the Seebohm Report; the setting up of a number of Community Development Projects throughout the country by the Home Office, as joint initiatives with local government, as a way of reaching communities not participating in Council services; the Government Urban Aid Programme, which financed innovatory projects in inner city areas, many of which then employed participatory approaches; the designation of certain areas as of Educational Priority; and so on.

At the same time contemporary social movements shaped the direction of these initiatives. The ways of working, principles and outcomes that many of the community development workers and projects followed, were informed as much by the social movements they were part of as by professional training. Empowerment was, for some, as crucial as participation. Furthermore, social movements such as the Civil Rights Movement, Black Power, Women's Liberation, the Student Movement, Anarchism and the New Left etc. played a major role in challenging the notion of community as something homogeneous, or something that ought to be homogeneous. In a very practical sense, the funding of a range of community centres and initiatives did, at the very least, help provide an infrastructure for small scale social movements, self help groups and community action groups, to develop and expand. A place to meet and resources to produce newsletters and publicity had an immediate effect on the ability of groups and individuals to network and organise.

The push and pull of these contradictory pressures are visible within contrasting public participation models today.

Public participation in health care

This same government led/influenced, social movement led/influenced, split or continuum can be seen today in the shift to more public participation in health care. The possibilities for greater involvement of communities in determining needs, policies and services have arisen because of the contracter/provider split opened up in many public services. It is now a requirement on many public bodies to consult with users and consumers in assessing need, drawing up plans, and meeting that need. How this consultation is to happen is not spelt out, but it has created a massive opportunity for effective partnership and strategic work.

This opportunity can more easily be taken up because the last fifteen years or so has seen a number of people and groups working within the health field to promote public participation, although until now without this statutory boost. The last decade has seen a mushrooming of community health initiatives, both supported by and outside of the NHS. For instance, in 1985 the Community Health Information and Resource Unit observed that there were over 10,000 community health initiatives in the UK which could legitimately be described collectively as a community health "movement".[3] It is interesting that the movement has sought to use the "Health for All" agenda of the World Health Organisation to support its campaigns, largely because of the three stated aims of Health For All - community participation, redressing inequalities, and intersectoral collaboration. These aims go hand in hand with other WHO statements which the movement felt it could support, such as: "It is the basic tenet of the Health for All philosophy that .....health developments in communities are made not only for but with and by the people" and that: "at the heart of this (health promotion) process is the empowerment of communities, their ownership and control of their own endeavours and destinies".[4] Other relevant Government sponsored reports, eg, the Cumberledge Report of 1986, have also emphasised the need for services to be more sensitive to the requirements of individuals, their families and their communities. This has helped to push other health professionals, including community nurses and health visitors, in the direction of experimenting with community participation approaches as a way of enhancing their work.

Empowerment versus consumerism

It is interesting that the ways different health bodies, whether contractors or providers, are responding to the requirement to involve "local voices" in their plans, can be seen along an "empowerment/consumerism" continuum. This seems to me a very similar continuum to the "empowerment/control" continuum present in the "government led/social movement led" push and pulls that characterise much of the work on public participation taking place throughout this century, as described above. Elements of two models can be seen in the ways health authorities are tackling community involvement. Our recent work [5] indicates that the model which is adopted tends to depend on whether the organisation has a history of public participation to draw on (eg funding community health projects, developing Health Promotion along Community Development lines), and whether key individuals have access to or experience of the

116

wealth of work on public participation carried on outside of the health service and can draw on this on developing their strategies.

The "consumerist" model is characterised by focusing on the information needs of the purchasers and their need to manage their agencies in a more efficient, effective and economic way, only seeking individual input to that end, seeing choice in individual ways, and ensuring that decision making stays within the hands of the purchaser.

The "empowerment' or democratic model is characterised by focusing on the needs of service users, listening to the new social movements that represent them, being concerned with whole lives not just services, wanting change and wanting service users involved in decision making.[6]

Working within an empowerment model

Our work to help build a Health Action Area in an inner city part of East Birmingham is an attempt to use an empowerment approach to tackling the opportunities and challenges of public participation.

In 1991 East Birmingham Health Authority, along with other agencies associated with Healthy Birmingham 2000, declared Saltley as one of five Health Action Areas in the city. This designation implied a recognition that this inner city area, which is an area of terraced housing with a predominantly Asian population, deserved priority status for action. The decision, led by the Health Promotion Unit and Healthy Birmingham 2000 Office, was taken to build this Health Action Area in a way in which community participation would be encouraged at every level in a realistic and thorough way. Labyrinth Training and Consultancy was brought in to guide and support the process.

At this stage the work was clearly management led: the community had not been involved in making the decision about the Health Action Area. The aim of our work was to build an infrastructure for Saltley so that the appropriate needs, roles, relationships, skills, knowledge and structures could be developed at all levels which would facilitate action for change in response to community needs. A vital part of this was to develop ownership and some control of the initiative by the Saltley communities.

We based our approach on a strategic model for community participation which we have developed over time.

117

COMMUNITY WORK
(support for grass roots work)
eg. grant aid to user groups

PROFESSIONAL
INFRASTRUCTURE
(healthy alliances)
eg. intersectoral working groups

COMMUNITY SECTOR
INFRASTRUCTURE
(networking)
eg. community health forums

ORGANISATION DEVELOPMENT
(managing change)
eg. workshops on developing corporate values

Figure 7.1 Strategic model for community participation

This model incorporates both "bottom up" and "top down" approaches to community involvement. The "bottom up" approaches are present in the first two elements - community work support and community infrastructure. They concern activities carried out directly within communities, at community level, to stimulate community initiative and participation. The "top down" approaches are present in the last two elements - professional infrastructure and organisation development. They concern activities carried out within and between organisations, usually statutory organisations, aimed at "opening them up" so that they are responsive to community initiatives and to managing the change required. All four elements require active resourcing by health authorities.

These four basic elements are interdependent and feed into and from each other. They imply a recognition that the effectiveness of a community based activity (the "bottom up" approach in the first two elements) will be limited if work is not also carried out within the statutory bodies themselves (the "top down" approach of the last two elements). Equally, the effectiveness of organisational change within statutory bodies and collaboration between them will be limited if community groups are not enabled to feed into and affect these structures and their decisions in an appropriate way. This is especially important in ensuring that the views and involvement of the most disadvantaged, discriminated against and oppressed, the "usually excluded", are taken into account.

Different people working at different levels such as grassroots, service delivery or management and policy, within organisations, and from different sectors, will be primarily involved with different elements. Therefore, an overview is required which ensures coherence, which needs to be carried by a particular team, working group or a specific individual.

Applying the community participation model to Saltley

It was decided that all agencies relevant to Saltley should be drawn in, from the community and voluntary sectors, the statutory sectors (especially the local and health authority), the private sector and academic institutions, because they all make decisions and take actions that are relevant to the health of people in Saltley, and therefore all need to be influenced. At the same time, it was decided to work at all levels. The grass roots and community development levels were important because of their key role in reaching out to the community and helping them organise. The service delivery level was important because of their key role in delivering services that are appropriate, and in an appropriate way, to Saltley people. The management level was important because of their key role in decision making and resource allocation affecting people in Saltley. Barriers and blocks at all levels needed to be worked on and overcome.

The different stages of this process, which for practical reasons have overlapped, are described below.

(a) Stage I May 1991-July 1992: Workshops were organised separately for community development workers, service delivery staff, and managers. They included representatives from all the different sectors. The purpose of these separate events was to enable each level to consider in detail what their role was in enabling and bringing about community participation, and how they could put it into practise. All groups decided to continue to meet regularly after their workshops, to pursue this work further, and to take practical action. Both community development workers and service delivery workers made an input into the managers' training day on community participation.

In addition, a day workshop on organising action to assess local health needs was organised for the local community and health workers. They felt by the end of the day that enough information about health needs was known about Saltley - if anything, the area had been over researched. Their two priorities for action were action to meet those health needs, and action to involve the community more in decisions about them.

(b) Stage II April 1992-August 1992: A Steering Group for the Health Action Area was set up. Representatives from the three levels, managers, service delivery staff, and community development workers, as well as, crucially, representatives of the wider community (with their involvement facilitated by the community development workers), were nominated by their groups to attend for a minimum of one year. They established, through participation, the draft aims and objectives of the Health Action Area as a basis for steering its actions.

(c) Stage III September 1992-January 1993: In this stage, "cascade" training was offered to people from all three levels. The purpose of this training was to develop strategies and action plans for meeting the initial aims and objectives of the Health Action Area through collaboration between the different levels and different sectors working and living in Saltley, and with strong community involvement and representation.

(d) Stage IV February 1993-ongoing: This is the stage at which the Health Action Area should be actively working to bring about change and improvements in people's health, based on needs assessment by the community. It will involve working together across sectors and levels, community participation, and actively redressing inequalities. The main vehicle for this success will be the development of an infrastructure for change within the area which to some degree, involves all those living and working in the area. The outcome should be healthy workers and communities in Saltley.

Key working principles

As a consultancy organisation, the approach we have taken to Government led initiatives aimed at promoting consumer involvement arises from our Community Development and Organisation Development backgrounds. Simply, we have developed four key working principles.

Firstly, we have felt it essential to work equally with all levels of organisations, which we loosely define as managerial level, service delivery level and community development level. The rationale is that all play an essential role in enabling community involvement but that their roles are different even though they may overlap.

Our second working principle is the need to pull people together across sectors so they work collaboratively, efficiently and without duplication. In practice for us this has mostly meant the local authority, the health authority and the voluntary/community sectors, although academic bodies and private industry have played important roles in some initiatives we have developed.

Thirdly, we use training in all of this work as an effective developmental tool. It can help build a process at the same time as developing commitment to that process and to the changes necessary at all levels to achieve effective community involvement.

Fourthly, it is essential to work with a co-ordinating group that can develop an overview of the whole process, and develop the strategic thinking and practise to maintain and promote it.

In practice, as in Saltley, at any one time within a particular piece of work, we may be working with one sector or one level only, to help them explore their particular individual role as part of a collaboration. This is always with the aim of bringing the different levels and sectors together at a later stage to take the work forward coherently and strategically, with the development of a shared overview and infrastructure that combines all sectors and all levels within the framework of greater community involvement.

Dealing with the contradictions

A number of issues emerged as the Saltley work progressed, which are common to most public participation initiatives of this type. Some of these are described below.

1   The Saltley initiative was initially management led. The service delivery workers had heard very little about it and the community people were cynical about yet another initiative when they felt none of the others had achieved real change for the area. (Although our research[7] indicated a number of things which had changed in the area as a result of previous community involvement). Over time and using a participatory training and development approach, the community has begun identifying strongly with the initiative. They

are using their resources and networks, in many practical ways, to make the Health Action Area work. At the same time, management commitment has waned and is being tackled now. This is much to do with the restructuring of health authorities that is taking place in Birmingham, as well as budget cuts within the local authority. Interestingly, it is the community that is enabled to have the long term view and vision necessary for large scale change: they live there, and that is unlikely to change. The managers find this more difficult.

2   In this situation, the role of the multi-agency, multi-level Steering Group is crucial and needs to be kept under constant vigilance if it is not to lose its overview and co-ordination because of the pulls from different agencies. At the end of its first year the Steering Group is about to review its aim, objectives, principles, membership and method of working, and this will need to be an annual activity.

3   Race is a big factor in the Saltley initiative. It is a predominantly Asian area with a number of different languages spoken. Practically, this has meant that some events have been held in more than one language. At the same time, direct experience of the Asian communities is much more common at community level than at service delivery level or management level: there are many Asian community development workers and activists but very few Asian service deliverers or managers. This has made it even more important that the different levels are present at meetings and can influence top decisions.

4   Public participation is a feasible, practical policy and aim but it is not one which is neutral or simply technical. It evokes emotions, including fears and anger at all levels, as well as, sometimes, exhilaration and confidence. Therefore a way of working which can recognise and deal with this, is crucial, at all levels. Managers are not always used to this experiential approach and yet it has been important that in Saltley, their workshops, as well as those for other levels, and the shared workshops, use this approach so that real blocks and barriers can be identified and worked on.

5   Resources are an issue here. Much of the Saltley work has been financed through the Urban Programme which will end in 1993, leaving a severe gap. Public participation work requires money.

6   The building of trust between different levels, especially between
        the community and managers, and between different agencies, has
        been a crucial factor. A cross-level and multi-agency approach -
        "healthy alliances" - has facilitated this, but more work remains to
        be done here. There is a tension around ownership of achievements
        which is fairly common when local initiatives are seen by some as
        feeding off a central initiative (in this case Saltley Health Action
        Area versus Healthy Birmingham 2000), and by others as
        developing out of intensive work at local level. This is an inevitable
        tension in public participation initiatives, and working through this
        tension requires building commitment to community participation
        from managers as well as community. Connected to this has been
        the confrontation between different cultures - race cultures but also
        organisational cultures. The result has been sometimes very
        creative, but may not have been without the training and
        organisation development support available.

7   The maintenance of an overview has, in practise, proved difficult.
        Whilst it is the role of the Steering Group to develop and maintain
        this overview, until recently they have not had a team or individual
        for whom that is a major part of their job remit. The funding by
        Inner City Partnership of a three year Health Liaison post with
        admin support for the Health Action Area, managed through the
        local authority, should facilitate this. However, the complexity of
        developing this overview and co-ordinating the infrastructure for
        change across levels and organisations, should not be
        underestimated.

Conclusion

The history of public participation in this country has helped to inform the
current debate and initiatives within the health field. Empowerment and
consumerism are two very different aims for public participation and our
experience in Saltley and elsewhere indicates that empowerment is possible
and does happen but that a properly resourced, facilitated and strategic
approach is vital if this is not to slip into control and exploitation.

Notes

1. NHS Management Executive (1992), "Local Voices" paper.

2. Georgina Webster (1988), paper to Health Education Authority, for Professional and Community Development Division 1988, unpublished.

3. Quoted in Jane Jones (1991), "Community Development and the Health Service", paper presented to the Open University Winter School on Community Development and Health.

4. Ottawa Charter 1986.

5. Jan Smithies and Georgina Webster, Labyrinth Training and Consultancy (1993), "Responding to Local Voices: A Guide to Training and Organisation Approaches" available from the NHS Management Executive.

6. From a talk by Peter Beresford of the Open Services Project at a symposium in Manchester on "Involvement and Empowerment" September 1992 held by Labyrinth Training and Consultancy.

7. Jan Smithies and Georgina Webster (1992) "Health Action in Saltley: A Guide to Available Reports" available from East Birmingham Health Promotion Unit.

8 The process of excluding 'education' from the 'public sphere'?

Janet McKenzie

The fact that this is published in a book about the Public Sphere, and that you are interested enough to read it, indicates some sort of recognition that education still retains a place as an important issue in the public sphere. However, only a small proportion of the British electorate have enough interest in education as a political issue for it to affect their political behaviour - so few indeed that I will argue that the place of education within the public sphere is weakened by lack of public interest and awareness.

Education seems to have an ambiguous place within public discourse. It is frequently displayed in the media as a controversial public issue, but is commonly experienced and perceived by the wider voting public as a mainly private concern. Our educational failures are generally perceived as our own responsibility, problems in our children's schools tend to be localised or blamed on individuals (often the local council or teachers), and central government is often regarded as too distant to be associated with, or blamed for, personal family predicaments. In this way, distinctions between "public" and the "private" responsibilities have become particularly obscure and recent British governments have benefitted from (and promoted) a public discourse in which the emphasis is placed on private liability, rather than government responsibility.

The cumulative effect of some recent, and not so recent, trends can be seen as a process of excluding education from the sphere of public debate. As a process it is not (and never could be) complete, because alternative discourses exist, and even within the Conservative Party there are a variety of conflicting views. However, New Right ideology has set the political agenda in Britain since the 1970s and generated a dominant educational discourse to which opposition has responded with varying degrees of success. The long term effects of this unequal power relationship can be seen in the combined impact of several factors. If we see potential public interest in education as a political issue as a large cake (see Fig. 8.1) it is clear that, when several trends are taken into account, such large slices of potential interest are removed that only a few fragments remain. Those remaining fragments of interest may themselves be fragmented by the lack of cohesion between political partisanship and attitudes to educational sub-issues.

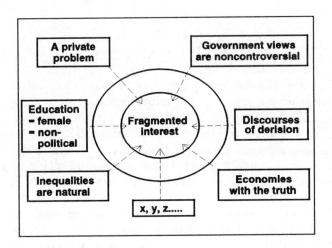

Figure 8.1 Factors in the elimination of potential interest in education

My research has been concerned with voters' attitudes to education as a political issue during the past 13 years. For this I analysed national and local survey data, including the British Social Attitudes Surveys (Jowell et al. 1983 onwards), the British Political Participation Study of 1984-5 (Parry, Moyser and Day 1992) and the Greater Manchester Study of 1980-4 (Edgell and Duke 1981, 1985, 1991). Analysis of this quantitative data resulted in the identification of significant variables, which were further tested via the collection of qualitative data. To do this I interviewed 52 informants in the summer of 1988[1] and, with the help of

Vic Duke and Christine Benney, interviewed 51 informants in April/May 1992 (including 37 of the people who had been interviewed in 1988).[2] These smaller samples involved quotas taken from the Greater Manchester Survey panel based on employment sector (equal representation of public employees, private employees, and people who were not employed), consumption of education (as in the wider population, two-thirds of the 1988 sample did not have children currently in full-time education), sex (both equally represented) and area (equal representation from "Torytown" and "Labourville", the two areas used in the GMS).

It was found that a low level of interest and activity in education as a political issue was indicated by all sources. For example, in their British Participation Study of 1984-5, Parry, Moyser and Day found that only 8.9 per cent of their sample had education on their, free response, personal agendas of "issues, needs or problems" which had been most important to them "over the past five years or so" and which they "might consider taking action on" (Parry, Moyser and Day 1992, p.243). Just 6.4 per cent of all of the issues mentioned were about education, which compares with 15.3 per cent about the environment and planning, 15 per cent about economic issues (excluding unemployment) and 9.6 per cent about unemployment.

Findings in the same survey also support my conclusion that the significance of education within the public sphere is mainly recognised by the relatively small proportion of the electorate who have an instrumental interest in the subject. Parry, Moyser and Day found that those respondents with college or degree qualifications were twice as likely as other members of the public to refer to the topic. Whilst constituting only 20.9 per cent of all respondents, those who had received higher education offered 42.3 per cent of the education issues. A British Social Attitudes report (Jowell et al. 1985) on personal action scores offered further verification of these findings; that those who had been longest in education were most willing to become actively involved in education and politics.

More will be said later about the complex relationship between attitudes to education and political partisanship, but for the moment it can simply be noted that, although voters cited education as one of the most important issues at the time of the 1987 and 1992 general elections, its actual influence on the election results was very limited.

Table 8.1
**Proportion mentioning an issue as one of the two most important
in influencing their vote in the general election.**

	1987	1992
	%	%
Unemployment	49	36
NHS/hospitals	33	41
Education	19	23
Taxation	7	10
Defence	35	3

Source: Gallup post-election survey, 10-11 June 1987; Gallup post-election
survey, 10-11 April 1992.

Crewe argued that, on the basis of declared attitudes to such issues,
Labour would have won the 1987 general election. However, his
well-known conclusion was that the influence of individual issues was
outweighed by an association between the Conservative Party and private
prosperity:

> When answering a survey on the important issues respondents think
> of public problems; when entering the polling booth they think of
> the family fortunes (Crewe 1987).

Again in 1992, Crewe noted that attitudes towards education could have
worked in Labour's favour but that they had little effect on the overall
vote.

> On the three issues that dominated voters' concerns - the health
> service, unemployment and education - Labour was preferred by a
> comfortable margin among those for whom the issue was
> important... Education was the only issue which both increased in
> importance (marginally) and moved in Labour's favour (Crewe
> 1992, p.7).

The election result came as a surprise after opinion polls indicated a win
for Labour and may have been swayed by the last minute decisions of
floating voters. A MORI poll (Curtice 1992) of floating voters taken after

128

the election found that, on the issue of education, there was a weak swing of opinion 1.5 per cent in favour of the Conservatives; not enough to be regarded as having a significant effect on the overall vote. In this respect my own quantitative and qualitative research could be seen as exploring attitudes that are particularly interesting because of their relative lack of influence.

My first interviews were carried out when what was to become the 1988 Education Reform Act was passing through its final stages in Parliament. It seemed logical to assume that the blanket coverage of educational issues by the media at that time would have been reflected in a relatively healthy public awareness of, and even interest in, educational issues. However, the majority of my informants in 1988 expressed little, if any, interest and (although analysis of the 1992 interviews has not been so well developed) it is already clear that there has been no sudden surge of public interest since then. Media coverage and high profile political debates about educational issues seem to be just as likely to generate or degenerate any potential interest in education as a political issue.

In 1988 I asked informants whether they had heard of, or had any interest in, seven subjects emerging from current local and national events.[3] Those who had heard of a subject were asked what they knew about it. The number giving any accurate details are listed in Table 8.2. Although based on a small, non-random sample, and not therefore generalisable, these exploratory findings generate possibilities for further research.

Table 8.2
Knowledge and interest frequencies
(interviewed in 1988)

Number of debates	Heard of	Interest	Detail
0	3	32	8
1	5	9	14
2	6	3	13
3	10	1	5
4	11	2	5
5	7	3	4
6	4	0	0
7	6	2	3
Total	52	52	52

People who were in some way consumers of education, or were public employees, were generally more aware of, interested in, and knowledgeable about educational issues. This finding has been supported in the early stages of analysis of the interviews carried out in 1992.

Table 8.3 shows the responses of informants in 1992 who were asked if they were interested in any of the subjects in a list of ten (housing, the police force, social benefits, unemployment, public transport, education, income tax, defence, the Poll Tax, health). In this small sample, a larger proportion of informants who were consumers of education (generously defined to include parents and students) or public employees expressed some interest in education.

Table 8.3
Expressed interest in education
(interviewed in 1992)

	Interested n=	Not interested n=
Consumers	19	10
Non-consumers	5	17
Public employees	13	6
Private employees	7	10
Not employed	4	11
Total	24	27

The most strongly supported finding from both quantitative and qualitative data is that interest in education is largely instrumental; ie. that individual interest is awakened by personal involvement.

Defining education as a private problem

There is a relatively short step between recognition of instrumental interest in education as a political issue and the emphasis on education as a private problem, rather than a public issue. Most social scientists are familiar with C. Wright Mills' differentiation between private troubles and public issues (Mills 1970, p.8-9). If this is applied to education, it can be seen that at a private, personal level troubles can involve the education of oneself or one's children, choice of school, choice of courses, examination results,

130

complaints about the institution, teachers and so on.

Many people do not seem to perceive education as relating to anything beyond their own private and localised arena. Indeed, several of my informants used the term "educational age" to support their lack of interest and reflect a common belief that education is not a lifelong experience:

> Education only lasts a short time but you pay tax all your life.
> Our daughter is a school secretary and my wife is a cleaner in the university. Now our sons are married and out of the way we don't seem to take much interest:

> As I'm not directly involved, I've very little interest. This is the whole point isn't it? How it affects you - and it doesn't.

Education may thus be associated with the private domain in which the family is nurtured and socialized. An "educational age" may be regarded as a stage in a natural process of personal growth that can be completed and left behind. From this perspective it may be seen as a non-controversial and therefore non-political fact of life.

At an issue level, in which education is regarded as a public matter, concern may be about the whole educational system, for example, teaching methods in general, types of school, the finance of schools, types of examinations, etc. This type of interest in education as a public issue is more commonly expressed by politicians, administrators, teachers, the media, and by only some of the parents of children currently in the education system. However, at any one time about two thirds of the electorate do not have any children at school, college or university. To many of them education only becomes and continues to be a significant issue when it is a personal problem, and it is only a personal problem when they have personal connections with the education system.

I am not implying any criticism of my informants by expressing regret at their lack of interest. Indeed, when the whole political climate is considered, the low priority accorded to education by many voters is quite understandable. The relative poverty experienced by many at a time of high unemployment, wage restraints and cuts in public spending also adds a further dimension. In 1987 I interviewed a local authority Education Officer who clearly explained what he saw as the nature of interest or lack of interest in education as a political issue:

> I happen to think that education's the most important thing in the world... It's easy for education to be vitally important if you're

living in a nice house, you've got a good job and you want to see your children in the same situation; education's vitally important isn't it? If you sit in the inner city where you see a certain amount of hopelessness about your own position and the fact that no matter how well your children might do at school - is that going to get them a job - education may not seem as relevant as it does to the middle class areas. I can understand that. I think that there are issues that are considered important. Housing is obviously important. Employment, or rather lack of employment, is extremely important to many. I think that support for one-parent families - the sort of support they need to sustain themselves in the city - is important. I think that those issues to those people are clearly more important. (Chief education officer, "Labourville")

The point is that as issues relating to personal survival (for example, unemployment, social security, housing) have assumed a more obvious and immediate importance to many people, education has been viewed as a luxury item on a personal issue agenda. Even at a personal level, education is often associated with long-term planning and short-term interests are, of necessity, regarded as most important.

Defining education as a "female" interest and "therefore" non-political

The main feminist complaint about artificial distinctions between private and public spheres is that, if the "private" sphere is not regarded as of public interest, no safety net is provided to combat potential abuses and injustices. In the present context, if education is defined as simply a personal problem, and not an important public issue, definitions of equal educational opportunities will be so weak that they are meaningless. Yet this process of associating education with individuals and their families in a supposedly private sphere clearly supports recent government policies of privatisation and individualisation. Moreover, the position of education within the public sphere has not been strengthened by the greater interest of women in educational issues. Using a feminist perspective we can see that it suffers a double blow via its association with the private sphere of the family, and with women's interests in particular, because women's interests are often seen as non-political.

Both quantitative and qualitative findings indicate that more interest in education is expressed by women than by men. For example, Parry, Moyser and Day (1992, p.262) found that over twice as many women as

132

men put education at the top of their issue agendas. After the first Greater Manchester Survey (in 1980-1) Edgell and Duke reported a greater cuts consciousness amongst parents in general and amongst mothers in particular. They found that the perceived impact of education spending cuts amongst women with dependents in all age groups was greater than that of men in the same situation. (It was noticeable that women without young dependents did not report a greater impact of spending cuts.)

According to the British Social Attitudes 1986 Report women (but not men) were becoming less likely to choose "smaller classes" as the main priority for improving primary schools (Jowell et al. 1986, Table 7.2). The writers claimed that the gradual drop in the proportion of large primary classes was a factor that was probably more apparent to women, because of their more direct contact with their children's schools. This impression that mothers knew more than fathers was reinforced during interviews in 1988 and 1992 when men frequently suggested that I interview their wives or tried to enlist the help of their wives or children in answering questions about education. The reverse was not the case, and women were generally prepared to deal with questions unaided.

Women tend to be more involved with the welfare state as producers as well as consumers. Edgell and Duke found that cuts in public spending affected women more than men in three ways: three-quarters of welfare state workers are women, women are the main users of collective social provision and "..as the major providers of care in the family - the less the welfare state does, the more is done by women." (Edgell and Duke 1992, p.118-9).

The association of education with the social role of the mother, and the greater involvement of women with the welfare state, can lead to a downgrading of education in political terms. Other "masculine" issues, associated with the workplace rather than the home, may take precedence in the public imagination; for example (male rather than female) unemployment, (male dominated) industrial action, and reductions in taxation. Indeed tax cuts could be seen to be potentially of more benefit to men, because of their higher average hourly rate of pay, and less beneficial to women because of their greater dependence on, and contact with, the public services that are to be "rolled back" in order to finance tax cuts.

Defining educational inequalities as "natural"

Most voters are aware of social class inequalities. For example, in analysing the responses of my interviewees, I created an index of support for Conservative policies by subtracting answers which did not favour Conservative policies from those which did. Thus, an answer with a plus sign indicated majority support and an answer with a minus sign indicated majority opposition. Of the 52 people interviewed in 1988, a majority of -32 were aware of social class. This majority increased to -35, out of the 51 people interviewed in 1992. The majority also felt that social class affected opportunities. Yet I also found that a majority of +28 in 1988, and +31 in 1992, were opposed to the abolition of private schools. This seemed odd!

When case study informants were asked in 1988 to explain their support for private schools the most common response (from 12) was that people should be free to spend their money as they chose and 10 said that a choice should be available:

> Let them that's got the money pay and let them that's not got the money go to others. If people don't have to rely on the state let them. Then there's more for them that do.

> State schools would suffer. There'd be more children in them and a higher ratio of children to teachers.

Several informants referred to the source of finance for private education, apparently believing that the government contributed nothing towards it:

> They [the Government] don't pay for them. We've got to have brains at the top otherwise we couldn't have brains in the middle. If I had the money I'd have sent mine. You've got to have highly educated people.

> If people want to send their children to private schools they're entitled to do so as long as they pay for it. They pay for it. There's nobody else.

However, from these small samples there emerged a large number of illustrations of the effects of relative deprivation on educational achievement. Many date back to the informant's childhood, or even to his/her parents' childhood, but they are particularly interesting in view of the Government's emphasis on parental "choice" in education. For example, a child's school leaving age was found to be largely determined by family income. To many of the informants, education beyond the usual

134

school leaving age was totally out of the question because of the family's need for an extra wage. One informant said that his mother left school at eleven:

... which was allowed in those days if you had a one parent family.

Another informant spoke of his mother leaving school at 14 to look after her mother who had had a stroke. His father ran away from home at 14 because his parents wanted him to work down the local mine. A strong Conservative identifier left school at 15 because of the financial needs of the family:

My father came out of work, so I was taken away and told to earn some pennies.

Financial constraints on the type of education children have appear to have been passed from generation to generation. For example, one informant talked about his mother's and father's education and how they tried to pay for him to have a private education:

[Fathers' education] He went to a boys secondary modern school because they couldn't afford to let him go to the grammar school because they had to buy their own books and were so poor that they couldn't afford them at that time. [Mothers' education] She went to grammar school but left at 14. They pulled her out before the end because they couldn't afford to keep her there.

[Informants' education] Instead of taking the 11+ I went to a boarding school because mum wanted me to. She had to pay to send me and my brother there. I went when I was 10 or 11 until I was 13. Then I went to a secondary modern school.

Another informant said that his mother left school at 12 and that he had to leave his elementary school at 14, although he would have liked to have had a better education:

They [his parents] were both from big families. They had to leave school to help keep the family.

[Why informant left at 14] Because I had to. Because I had to go and get a job and start work to help keep me brothers and sisters.

135

[His preferred education] I would rather have gone to an all boys school. In them days there was no such thing because you're parents couldn't afford it. Mine couldn't anyway.

Other families tried to pay for their children to be privately educated but had problems in keeping up the payments:

[Mother's education] For a while she was at a girls' private boarding school. Her father died. Therefore she left and I don't know where she went. She got some further education and a Pitmans shorthand typing qualification.

[Informant left private school at 15] It was just at the end of the war and I was off school a lot. Mother was ill and I wasn't doing well in my exams, so dad said I'd better get out and go to work.

When a family had enough money a child could stay at school after the school leaving age despite examination failures. The following informant, for example, had an affluent, self-employed father. He stayed at his grammar school until he was 19, later graduating and becoming a teacher.

I left school at 19 because I failed my O'Levels the first time and had to take an extra year. I was sport mad and spent more time on that than in the classroom.

This can be contrasted with one informant who was a single-parent. Her daughter was eligible for free school meals:

She [daughter] could have had them but I wouldn't embarrass her. We made sandwiches instead.

Those informants who had recently consumed private education also had problems. A self-employed Torytown builder had one child with an Assisted Place to which he contributed:

If my income was fixed I'd be laughing. It fluctuates and therefore there's just enough to maintain the house. I'm in debt and therefore living above my means.

When this man was interviewed again in 1992 it was found that his business was just about to close, he was expecting to have to sell his house and did not know how the family would cope.

Another informant went to a direct grant school herself but would not want her own children to have the same sort of education because of the distance she had to travel to school:

> There are a lot of benefits in being educated locally. I had to travel a long way to the direct grant school and my contemporaries at school were not otherwise known to me.

However, whilst the majority perceived the existence of social class, many deferential statements were made during the interviews. Several seemed to regard class distinctions as natural phenomena rather than social constructions:

> [About social class affecting opportunities.] It does. There's the rich, the middle class and the poor - so it does seem to have some effect. Naturally the poor can't be like the middle class and the middle class can't live up to the rich - so you've all got your own grades.

The emphasis of recent Conservative governments on parental choice means that the educational inequalities experienced by my informants will not be confronted by systematic political action. Indeed, I found over and over again that the idealized image of the parent was challenged by the data. In particular, educational decisions made by parents were often based on financial constraints, lack of information about the possibilities available or sometimes convoluted reasoning. For example, some parents regarded their daughters' education as less important than that of their sons' and made decisions accordingly. If the compounding of educational inequalities regarding gender and race were also considered in full, the fallacy in labelling inequalities as natural would be even more apparent.

Defining Government views as non-controversial

Any government, of whatever political perspective, is likely to present its own policies as non-controversial and will adopt a range of strategies in order to do so, ranging from overt force to the more covert legitimization of its own perspective as "common-sense" reality. Recent Conservative governments have tended to focus on the latter by defining changes in the education system as technical, rational and non-political. Broadfoot (and other social scientists) saw the rhetoric used and its emphasis on administration and efficiency as a means of legitimating Conservative ideology.

> The effect of this trend is not only to preclude explicit discussion of the different educational values that might be involved in any particular issue, but also to conceal a growing lack of consensus over educational priorities in general by defining them off the agenda of debate. (Broadfoot 1985, p.273)

It can even be claimed that politics should be taken out of education, as though education were purely a technical problem and solutions could be arrived at objectively. In his critique of what he called the "economic utility challenge" to education, Bailey argued that, by virtue of its implicit assumption of consensus about society, the economic utility model of education favoured by recent governments is essentially indoctrinary (Bailey 1984). To Conservatives, and the largely Conservative press, Government views have represented the status quo and not therefore a political bias. Where bias is identified as a problem in the education system it is, from this dominant perspective, most obviously an unacceptable left-wing bias. At the moment the most widely publicised pressure to keep politics out of education appears to come from the right-wing because a long-established government has the means to persuade (rather than coerce) voters to accept its definitions of reality through its determination of the agenda for educational debate.

We can see this production process in many statements by Conservatives. Margaret Thatcher regularly claimed a monopoly of traditional virtues for the Conservative party and interchanged expressions of truth and value to suggest that they had the same meaning:

> Most of us were brought up to respect these values. I respect them today, for they are the traditional values of British life. And as the false values of Socialism fade, so those true and traditional values are returning to our country. (Thatcher, Conservative Women's Conference 1988, quoted in *The Guardian*, 26 July 1988)

In 1987 the *Salisbury Review* described the Department of Education as, "..rotten with leftist ideology, and well-stocked with conspirators anxious to impose that ideology throughout the world of education". Baroness Cox, Conservative education spokeswoman in the House of Lords, claimed that:

Education has been turning into indoctrination. There are a growing number of education authorities and teacher groups who are committed to politics in the classroom. (Baroness Cox, Addressing the Freedom Association in 1987)

When making such criticisms Conservatives tend to ignore or sanction possible right-wing indoctrination. For example, during the 1987 General Election campaign, Margaret Thatcher visited Waldersdale Secondary Modern School, where Conservative hats, stickers and flags were handed out to pupils. The introduction of a National Curriculum also increases government control over the knowledge that is produced in schools.

Discourses of derision

Ball has described the critical tone of educational debate generated by recent governments as "discourses of derision". In other words the presentation of Conservative values as non-controversial is supported by the ridicule or denigration of alternative views and of British education itself. The education system itself, and teachers in particular, are derided as in some way failing the nation. Radical changes have been legitimized by the labelling of the education system as defective because of the influence of dangerous left-wing views.

Some aspects of the once unproblematic consensus are now beyond the pale, and policies which might have seemed like economic barbarism twenty years ago now seem right and proper. (Ball 1990, p.38)

Set in sharp relief with this new "consensus" or politically sponsored normative paradigm is the previous normative paradigm.

The false prophets of the 1960s gravely damaged British education. Instead of concerning themselves with standards and skills, they preached the virtues of "progressive" education and "spontaneous self-expression". They tried to use schools as an instrument of social engineering. (Conservative Research Department 1985, p.282)

Thus, the rhetoric used and methods favoured in the past are presented as false and "social engineering" equated with spurious attempts to generate a supposedly unnatural level of social equality rather than with the

139

Conservative government's version of social engineering via an increase in parental (and therefore social class) influence on educational outcomes.

Implicit in this derision is the suggestion that central government is not responsible for faults in the education system. If education is to be a private issue, rather than a public issue for which the Government has responsibility, then any liabilities have to be denied. Yet the effect of privatising the education system is to centralise control of education even further, in order to "protect" right-wing ideals. For example, at the Conservative Party Conference in 1987, Margaret Thatcher provided a long list of criticisms of an education system that her government had already been responsible for for eight years. She claimed that often children were deprived of an adequate education because of left-wing influences:

> And in the inner cities - where youngsters must have a decent education if they are to have a better future - that opportunity is all too often snatched from them by hard-left education authorities and extremist teachers. (Thatcher, quoted in the *Times Educational Supplement*, 16 October 1987)

A result of the more recent "Back to basics" campaign by the Government has been the rather unexpected (in view of the repeated emphasis on parental choice) blaming of parents for inadequacies in their children's education. John Patten announced in January 1994 that advice on morality, discipline, citizenship and family values would be sent to about 20 million homes. Margaret Morrissey was quoted as responding:

> Parents in our association have run around flogging themselves to death to keep schools resourced and in some cases to keep teachers. Now they are told that Mr Patten is spending £2 million sending out a leaflet telling them how to bring up their children. I think somebody is going to kill him. (Margaret Morrissey, secretary of the National Association of Parent Teacher Associations, quoted in *The Guardian*, 8 January 1994)

Implicit in such discourses is the assumption that only a Conservative government can be trusted to manage the British system of education and to defend it against the threat of dangerous political (ie. left-wing) and immoral elements. After 13 years in power the Government has achieved some success in its efforts to assume more control, whilst disassociating itself from faults in the system by laying the blame elsewhere.

Being "economical with the truth"

The phrase "economical with the truth" is being used here in order to avoid the suggestion that there is some absolute notion of truth that can be understood, communicated and accurately reproduced. In the framework of educational debate the "truth" is a very elusive concept indeed. Knowledge of educational sub-issues is acquired after a process of communication in which some facts are omitted (intentionally or not), some distorted and many are reinterpreted several times. As far as the "truth" is concerned a sort of economic scarcity, or vagueness, tends to favour the interests of the Government in that the various alternatives are not supported by a substantial information base. Examples at the time of my 1988 interviews included the continuing debate about educational standards, media reports of the *MacDonald Report* into the murder at Burnage High School, problems in administering an 11+ system in two Local Education Authority areas, and public ignorance about the Assisted Places Scheme.

Arguments about a supposed fall in educational standards are, for example, contradicted by statistics concerning the proportion and level of examination passes but supported by subjective views about discipline and literacy. Before a debate on that subject could be reasonably attempted, agreement would have to be reached about how to measure "standards", and elements of bias identified. Yet the identification of bias again assumes some recognition of the truth, some firm ground or framework within which the debate can take place, and this poses problems of its own. It is common for favourable/unfavourable measures (the firm ground) of "standards" to be chosen according to the perspectives of the combatants; examination passes and school league tables may, for example, be considered sufficient evidence from one perspective but not from another.

In 1988, I tried to assess informants' "knowledge" about the murder, in a Manchester school playground, of a schoolboy from an Asian family. Although the authors of the *MacDonald Report* into the murder and the Government at Westminster favoured publication, the local authority refused to publish the report because of anticipated legal problems. Parts of the report were released to the press and some newspapers (who had already defined the concept of anti-racial education as wrong) interpreted the released parts as a criticism of anti-racial education in general. Limited information about the report was therefore distorted by a biased media before reaching the public, who then imposed on it their own definitions of reality. Myths emerged, based on distorted media reports, hearsay or sometimes half understood messages. Analysis of the interviews in "Torytown" and "Labourville" in 1988 showed that it was the interviewees with the least knowledge about the murder of Abdul Ullah who tended to make racist comments, when asked about recent "events" at Burnage High School. Indeed right-wing fears that political education can result in the propagation of left-wing views can be countered by fears that political ignorance could make voters particularly vulnerable to fascist arguments.

A system of selection at 11+ continues in Torytown and it has been beset by problems every year. It has for a long time depended upon most parents' relative ignorance of the system. For example, until the 1970s the grade necessary for a pass varied from school to school. As relatively few families appealed against results it could be assumed that they trusted the decisions of experts, felt incapable of taking action or simply regarded educational successes or failures as personal and private. Since the reorganization of local authority boundaries in 1974 there has been a standard pass rate throughout the borough, all children having to achieve the same standard in tests and assessment in order to get a grammar school place. As a result the proportion of 11+ passes in some particularly deprived areas of the borough is now very low indeed.

A little known and complicated system of ranking pupils according to the performance of other pupils existed in Torytown until 1989. Teachers placed pupils in a numerical rank order for their class or school. For example, if a child was ranked 10th by the teacher and came 5th in the test, his/her actual examination mark would be added to the test mark of the child who actually came 10th. The final mark was a combination of the two and therefore depended on the child's own examination result and the result of the child coming 10th. Teachers could underestimate a child and the result of the child who got the mark that teachers predicted for another child could be particularly low. A child's parents would not know this and could not therefore appeal on such grounds.

Gender inequalities have their own implications regarding selection for secondary schools. The old practice of compensating for the supposed earlier maturation of girls than boys by raising the grade necessary for girls to pass the 11+, has now been declared illegal. Yet, in 1992, Birmingham City Council was still appealing against the ruling that it had discriminated against girls by providing fewer grammar school places for them. Again the significant point is that most families have known nothing about systematic sex discrimination and have regarded successes or failures as personal and private.

Most Torytown voters were aware of the continuing debate about systems of secondary education but few had any detailed knowledge about the selection process. This is not peculiar to Torytown, or to this point in time, as most of us (myself included) who were selected for a particular type of education at $11+$, have little knowledge about how the process in which we were involved worked.

Indeed strong opinions often emerged from a very weak knowledge base and were often apparently unrelated to personal experience. Attitudes to comprehensive schools and private schools show this quite clearly. Many interviewees had no personal experience of comprehensive schools but had negative attitudes towards them. The majority of informants were against the abolition of private schools, without any personal experience of them, and despite the fact that many thought of them as out of reach for low income families. Few had heard about Assisted Places (either by their correct name or as an opportunity for children from less affluent families to go to independent schools).

Some politicians may see the administration of education as less difficult if consumer sovereignty is not encumbered by a critical awareness of the finer points of the system. In this way lack of public knowledge considerably weakens the position of education within the public sphere. Yet when individuals do take an interest in education, and public debates do take place, they are severely handicapped by the scarcity of any identifiable "truth" within the discursive arena.

Lack of cohesion in attitudes to education

It has been argued that the trends considered above (and probably others not mentioned) have combined to reduce potential interest in education and weaken its status within the public sphere. Here I will look at the remaining fragments of interest in education and how they are themselves fragmented by the lack of cohesion between political partisanship and attitudes to educational sub-issues. In other words, although there are many educational pressure groups and individuals with a genuine interest in education as a political issue, voters' attitudes to education are so diverse that recent governments have been relatively free to pursue their own policies without feeling the constraints of the ballot-box.

Table 8.4 is based on analysis of the second phase of the *Greater Manchester Study* (1983-4 survey) and the 1983 *British Social Attitudes Survey* (reported in 1984, Jowell et al). It indicates a weak association between consumption of education and voting behaviour. Here we can see that in the early 1980s the Labour Party received more support from educational consumers in the Greater Manchester area than did the

Conservative Party. At a national level the Conservative Party received more support from both consumers and non-consumers, although consumption still seemed to have a slight influence. This tendency has continued, although we cannot be sure that a confounding variable has been excluded.

Table 8.4
Education consumption and party identification:
Torytown, Labourville and national data compared
GMS 1983/4 and BSA 1983/4

	n=	Conservative %	Labour %	Alliance %
Torytown:				
Consumers	84	33	40	26
Not consumers	204	45	30	25
Labourville:				
Consumers	103	29	55	16
Not consumers	200	38	47	15
BSA 1983/4:				
Consumers	682	44	39	17
Not consumers	835	45	38	17

Source: Edgell and Duke, GMS2, computer analysis; BSA, 1983

It was noticeable however, that many individual voters did not seem to have consistently left-wing or right-wing attitudes to the large range of individual sub-issues within the field of education. In order to assess the cohesion of attitudes to a variety of sub-issues I created two exploratory scales of educational radicalism (McKenzie 1993, pp209-217) for the analysis of the survey data that was available before I carried out my first interviews in 1988. My interest was in discovering the extent to which voters expressed consistently left-wing (most radical) or consistently right-wing views (least radical). In this I was obviously limited by the questions other researchers had chosen to ask. The first scale (Ed Rad I) used three questions that were asked in the *Greater Manchester Study*. A second scale of educational radicalism (Ed Rad II) was created by using three questions asked in the *British Social Attitudes Survey* of 1983 (Jowell et al. 1984).

In the analysis of both scales it was found that consumers of education reinforced when the scales of educational radicalism were cross tabulated with political partisanship. Again the modal response was also skewed to the politically right of centre, although there was again a weak association between educational radicalism and political partisanship.

The findings have so far been supported by more recent qualitative (and small-scale quantitative) data from the interviews carried out in 1988 and 1992. Very few informants expressed views that consistently supported the education policies of any one political party, although consumption of education and political partisanship have been found to have some influence.

Defending the place of education in the public sphere

It has been argued that, although this may not have been a systematic process, the trends identified have operated in the interests of Conservative governments by helping to define education as a private rather than a public issue. This has helped to legitimize the radical changes in education that have taken place since 1979. British governments have actually been able to increase their claims to knowledge and authority over the education system whilst promoting a theoretical and superficial movement towards consumer sovereignty. Legislation passed by Conservative governments since 1979 has increased the powers of central government over education to an unprecedented extent. At the same time education has gradually been squeezed out of public discourse via the promotion of public ignorance (economies with the truth) about education as a political issue.

However, the process is not complete, as a relatively small proportion of the population continue to challenge the dominant ideology and insist that education is still a controversial issue. These dogged individuals and groups are confronted by the Government's insistence that it knows best and that they have no argument to make. There has, nevertheless, been resistance at the grass roots level of policy implementation; examples being seen in the reluctance of many schools to apply for Grant Maintained status and teachers' refusal to administer some National Curriculum tests. Efforts have also been made to set alternative agendas; for example, the report of the *National Commission on Education* (1993). However, these are still responses to an agenda set by the Government and, as the official Opposition, the Labour Party has frequently been criticised for its failure to set a strong alternative agenda in order to seize the initiative.[4] Yet, whatever the agenda, a process by which an issue is gradually excluded from the public sphere should cause concern, and this is especially true in the case of education. The public has a vested interest in the control of knowledge and in a system of education that has such an incalculable positive or negative effect on individual lives.

Notes

1. Data collected during the 1980s was used for Janet McKenzie's Ph.D. thesis, Education as a Political Issue, University of Salford, 1990, ESRC award No. A00428624318. A version of this has now been published by Avebury. See References.

2. The fieldwork carried out in April 1992 was supervised by Janet McKenzie and Vic Duke and was financed jointly by Liverpool Institute of Higher Education and the University of Salford. The interviewing was shared between Janet McKenzie and Christine Benney. Both Vic Duke and Christine Benney are based in the Sociology Department, University of Salford.

3. The seven subjects were:
    a) Changes or proposed changes in the local provision of education.
    b) The Assisted Places scheme.
    c) City Technology Colleges.
    d) The Education Reform Bill (currently passing through Parliament.
    e) Proposals to let schools opt out of Local Education Authority control.
    f) The proposed abolition of the Inner London Education Authority.
    g) Recent events at Burnage High School in Manchester (the MacDonald Report into the murder of a pupil in the playground had received extensive press coverage in recent months).

4. See for example, Lawton 1992, p.30.

9 Green consumerism: Blurring the boundary between public and private

Peter Simmons

[1]From the perspective of science and policy, environmental issues represent a complex of inter related natural processes and effects which result from the physical "impacts" of human activity. They present a challenge to be resolved by the application of our problem solving and technological capabilities. However, this is only one side of the story. Far from being simply a cluster of objective problems to be remedied by the instrumentality of science, the problematic of the environment brings into existence a new public space in which the dominant values of our society are brought into question, a new space for democratic debate (Ewald 1992). The distinction between the public and private spheres is deeply embedded in the political organization of liberal democratic societies. Yet the global environmental problems in which the consumption patterns of advanced industrial societies are implicated force us to question the social robustness of a distinction that consigns market activity with profound public and environmental consequences to the sphere of private interests.

If we look more closely, however, we find situations where the distinction between public and private, and more specifically between polity and market, is increasingly unclear and where the identities of citizen and consumer blur. We find such an example in the introduction of market relationships into domains of public life and the political reconstruction of the citizen as a consumer of public services, what might be termed a consumer-citizen, which has been the focus of much recent debate.[2] At the same time though, public interest concerns have also led to the politicization of relationships in the economic sphere, in a way that casts the individual as a citizen-consumer. Although a wide range of issues have led to forms of political action by consumers none has mobilized such widespread involvement or raised such fundamental questions about the values of the industrial market economy as the environment. In this chapter I examine the significance of the emergence of the environment as a major consumer issue in Britain in the late 1980s and of the practice which became known as "green consumerism".[3]

Central to this development is the figure of the "green consumer". The account presented here adopts the view that green consumer activity cannot be explained purely in terms of the expression of utilitarian preferences in the choice of products within the market place, but that it also expresses an identification with wider moral and political values, including conceptions of the good society as one in which the natural environment is not despoiled, which does not harm other cultures or species, and which bequeaths the resources for future well being to its own offspring. Writers such as Sagoff (1988) argue against treating citizens as consumers by using the language and tools of economic valuation as a surrogate for public debate; and emphasises the fundamentally political questions of value that inhere in environmental issues. Yet the analytical distinction between spheres of action elides the complexity and ambivalence of individual experience. At the level of cultural practice, as ethnographers have found, "drawing the artificial boundaries between economy and culture, economy and religion, economy and language, economy and ecology, and so on, is an extremely difficult task" (Gregory & Altman 1989, p.197). Green consumerism is a case in point. By treating consumers as citizens it represents a blurring of the distinction between economy and politics, between private and public. Nevertheless, what I wish to argue is that, despite this conflation of the roles of consumer and citizen, the expression of non market values in consumer practice is constrained by the economic, str ctural and cultural conditions to which individuals are subject within the institutional context of the market.[4] In this chapter I will, first of all, outline the conceptual and political context from which green consumerism emerged in the 1980s and review briefly the evidence for the phenomenon. I then consider the tensions and conflicts experienced by green consumers and critically examine some of the mechanisms for enabling green consumer action. I conclude by identifying a number of problems inherent in prevailing constructions of green consumerism that need to be addressed if we are to formulate strategies that enable individuals to participate actively in developing sustainable patterns of consumption.

Sovereign consumers and environmental concern

More than twenty years ago UK Friends of the Earth put its name to a book entitled *Consumers' Guide to the Protection of the Environment*. The final chapter, "Consumer Power", concludes that:

> The conversion to a lifestyle more related to the ability of the Earth to supply our needs must start by the consumer regaining the political power of the individual to have real choice in the market place (Holliman 1971).

The question of what might constitute "real choice" is one to which we shall return below, but the connection that it makes between consumer power and consumer choice invokes the notion of consumer sovereignty.

Consumer sovereignty is a market ideology which draws an analogy between an individual's political vote as citizen at the ballot box and her economic "vote" as consumer in the market place. It holds that consumers possess the power to remedy inadequacies in the products sold to them by bringing economic pressure to bear upon producers through the aggregation of their market choices. There has been long-running debate about the potential for extending consumer sovereignty to bring about increased corporate accountability on wider social issues.[5] "Ecologically responsible" or "green" consumption represents one distinct form that the attempt to extend consumer sovereignty has taken:

> As environmental concern increases, there is a tendency - still more celebrated than measurable - for "ecologically responsible" citizens to express their identification with the public interest by their private purchasing decisions. People can thus influence environmental issues by "voting" with their dollars, as well as with their ballot. In effect, they are taking seriously the analogy between "dollar" votes and political votes, which forms the basis of the corporate defence of consumer sovereignty. (Vogel 1975, quoted in Smith 1990, p.183).

This extended notion of consumer sovereignty goes beyond analogy and treats consumer choices as an instrument not merely for the expression of product-related preferences but also of popular political will.

Although reported levels of environmental concern have continued to increase over the years, the tendency described in Vogel's account and rooted in the ideology of consumer sovereignty, did not achieve notable prominence in Britain until the late 1980s, when it appeared under the banner of "green consumerism". The emergence of green consumerism at this time has to be seen in the context of a conjunction of social and political conditions and events.[6] The ideological climate was, to a great extent, conditioned by the political ascendancy of neoliberalism and its social expression in the discourse and values of the "enterprise culture" of the 1980s (Keat and Abercrombie 1991, Heelas and Morris 1992). As the politics of Thatcherism transformed the political agenda, so increasingly the market was upheld as the solution to a whole range of public problems. At the same time, environmental movement campaigning throughout the 1980s had focused media and public attention on a succession of high profile issues, highlighting the shortcomings of government policy and undermining its public credibility. One issue in particular, the link between the CFC propellants used in aerosols and stratospheric ozone depletion, with its well-publicized risks to human health, focused attention on the consumption nexus. Friends of the Earth launched a campaign in August 1987, calling for consumers to boycott aerosol products that contained CFCs and to seek out those alternatives which did not, such as pump action sprays or those using hydrocarbon propellants. The subsequent announcement in February 1988 by a group of leading aerosol manufacturers that they would discontinue the use of CFCs in 95 per cent of their products by the end of 1989 was widely seen as a triumph of consumer power.[7] This episode played a crucial role in alerting business to the changes in consumer expectations and, by appearing to offer a new model of political agency expressed via the market, it primed consumers for a more active role.

It is against this backgound that green consumerism emerged as a putative movement, championed by environmental consultants John Elkington and Julia Hailes who, together with a coalition of market researchers, environmentalists and retailers, were responsible for a number of national promotional events and publications aimed at enrolling both business and the general public. These began in September 1988 with a national Green Consumer Shopping Week and the publication of The Green Consumer Guide (Elkington and Hailes 1988), and were followed by a second promotion and publication the following year.[8] Quite fortuitously for its promoters the event coincided with the highly publicised "green conversion" of Prime Minister Margaret Thatcher, who made major speeches to the Royal Society and to the Conservative Party conference on the need for urgent action to address global environmental problems and in particular stratospheric ozone depletion, which served to endorse public concern and the message of green consumerism. Green consumerism differs from the widely used boycott approach in that it

150

attempts to direct consumer choice toward certain products rather than away from them. It aims to encourage manufacturers by building a market for products that are deemed to be less harmful to the environment, rather than sanctioning those which are not. Underlying this market-building approach is a shift of emphasis from the predominant environmentalist theme of consuming less and to one of consuming differently. The issue ceases to be framed as one of changing lifestyles, in other words, whether one consumes, to one of changing products, that is, what one consumes, an ideology to which business can much more readily adapt. The widespread media attention received by the promotional events and surrounding publications helped to mobilize business concern. As business sought to understand the implications of the changes in consumer expectations, highlighted by the events in the aerosols market, market researchers attempted to delineate this new force in the market place.

The green consumer in Britain

Surveys of public environmental attitudes recorded a marked rise in levels of environmental concern among the British public during the latter half of the 1980s (Department of the Environment 1992). This was undoubtedly stimulated by media coverage of a succession of major environmental issues brought into the public arena by the environmental groups, who showed themselves to be adept at tuning into and focusing public concerns and who experienced a dramatic increase in membership in 1988 and 1989 (Grove-White 1991, Cairncross 1991). This growing environmental concern was accompanied by changes in the attitudes of individuals as consumers.

The first market research report to attempt a qualitative assessment of this new phenomenon, produced by one of the promoters of green consumerism, suggested that it was a minority activity that could very rapidly grow to a mass market trend (Brand New Product Development 1988). Surveys by Market and Opinion Research International (MORI), which attempted to go beyond the study of attitudes by asking people what they actually do about environmental problems - rather than simply what they think or what they say that they would be prepared to do - have been the basis for claims that a significant proportion of the population are "green consumers".[9] The proportion of respondents identified as green consumers in MORI's regular national surveys grew from 19% at the time of the first "Green Consumer Week" in September 1988 to 47% by July 1989 and has fluctuated around that level ever since. In a MORI survey of a representative sample of more than 2,000 British adults conducted in late 1991 this rose as high as 54%, a figure which tallies closely with the 58% recorded by a major European survey early the following year (EUROBAROMETER 1992), but was followed by a 25% decrease to just 40% in July 1992.[10] Although the MORI studies found that certain sections of the public - women, people from social classes AB and, to a slightly lesser extent, C_1, and people in the 25-44 age group - were more likely than others to be green consumers, its research shows green consumers across all social categories. These figures are based, however, on an extremely minimal definition of the green consumer: that is, that an individual had chosen, sometime in the past year or two, one product over another in the belief that it is in some way less environmentally harmful. They give no indication of the frequency or intensity of the behaviour and tend to raise as many questions as they answer about the incidence of green consumer activity.

In an attempt to link green purchasing behaviour to other, non-market behaviours, such as recycling, the MORI studies also asked individuals to indicate which from a list of consumption-related "green" activities they had performed in the last twelve months. A recent study (MORI 1992) also asked which of these had been done out of concern for the environment. For all of the listed activities the number of people claiming to have been motivated by environmental concern was lower. In many cases this result might be expected, as some of the actions could equally well be attributed to economic motivations (for example, buying lead-free petrol, which is cheaper than the leaded variety, buying energy-efficient appliances or reducing energy use in the home). The same could also apply to "buying products made from recycled material". For example, one of the most commonly purchased products, toilet rolls made from recycled paper, are often cheaper than many competing products. On the other hand, when only 75% of those who said that they "bought a different product because it was less damaging to the environment than [their] usual brand" or who had "joined/been a member of an environmental group" claimed to have done so out of concern for the environment the explanation for the discrepancy is less clear. At the very least it suggests some ambiguity in the respondents' interpretation either of the question or of their own actions. It also highlights the limitations of survey research as a means of investigating meaning and ambiguity in human behaviour. In order to obtain a better sense of the dilemmas and conflicts that they experienced, the author conducted a series of interviews and group discussions with "green consumers" during 1993.[11]

152

The dilemmas and conflicts of green consumerism

It emerged clearly from the interviews that when individuals engage in market transactions they very often experience a conflict between the different values which they hold. Thus, even for consumers expressly motivated by some form of environmental concern, price still remained a predominant issue. Significantly few of those interviewed saw a reduction in their level of consumption as an alternative course of action that was not price dependent. Some resisted the implications of such an alternative quite strongly, expressing a reluctance to relinquish the comfort and convenience afforded by the hard won commodities which they had come to associate with an acceptable standard of living. Some expressed a distrust of others, a concern that if they themselves made sacrifices others could not be relied upon to follow suit, thus rendering their efforts meaningless.[12] Above all, however, the views of many of these individuals revealed a deep ambivalence about the value of the green consumer activities in which they engaged. Scepticism about the environmental claims made for products by their manufacturers or about the extent to which the actions in which they as consumers engaged actually made any difference existed alongside a sense of nonetheless "feeling better" because they were "doing something". For some of them the suspicion that their individual efforts were simply licensing industry to continue business as usual deepened at times to a profound cynicism.

Part of the problem here can be traced to the structure of the green consumer's relationship to the producer. The individualized "responsible shopper" approach, which does not have the visibility of public mounted consumer boycott campaigns, is dependent on the market mechanism to aggregate individual consumer choices as "revealed preferences" and communicate them to a multiplicity of individual companies. Consequently, even where altered patterns of consumption begin to have some impact in a particular market, the effect upon industry and the environmental consequences may not be directly visible to the consumer. The link between consumer action and its outcome is mediated in both directions by market institutions. Information about changes that result either directly or indirectly from consumer action is controlled by manufacturers and retailers, and usually presented to promotional ends. Yet survey research has shown that business is not generally trusted as a source of environmental information (MORI 1992). Our own research found that whilst many of the green consumers interviewed were distrustful of business, they also tended to be dependent on producer-supplied environmental information when making purchasing decisions.

For many of the green consumers to whom we spoke, therefore, there was a tension between the perception that firms cannot be trusted to embrace non-market values and a dependency on the producer as a source of transactional information. The absence of alternative sources of information constrained these individuals to act **as if** they trusted the information provided by industry even when they believe that information to be inadequate or misleading, a situation that compounded the sense of powerlessness experienced by several of those interviewed.

Despite arguments that one outcome of post-fordist developments in the economy has been an enabling of consumer choice (Abercrombie 1992), which would seem to support the possibility of an extended consumer sovereignty, these green consumers continued to experience an imbalance of power between themselves and business. Although all of them engaged in forms of consumption-related environmental activity, from buying products that were less environmentally harmful to recycling packaging, most believed that without other constraints upon industry the effect of their individual actions would be limited, if not insignificant. Whilst there was some faith in the power of individual consumer action to affect the behaviour of firms, they displayed little or no confidence in the power of market forces alone to realize the values that they held. Rather than relying on the invisible hand, the majority of those interviewed identified a need for intervention in the market opportunity structure to facilitate the growth of the market in less environmentally damaging goods combined with strong regulation to curb corporate environmental irresponsibility.

Although many of the green consumers who participated in the study expressed the view that the authority to bring about changes in a market populated by large corporations lay not with a sovereign consumer but with the state, this view was complicated by scepticism and distrust, based on their perceptions of the government's environmental record and political self interest, and on the belief held by some that a convergence of interests tended to engender a collusive relationship between industry and government. Thus these green consumers felt impelled, for a variety of reasons, both instrumental and expressive, to take personal action of some sort, but found themselves dependent in various ways upon organizations which they distrusted and over which, individually, they have little influence or control.

Beyond private action: empowering the green consumer

The dilemmas facing green consumers highlight the problems of attempting

154

to use the market as the institutional means for connecting the individual to larger social identities and goals. With many markets dominated by a handful of very large companies, the individual consumer finds herself in an unequal relationship with powerful economic actors. For consumers to have the power to influence corporate behaviour to any significant degree the relationship between consumer and corporation has to be institutionally mediated by some form of co-ordinating mechanism.

The most notable attempts at instituting formal mechanisms to encourage green consumerism have been the various environmental labelling schemes, which include national product and packaging labelling schemes, and the European Union's eco-labelling scheme (EEC 1992). Although framed primarily in terms of market transparency and consumer protection, and serving to reduce consumer dependence on producer-supplied information, state-sanctioned environmental labelling does not simply constitute a form of product information but, by its very presence, also communicates a normative signal to consumers. In the British Government's Sustainable Development Strategy eco-labelling appears as one of the few specific mechanisms for enabling individuals to contribute to achieving societal goals (HM Government 1994). However, from the perspective of consumer empowerment, environmental labelling suffers from a number of inherent limitations. In the first place, the voluntary nature of producer participation in current schemes reduces their potential for giving consumers greater influence over producers. More fundamentally however, policies that rely mainly on environmental product labelling to stimulate changes in consumption patterns tend to assume an individualized, rational, relatively unconstrained consumer and do not address the "exogenous" conditions that shape consumption patterns and constrain behavioural change.[13]

The other main source of mediating institutions is consumer organization (Winward 1994). Historically, consumer organisations have assumed a representational role on issues of consumer rights and safety, as well as increasing market transparency by product testing and providing information to enable consumers to make informed choices. In Britain, however, established consumer organizations have tended not to give environmental concerns a high priority.[14] Newer not-for-profit organizations, such as New Consumer and Ethical Consumer, have been established to provide information services similar to those of traditional consumer organizations such as the Consumers' Association, publishing magazines and shopping guides. Unlike the older consumer organizations, and unlike the authors of the Green Consumer Guide, they have concentrated on assessing the ethical performance of the company rather

155

than the performance of individual products.[15] These initiatives represent an important source of information about the producers of goods that complements environmental assessments of the products themselves. However, the wide range of ethical issues which they address lacks the focus of the environment as a package of issues and does not command such widespread support. This weakens their capacity to mobilize a large body of consumer concern, which may be reflected in the difficulties that they have experienced in expanding their circulation to reach a wider public. At the same time, whilst they perform a valuable role in the struggle to increase corporate responsiveness to ethical concerns, they do not play a representational role analogous to that performed by traditional consumer organizations. Self-organizing consumer co-operatives also have a long history in Britain and appear to offer a means of collectivizing green consumers to give them more power in the market place. Unfortunately, most locally organized ventures have tended to be short lived and an attempt by the publishers of New Consumer magazine to form a national ethical consumer co-operative, aimed initially at building a stronger market for organically grown produce, also proved unsuccessful. Environmental groups have, at times, also co-ordinated consumer action. Through consumer campaigns, such as those mounted by Friends of the Earth and the Women's Environmental Network, they provide consumers with information and a means of collectivizing their action. These campaigns almost invariably take the form of boycotts, however, rather than directing action towards the green consumer goal of developing more sustainable markets.[16] Whilst these are an effective way of attracting attention to an issue, they tend to be rather episodic and do not provide a consistent means for channelling consumer action; in fact, overloading the public with anxiety-provoking environmental campaigns may even be counter-productive, running the risk of inducing "issue fatigue".

Conclusion

At the heart of green consumerism is the idea that a politicized market can create an economic "democracy of small decisions", in which the purchasing decisions of individual consumers constitute an expression of popular political will that can play a part in regulating the environmental consequences of consumption.[17] Yet it is this market-based construction that also gives rise to the tensions and conflicts experienced by would-be green consumers. Many of the problems that have been identified can be seen to be an inherent consequence of framing green consumerism in terms of consumer sovereignty. Most importantly, even though it brings non-market values into the market place, green consumerism tends to individualize the consumer and does not take account of the social context within which consumption decisions are made. In this respect it embodies a model of the consumer derived from neoclassical economic thinking. A related problem is that market-based green consumerism places an increased onus of responsibility on the individual, whilst at the same time the institutional structure of the market isolates the individual consumer. Attempts to collectivize consumer action represent a strategic response that attempts to mitigate the conditions of this inimical institutional environment. At the same time, however, recognition of the conflict between the profit-maximizing rationality of the market and the values of environmental protection also leads to consumer scepticism of market institutions as a means for achieving the goal of sustainability. This is further complicated by various forms of consumer dependency. On the one hand, as we have seen, many consumers find themselves dependent on producers for information, something that can be overcome to some extent by the provision of alternative sources of information by consumer and environmental organizations. On the other hand, there can also be technological dependency, as in the case of automobile use which, due to its social embeddedness and the gradual erosion of alternative forms of infrastructural provision, cannot realistically be addressed by individual action but which nonetheless is a source of individual concern. Thus consumer inaction cannot be assumed simply to denote a lack of awareness or concern about the environmental consequences of consumption - that is, a problem for environmental education - but may represent the outcome of less visible processes involving institutional distrust, dependency relations, and conflicts between institutional contexts and social values.

One further consequence of framing the "greening" of consumption in terms of participation in increasingly globalized commodity markets is that it tends to preclude the consideration of forms of non-market or local provision and limits the scope for mobilizing the creative resources of consumers themselves. To return to the earlier quotation from Holliman, fostering a diversity of institutional arrangements would represent a genuine extension of consumer choice and would open up new possibilities for developing more sustainable patterns of consumption. Under the ideological sway of market thinking, however, there is a lack of political commitment to fostering the conditions under which such alternatives might more readily develop and prosper.[18]

To recap, historically the roles of citizen and consumer have been located on either side of the divide between public and private. At the heart of the market ideology of consumer sovereignty is an analogy between the role of citizen and the role of consumer, but as long as this refers only to the expression of the consumer's commodity values it remains an analogy and does not alter the boundary between politics and economy. That boundary does become blurred when consumers are encouraged, and attempt, to extend their authority over producers to embrace fundamentally political issues such as environmental protection through the practices of green consumerism. What though is the significance of this blurring of the distinction between politics and the market? In its sustainable development strategy document, under the heading "Green Consumerism", the British Government claims that "one of the most powerful ways in which individuals can influence environmental matters is through the products they buy" (HM Government 1994, p.212). Green consumerism undoubtedly draws attention to the public environmental consequences of private consumption but, as we have seen, far from unambiguously empowering the individual, it has left many individuals feeling powerless and cynical. Green consumerism, conceived as a form of consumer sovereignty and as it is expressed in public policy, ironically is disempowering precisely because it individualizes the issues and ignores the contextual constraints upon consumer action.

Thus the tensions and contradictions experienced by green consumers are not merely an individual problem - they are a consequence of the way in which green consumerism itself is constructed. Making progress towards developing sustainable patterns of production and consumption depends upon individuals playing an active part. The Government recognizes that encouraging individuals to translate their environmental attitudes into action is a key challenge for the future of its sustainability strategy and suggests that "there may be more that could be done to encourage individual commitment, to give incentives or to remove obstacles" (HM Government 1994, pp.211-12). But if this strand of the Government's strategy fails to elicit the desired response it is perhaps unfair to lay the blame at the door of the individual consumer. The argument that has been advanced in this chapter is that framing the "problem" of unsustainable consumption in terms of the characteristics of the individual consumer (typically ignorance, "confusion", self interest or inertia) or framing the response primarily in terms of individual incentives and obstacles can be seriously counter productive, because a more fundamental, if unavoidably difficult, problem remains unaddressed: that of the institutional and cultural conditions that shape both patterns of consumption and the possibilities for consumer action.

Notes

1. The research on which this chapter draws was funded by the UK
    Economic and Social Research Council under its Global
    Environmental Change Initiative, grant number Y320283001. I
    should like to acknowledge the helpful comments on an earlier draft
    of this chapter received from colleagues at the Centre for the Study
    of Environmental Change and from Stephen Edgell. Its remaining
    faults are all my own work.

2. In addition to the discussions in this volume see also Keat and
    Abercrombie 1991, and Keat, Whiteley and Abercrombie 1994.

3. The word "consumerism" has two usages. The first, often negative
    sense in which it is used refers to commodity consumption as a
    cultural end in itself. The sense in which it appears in "green
    consumerism" originated with the consumer movement in the USA
    and refers to the principle of consumer organization. The ambiguity
    of the term captures something of the ambiguities of green
    consumerism itself.

4. The phrase "non-market values" is used here to refer to social
    values other than those concerned with individual utility, particularly
    exchange value and use value, which usually are associated with
    market transactions. The term is used in contrast not simply with
    utilitarian "commodity values" of price and efficiency, but also with
    the social positional values associated with the symbolic
    consumption of certain goods (Hirsch 1976, Bourdieu 1984).
    "Environmental values" would be more specific to the example
    under discussion but begs the question as to what is being valued
    when citizens act in this way.

5. See Smith (1990) for a recent discussion of the literature on
    consumer sovereignty and its extension to issues of social concern.

6. There is insufficient space here to examine the conditions of its
    emergence. For an account of the history and dynamics of green
    consumerism in Britain, see Simmons (1993b). There are also a
    number of other issues which I have been unable to discuss here; in
    particular, environmentalist criticisms that green consumerism does
    not tackle the "real" issue of need - that is, of the use value of
    commodities as opposed to their exchange value - (Irvine 1989) and

that it represents a futile but costly diversion of resources from the "real" business of environmental protection carried on by the NGOs (Rose 1990).

7.   In fact, the picture was considerably more complex than that and organizational and technological factors played a considerable part in the changes that took place. The point here, however, is that the outcome was widely perceived to be a result of consumer pressure. The episode is analyzed in detail in Simmons (1993a).

8.   Elkington & Hailes' book, which sold 95,000 copies in its first three months of publication and found its way into the non-fiction bestseller lists, became the "bible" of green consumerism. Its successor, *The Green Consumer's Supermarket Shopping Guide* (Elkington & Hailes 1989), published the following year, enjoyed even greater public success, selling 75,000 copies in its first week.

9.   It suggests that market researchers simply "measured" an objectively given phenomenon. But, the categories produced by market research firms were themselves part of the process through which "the green consumer" was constituted as a focus for organizational action. This process is examined in more detail in Simmons (1993b).

10. Discussions of the 1988 and 1989 surveys can be found in Corrado (1989) and Corrado and Ross (1990). A summary of data from 1990-1992 can be found in Worcester (1993). I am grateful to MORI for making these reports available to me.

11. More than eighty people participated in the interviews, which were carried out in the Midlands and the North West of England, and involved roughly equal numbers of men and women drawn from all socio-economic and age groups. The basic criterion for inclusion was that the individuals should have engaged in at least two from a list of fifteen consumption-related activities in the previous twelve months. On average participants had engaged in seven or eight of the listed activities, which included both purchasing products that were believed to be less environmentally harmful and other consumption-related activities such as recycling.

12. This classic prisoner's dilemma in the face of the free rider problem confronts any attempt to resolve collective problems through individual action in the market.

160

13. For a fuller discussion of some of the difficulties faced by the European eco-labelling scheme, particularly credibility problems associated with the production of criteria for the award of an environmental label, see Simmons (forthcoming).

14. This is beginning to change. For example, the Consumers' Association has begun to include assessments of environmental performance in the product tests reported in its magazine *Which?* and a representative of the National Consumers' Council sits on the UK Ecolabelling Board. In general, however, traditional consumer protection concerns prevail over broader environmental issues.

15. Although *Ethical Consumer* magazine proposes to include an environmental assessment of individual products in future issues. (*Ethical Consumer* 27 January 1994, p.3).

16. An exception to this was Friends of the Earth's campaign against the use of rainforest hardwoods which, during the latter part of the 1980s, encouraged consumers to buy hardwood products from sustainably managed sources in order to build the market for alternatives. The Women's Environmental Network, which already provides consumer information as part of its campaigns, notably on paper products, also encourages the use of reusable alternatives to disposable products.

17. On small decisions, see Hirsch 1977.

18. For recent discussions of alternative forms of economic organization, see Ekins & Max-Neef 1992, Chapter 11, Wainwright 1994, Chapter 6, and the journal *New Economics*. On the successful Japanese Seikatsu Club, which provided the model for the New Consumer co-operative, see Maruyama 1991.

Part 3
THE EXPERIENCE OF THE PUBLIC SPHERE

10 Bodily experience in public space

Richard Sennett

Western civilization has had persistent trouble in honouring the dignity of the body and diversity of human bodies; I have sought to understand how these body troubles have been expressed in architecture, in urban design, and in planning practice.

I was prompted to write this history out of bafflement with a contemporary problem: the sensory deprivation which seems to curse most modern building; the dullness, the monotony, and the tactile sterility which afflicts the urban environment. This sensory deprivation is all the more remarkable because modern times have so privileged the sensations of the body and the freedom of physical life. When I first began to explore sensory deprivation in space, the problem seemed a professional failure - modern architects and urbanists having somehow lost an active connection to the human body in their designs. In time I came to see that the problem of sensory deprivation in space has larger causes and deeper historical origins.

The passive body

Some years ago a friend and I went to see a film in a suburban shopping mall near New York. During the Vietnam War a bullet had shattered my friend's left hand, and the military surgeons had been obliged to amputate above the wrist. Now he wore a mechanical device fitted with metal

165

fingers and thumb which allowed him to hold cutlery and to type. The movie we saw turned out be a particularly gory war epic through which my friend sat impassively, occasionally offering technical comments. When it was over, we lingered outside, smoking, while waiting for some other people to join us. My friend lit his cigarette slowly; he then held up the cigarette in his claw to his lips steadily, almost proudly. The movie partons had just sat through two hours of bodies blasted and ripped, the audience applauding particularly good hits and otherwise thoroughly enjoying the gore. People streamed out around us, glanced uneasily at the metal prosthesis, and moved away; soon we were an island in their midst.

When the psychologist Hugo Munsterberg first looked at a silent movie in 1911, he thought the modern mass media might dull the senses; in a film; "the massive outer world has lost its weight", he wrote, "it has been freed from space, time, and causality"; he feared that "moving pictures ... reach complete isolation from the practical world". (Hugo Munsterberg, *The Film: A Psychological Study: The Silent Photoplay in 1916*, New York: Dover Publications, 1970, pp. 95, 82). Just as few soldiers taste the movie pleasures of ripping other bodies apart, filmed images of sexual pleasure have very little to do with real lovers' sexual experience. Few films show two elderly naked people making love, or naked fat people; movie sex is great the first time the stars get into bed. In the mass media, a divide opens up between represented and lived experience.

Psychologists who followed Munsterberg explained this divide by focusing on the effect of mass media on viewers as well as on the techniques of the media themselves. Watching pacifies. Though perhaps some few among the millions addicted to watching torture and rape on screen are aroused to become torturers and rapists themselves, the reaction to my friend's metal hand shows another, certainly larger response: vicarious experience of violence desensitizes the viewer to real pain. In a study of such television watchers, for instance, the psychologists Robert Kubey and Mihaly Csikszentmihalyi found that "people consistently report their experiences with television as being passive, relaxing, and involving relatively little concentration", (Kubey and Csikszentmihalyi 1990, p.175). Heavy consumption of simulated pain, like simulated sex, serves to numb bodily awareness.

If we look at and speak about bodily experiences more explicitly than did out great grandparents, perhaps our physical freedom is not therefore as great as its seems; through the mass media, at least, we experience our bodies in more passive ways than did people who feared their own sensations. What then will bring the body to moral, sensate life? What will make modern people more aware of each other, more physical responsive?

166

The spatial relations of human bodies obviously make a great deal of difference in how people react to each other, how they see and hear one another, whether they touch or are distant. Where we saw the war film, for instance, influenced how others reacted passively to my friend's hand. We saw the film in a vast shopping mall on the northern periphery of New York City. There is nothing special about the mall, just a string of thirty or so stores built a generation ago near a highway; it includes a movie complex and is surrounded by a jumble of large parking lots. It is one result of the great urban transformation now occurring, which is shifting population from densely packed urban centres to thinner and more amorphous spaces, suburban housing tracts, shopping malls, office campuses, and industrial parks. If a theatre in a suburban mall is a meeting place for tasting violent pleasure in air conditioned comfort, this great geographic shift of people into fragmented spaces has had a larger effect in weakening the sense of tactile reality and pacifying the body.

This is first of all so because of the physical experience which made the new geography possible, the experience of speed. People travel today at speeds our forbears could not at all conceive. The technologies of motion, from automobiles to continuous, poured-concrete highways, made it possible for human settlements to extend beyond tight packed centres out into peripheral space. Space has thus become a means to the end of pure motion. We now measure urban spaces in terms of how easy it is to drive through them, to get out of them. The look of urban space enslaved to these powers of motion is necessarily neutral: the driver can drive safely only with the minimum of idiosyncratic distractions; to drive well requires standard signs, dividers, and drain sewers, and also streets emptied of street life apart from other drivers. As urban space becomes a mere function of motion, it thus becomes less stimulating in itself; the driver wants to go through the space, not to be aroused by it.

The physical condition of the travelling body reinforces this sense of disconnection from space. Sheer velocity makes it hard to focus one's attention on the passing scene. Complementing the sheath of speed, the actions needed to drive a car, the slight touch on the gas pedel and the brake, the flicking of the eyes to and from the rearview mirror, are micro motions compared to the arduous physical movements involved in driving a horse drawn coach. Navigating the geography of modern society requires very little physical effort, hence engagement; indeed, as roads become straightened and regularised, the voyager need account less and less for the people and buildings on the street in order to move, making minute motions in an ever less complex environment. Thus the new geography reinforces the mass media. The traveller, like the television viewer,

167

experiences the world in narcotic terms; the body moves passively, desensitized in space, to destinations set in a fragmented and discontinuous urban geography.

Both the highway engineer and the television director create what could be called "freedom from resistance". The engineer designs ways to move without obstruction, effort, or engagement; the director explores ways for people to look at anything, without becoming too uncomfortable. In watching the people withdraw from my friend after the movie, I realised he threatened them, not so much with the sight of a wounded body as with an active body marked and constrained by experience.

This desire to free the body from resistance is coupled with the fear of touching, a fear made evident in modern urban design. In siting highways, for instance, planners will often direct the river of traffic so as to seal off a residential community from a business district, or run the river through residential ares to separate rich and poor sections or ethnically divergent sections. In community development, planners will concentrate on building schools or housing at the centre of the community rather than at its edge where people might come into contact with outsiders. More and more, the fenced, gated, and guarded planned community is sold to buyers as the very image of the good life. It is thus perhaps not surprising that, in a study of the suburb near the mall where we saw the war film, the sociologist M. P. Baumgartner found, "on a day to day basis, life is filled with efforts to deny, minimise, contain, and avoid conflict. People shun confrontations and show great distaste for the pursuit of grievances or the censure of wrongdoing" (Baumgartner 1988, p.127). Through the sense of touch we risk feeling something or someone as alien. Our technology permits us to avoid that risk.

Thus, a great pair of engravings William Hogarth made in 1751 appear strange to modern eyes. In these engravings, *Beer Street* and *Gin Lane*, Hogarth meant to depict images of order and disorder in the London of his time. *Beer Street* shows a group of people sitting close together drinking beer, the men with their arms around each other's shoulders, or touching the women's forearms. For Hogarth, bodies touching each other signalled social connection and orderliness, much as today in small southern Italian towns a person will reach out and grip your hand or forearm in order to talk seriously to you. Whereas *Gin Lane* displays a social scene in which none of the bodies touch, each person catatonically withdrawn in him, or herself and drunk on gin; the people in *Gin Lane* have no corporeal sensation of one another, nor of the stairs, benches, and buildings in the street. This lack of physical touch was Hogarth's image of disorder in urban space. Hogarth's conception of bodily order and disorder in cities was far different from that purveyed by the builder of sealed communities to his crowd fearing clients.

It is evidence of this sort, the stretched out geography of the modern city, in concert with modern technologies for desensitising the human body, which has led some critics of modern culture to claim that a profound divide exists between the present and the past. Sensate realities and bodily activity have eroded to such an extent that modern society seems a unique historical phenomenon. The bellweather of this historical shift can be read, these critics believe, in the changed character of the urban crowd. Once a mass of bodies packed tightly together in the centres of cities, the crowd today has dispersed. It is assembled in malls for consumption rather than for the more complex purposes of community or political power; in the modern crowd the physical presence of these human beings feels threatening. In social theory, these arguments have been advanced by critics of mass society, notably Theodor Adorno and Herbert Marcuse. (See, especially, Max Horkheimer and Theodor Adorno, 1992;1944 "The Culture Industry: Enlightenment as Mass Deception", *Dialectic of Enlightenment*, trans. Hohn Cummings, Continuum, New York, pp. 120-67: Theodor Adorno, 1975, "Culture Industry Reconsidered", *New German Critique*, Vol. 6, pp. 12-19: and Herbert Marcuse, 1964, *One Dimensional Man: Studies in the Ideology of Advances Industrial Society*, Beacon Press, Boston).

Yet it is exactly this sense of a gulf between past and present I wish to challenge. The geography of the modern city, like modern technology, brings to the fore deepseated problems in Western civilisation in imagining spaces for the human body which make human bodies aware of one another. The computer screen and the islands of the periphery are spatial aftershocks of problems before unsolved on streets and town squares, in churches and town halls, in houses and courtyards packing people close together, old constructions in stone forcing people to touch, yet designs which failed to arouse the awareness of flesh promised in Hogarth's engraving.

Civic bodies

For people in a multi-cultural city to care about one another, I believe we have to change the understanding we have of our own bodies. We will never experience the difference of others until we acknowledge the bodily insufficiencies in ourselves. Civic compassion issues from that physical awareness of lack in ourselves, not from sheer goodwill or political

169

rectitude. If these assertions seem far from the practical realities of New York, perhaps it is a sign of how much urban experience has become divorced from religious understanding.

These lessons to be learned from the body are one of the foundations of the Judeo-Christian tradition. Central to that tradition are the transgressions of Adam and Eve, the shame of their nakedness, their exile from the Garden, which lead to a story of what the first humans became, as well as what they lost. In the Garden, they were innocent, unknowing, and obedient. Out in the world, they became aware; they knew they were flawed creatures, and so they explored, sought to understand what was strange and unlike; they were no longer God's children to whom all was given. The Old Testament recounts over and over stories of people who mirror this sorrowful awakening of the first humans. people who transgress in their bodily desires the commandments of God, are punished, and then, like Adam and Eve in exile, awaken. The first Christians made from Christ's passage on earth such a story; crucified for man's sins, His gift to men and women is to rouse a sense of the insufficiency of the flesh; the less pleasure His followers take in their own bodies, the more they will love one another.

Pagan history told this ancient truth in another way, as the story of what bodies experience in cities. The Athenian agora and Pnyx were urban spaces in which citizens felt bodily insufficiency: the ancient agora stimulated people physically, at the price of depriving them of coherent speech with others; the Pnyx provided continuity in speech and so gave the community experiences of narrative logic, at the price of rendering people vulnerable to the rhetorical stimulation of words. The stones of the agora and the Pnyx put people in a state of flux, each of the two centres a source of dissatisfaction the other could resolve only by arousing dissatisfactions of its own. In the dual centred city, people knew incompleteness in their bodily experiences. Yet no people more self consciously valued civic culture than these same Athenians: "human" and "polis" were interchangeable words. Intense civic bonds arose from the very play of displacement, people cared strongly about one another in spaces which did not fully satisfy their bodily needs, indeed, a Jewish contemporary might have said, **because** these spaces did not satisfy bodily needs. Yet the ancient city was itself not like a monument to stability. Not even the most binding of human acts, ritual, could guarantee its cohesion.

It is a modern habit to think of social instability and persona insufficiency as pure negatives. The formation of modern individualism has in general aimed at making individuals self sufficient, that is to say, complete rather than incomplete. Psychology speaks the language of people finding a centre for themselves, of achieving integration and wholeness of the self. Modern social movements also speak this language, as though communities ought to become like individuals, coherent and whole. In New York, the pains of being left behind or left out have inflected this individual-communal language; racial, ethnic, and social groups turn inward in order to cohere, and so to heal. The psychological experience of displacement, of incoherence, the domain of what the psychoanalyst Robert Jay Lifton calls a "protean self", would seem only a recipe for deepening those social wounds. (See Robert Jay Lifton, 1993, *The Protean Self: Human Resilience in an Age of Fragmentation*, Basic Books, New York).

However, without significant experiences of self displacement, social differences gradually harden because interest in the Other withers. Freud pointed to this sociological truth as a bodily truth in *Beyond the Pleasure Principle*, the short essay he published in 1920. He contrasts the bodily pleasure in wholeness and equilibrium to more reality centred bodily experience which transcends that pleasure. Pleasure, Freud wrote, "is invariably set in motion by an unpleasurable tension ....[and] its final outcome coincides with a lowering of that tension", (Freud 1961, p.1). Pleasure, that is, is not like sexual excitement, which involves an arousing disturbance of the senses; pleasure instead seeks to return to a state which Freud imagined ultimately to be like the comfort of a foetus in the womb, safe and unknowing of the world. Under sway of the pleasure principle, people wish to disengage.

Freud speaks to us as a worldly realist rather than as a religious ascetic because he knows the desire for comfort expresses a profound biological need. "**Protection against** stimuli", he writes, "is an almost more important function for the living organism than **reception of** stimuli", (Sigmund Freud, *Beyond the Pleasure Principle*, trans. James Strachey, New York: W.W. Norton, 1961. Emphasis in original). But if protection rules, if the body is not open to periodic crises, eventually the organism sickens for lack of stimulation. The modern urge for comfort, he said, is a highly dangerous impulse for human beings; the difficulties we seek to avoid do not therefore disappear.

What could defeat the urge to withdraw into pleasure? In *Beyond the Pleasure Principle*, Freud envisaged two ways. One he called the "reality principle": a person faces up to difficulties physical or emotional by force of sheer will. Under the sway of the reality principle, a person resolves to know "unpleasure", (Freud 1961, p.4). That "unpleasurable" (*Umlust*) we know in everyday life as courage. But Freud is also a realist because he knows the reality principle is not a very strong force, courage a rarity.

171

The other defeat of pleasure is more certain and more enduring. In the course of a person's experience, he writes, "it happens again and again that individual instincts or parts of instincts turn out to be incompatible in their aims or demands with the remaining ones" (Freud 1961, p.5). The body feels at war with itself; it becomes uncomfortably aroused; but the incompatibilities of desire are too great to be resolved, or to be pushed aside.

This is the work civilisation does: it confronts us, in all our frailty, with contradictory experiences which cannot be pushed away, and which make us feel therefore incomplete. Yet precisely in that state of "cognitive dissonance", to use the term of a later critic, human beings begin to focus upon, to attend to, to explore, and to become engaged in the realm where the pleasure of wholeness is impossible. The history of the Western city records a long struggle between this civilized possibility and the effort to create power as well as pleasure through master images of wholeness. Master images of "the body" have performed the work of power in urban space. The Athenians and pagan Romans made use of such master images; in the evolution of the Judeo-Christian tradition, the spiritual wanderer returned home to the urban centre where his suffering body became a reason for submission and meekness, the spiritual body thereby becoming flesh and stone. At the dawn of the modern scientific era, the centre served a new master image of "the body", the body a circulating mechanism and the centre its heart-pump and lungs, and this scientific body image evolved socially to justify the power of the individual over the claims of the polity.

Yet, as I have tried to show, this legacy contains deep internal contradictions and strains. In the Athenian city, the master image of male nakedness could not fully control or define the clothed bodies of women. The Roman centre served as the mythic focus of a fiction of Rome's continuity and coherence; the visual images which expressed this coherence became the instruments of power. Yet, if in the democratic centre, the Athenian citizen became a slave of the voice, in the imperial centre the Roman citizen became a slave of the eye.

When early Christianity took root in this city, it reconciled its relation to this visual and geographic tyranny so antithetical to the spiritual condition of the wandering people of the Judeo-Christian Word and Light. Christianity reconciled itself to the powers of the urban centre by dividing its own visual imagination in two, inner and outer, spirit and power; the realm of the outer city could not fully conquer the need for faith in the inner city of the soul. The Christian cities of the Middle Ages continued to experience this divided centre, now built in stone as the differences

172

between sanctuary and street. Yet not even Christ's body, meant through imitation to rule the Christian city, could rule the street.

Nor could the centre hold by acts of purification. The impulse to atone and to cleanse the polluted Christian body which animated the segregation of the Jews and other impure bodies in Christian Venice could not restore its spiritual core. Nor could the ceremonies of revolution make the core cohere. The impulse to clear away obstacles, to create a transparent space of freedom at the urban centre of revolutionary Paris, became mere emptiness and induced apathy, helping defeat the ceremonies aiming at a durable civic transformation. The modern master image of the individual, detached body has hardly ended in triumph. It has ended in passivity.

In the crevices and contradictions of master images of the body in space, there have appeared moments and occasions for resistance, the dignifying resistances of the Thesmophoria and the Adonia, the rituals of the dining room and the bath in the Christian house, the rituals of the night in the Ghetto, rituals which did not destroy the dominant order but created a more complex life for the bodies the dominant order sought to rule in its own image. In our history, the complex relations between the body and city have carried people beyond the pleasure principle, as Freud described it; these have been troubled bodies, bodies not at rest, bodies aroused by disturbance. How much dissonance and unease can people bear? For two thousand years they sustained a great deal in places to which they had been passionately attached. We might take this record of an active physical life conducted in a centre which does not hold as one measure of our present estate.

In the end this historic tension between domination and civilization asks us a question about ourselves. How will we exit from our own bodily passivity, where is the chink in our own system, where is our liberation to come from? It is, I would insist, a peculiarly pressing question for a multi-cultural city, even if it is far from current discourse about group injuries and group rights. For without a disturbed sense of ourselves, what will prompt most of us, who are not heroic figures knocking on the doors of crackhouses, to turn outward toward each other, to experience the Other?

Any society needs strong moral sanctions to make people tolerate, much less experience positively, duality, incompleteness, and otherness. Those moral sanctions arose in Western civilisation through the powers of religion. Religious rituals bonded, in Peter Brown's phrase, the body to the city; a pagan ritual like the Thesmophoria did so by literally pushing

173

women out of the boundaries of the house, into a ritual space where both women and men confronted the gendered ambiguities in the meaning of citizenship.

It would be crass to say that we need, in a utilitarian fashion, religious ritual again in order to turn human beings outward, and the history of ritual spaces in the city will not allow us to think of believing in so instrumental a way. As the pagan world disappeared, the Christian found in the making of ritual spaces a new spiritual vocation, a vocation of labour and self discipline that eventually put its mark upon the city as it had earlier upon the rural sanctuary. The gravity of these ritual spaces lay in ministering to bodies in pain, and the recognition of human suffering inseparably bound in the Christian ethos. By a terrible twist of fate, when Christian communities found they had to live with those unlike themselves, they imposed this conjoint sense of place and burdens of a suffering body on those, like the Venetian Jews, whom they oppressed.

The French Revolution played out this Christian drama again, and yet not again. The physical environment in which the Revolution imposed suffering, and in which the revolutionaries sought to recuperate a maternal figure incorporating and transforming their own sufferings, had lost the specificity and density of place. The suffering body displayed itself in empty space, a space of abstract freedom but no enduring human connection.

The drama of the revolutionary rituals echoed a pagan drama as well, the attempt deeply rooted in ancient life to deploy ritual, to guide it in the service of the oppressed and the denied. On the Champ de Mars this effort at the design of ritual also aborted; the ancient belief that ritual "comes from somewhere else" now seemed to mean that its powers were beyond design, beyond human agency, inspired by forces which lay beyond the powers of a humane and civilized society.

In its stead, design turned to the shaping of pleasure, in the form of comfort, originally to compensate for fatigue, to lighten the burden of work. but these powers of design which rested the body came as well to lighten its sensory weight, suspending the body in an ever more passive relation to its environment. The trajectory of designed pleasure led the human body to an ever more solitary rest.

If there is a place for faith in mobilizing the powers of civilization against those of domination, it lies in accepting exactly what this solitude seeks to avoid: pain, the kind of lived pain evinced by my friend at the cinema. His shattered hand serves as a witness; lived pain witnesses the body moving beyond the power of society to define; the meanings of pain are always incomplete in the world. The acceptance of pain lies within a realm outside the order human beings make in the world. In a magisterial work, *The Body in Pain*, the philosopher Elaine Scarry has drawn upon Wittgenstein's insight. "Though the capacity to experience physical pain is as primal a fact about the human being as is the capacity to hear, to touch, to desire", she writes, pain differs "from every other bodily and psychic event, by not having an object in the external world" (Scarry 1985, p.161).

The vast volumes which appear in Boullee's plans serve as one marker of the point at which secular society lost contact with pain. The revolutionaries believed they could fill an empty volume, free of the obstacles and litter of the past, with human meanings, that a space without obstructions could serve the needs of a new society. Pain could be erased by erasing place. This same erasure has served different ends in a later time, the purposes of individual flight from others rather than moving closer toward them. The French Revolution thus marked a profound rupture in our civilization's understanding of pain; David placed the body in pain in the same space that Marianne occupied, and empty, homeless space, a body alone with its pain, and this is an unendurable condition.

Lurking in the civic problems of a multi-cultural city is the moral difficulty of arousing sympathy for those who are Other. And this can only occur, I believe, by understanding why bodily pain requires a place in which it can be acknowledged, and in which its transcendent origins become visible. Such pain has a trajectory in human experience. It disorients and makes incomplete the self, defeats the desire for coherence; the body accepting pain is ready to become a civic body, sensible to the pain of another person, pains present together on the street, at last endurable, even though, in a diverse world, each person cannot explain what he or she is feeling, who he or she is, to the other. But the body can follow this civic trajectory only if it acknowledges that there is no remedy for its sufferings in the contrivings of society, that its unhappiness has come from elsewhere, that its pain derives from God's command to live together as exiles.

11 Going to town: Routine accommodations and routine anxieties in respect of public space and public facilities in two cities in the north of England

Karen Evans, Penelope Fraser and Ian Taylor

This paper emerges out of an ESRC - financed research project into the "Public Sense of Well-being" in two old industrial cities in the North of England.[1] It rests on a set of empirical findings derived from a survey completed in Manchester and Sheffield during 1992, which were later further explored in detailed focus group enquiries with particular groups of residents and users of these two cities. The research is particularly concerned to identify patterns of use and practical appraisal of public spaces, by different sections of "the public", and public facilities in these two cities.

   The findings which we report here are relevant to theoretical and policy debate taking place in the field of criminology in respect of the problem of fear in urban areas, but they also touch on the issue of the "urban experience" which has been at the heart of much recent writing in the area of "urban sociology".[2] We are also concerned to contribute to a series of theoretical debates between social theorists and urban geographers on the viability of the ideas of "space" as an object of analysis initiated by Peter Saunders (1981), carried forward by Derek Gregory and John Urry (1985), and most recently taken up by Benno Werlen (1993). Much of this literature is theoretical and speculative (often in the very best sense), and sometimes rather generalised (suggesting, if only by default, that there is a universal urban experience common to all conurbations, whether in Milan, Montreal or Manchendster). In contrast the research in which we are engaged is an attempt at what we would call a grounded exploration of urban use and urban experience in relation to these cities in the North of England, both of which exemplify a vital industrial history from the early nineteenth century but are now at a different stage of economic reorganisation, in the aftermath of a decade and a half of "de-industrialisation".[3] Where some of the recent literature on the urban experience must be read as the commentator's own "writing in" of his or her own experience of the city as **the** urban experience, whether in the form of a celebration or a critique of the city, our particular concern has been to attempt to construct the elements of a **sociology of urban experience**, sensitive to the very different uses that are made of particular urban spaces and facilities, and the diffuse definitions held of those cities by populations within them. Our research was conducted in the North of England, one of the least prosperous regions, in what is, in any case, an extremely, and increasingly, unequal society at its national level, divided by class, gender, age and ethnicity. We therefore wish to see our research as a contribution towards debates on urban experience whilst recognising that the findings of our research may not be generalisable to all conurbations, even in the one national formation, England.

Our research may best be understood as an attempt to provide a grounded sociological dimension to "space and time geography" of individuals' use of the city pioneered by Hagerstrand (1970, 1975), more recently subjected to a theoretical reformulation by David Harvey (1989b), following the work of Henri Lefebvre (1974), and Tony Giddens (1984 c.3). We are interested too in de Certeau's idea of walking through the city as a mundane, but quite complex, practical accomplishment (de Certeau 1984, pp.99-110) and also in Bourdieu's earlier insistence on understanding the ways in which objective structures (like the architecture of urban space) are always linked to actual social practices through the *habitus*, which he defined as "a durably installed generative principle of regulated **improvisations**" (Bourdieu 1977, p.95, our emphasis).

In the context of a conference dedicated to exploring the idea of "*The Public Sphere*", held nearly fourteen years after the election of a government committed to a radical and, from its point of view, utopian experiment in free market economics, we would also want this presentation to be read as an exploration of the character of **lived social relations** in public places in these two northern cities. In particular, in the sense of well-being and/or anxiety and fear in evidence across different sections of these cities' populations. An inescapable feature of this period in Britain has been the withdrawal of national Government from many spheres of public activity and public responsibility. Deprived of subsidies from national government, public local authorities have withered on the vine as instruments of any larger idea of the Public Interest vis-a-vis the City. Increasingly, have been forced into strategic alliances with private interests, often involved in sectoral commercial redevelopment of part of the city. The resulting transformation of the English city in the 1980s has involved the development in certain places of "temples of private consumption" in the form of enormous self contained, enclosed shopping malls on a North American model (Gardner and Sheppard 1989). Or shopping centres on the "edge" of several conurbations with resulting implications for the existing centres of nearby cities (Garreau 1991). The urban transformation in England during the 1980s has taken place at the same time as we have witnessed a massive withdrawal of Public Authority from its accustomed role in the supervision and regeneration of urban spaces. This is perhaps most apparent to the public at large in England in respect of the withdrawal of Government support for "monopolistic" provision of local bus services (signalled in the deregulation of local bus services in the Transport Act of 1985),[4] but it has also been apparent to many commentators in respect of the level of litter routinely covering the streets of English cities,[5] and in respect of the level of vandalism and neglect in public parks and in other areas of public resort and public leisure (municipal swimming pools, libraries and information services, etc.). All of which is, in some vital respect, a measure of the declining capacity and politically approved mandate of local government.

It is by no means our intention to suggest that the generally grubby and tatty condition of English cities is **a direct** and unmediated expression of the withdrawal of national Government, for reasons of free market ideology, from the exercise of its public responsibilities: neither do we want to suggest, that there is some direct and uncomplicated relation between the well-being of the various publics in any urban setting and the commitment of a national and local government to some notion of the Public, as distinct from the Private, Good. What is apparent from our work, as well as that of many other sociological and criminological commentators on the aesthetic and moral character of urban space, is that it is precisely those pieces of urban development and innovation supported by civic and municipal authority in the 1950s and 1960s (e.g. the urban underpass, underground carparks, bus stations, and the public estates bordering on the city centre core) which appear to evoke most distaste and/or fear in the minds of many urban residents. What we do want to suggest is that the strains and stresses which, historically speaking, have always been placed on the idea of shared public provision in an unreformed, class divided and, in many ways, unmodernised English society, have been exacerbated, in a fundamental fashion, by the last

179

fourteen years' of free market experimentation, underpinned as they have been by a theological dislike of local authority provision of public goods (reliable, modern transport, clean urban centres and local streets)[6].

Private/public enterprise and urban redevelopment in Manchester and Sheffield in the 1980s and 1990s

It is the Urban Development Corporations, created, initially in Liverpool and London Docklands, as a result of the Local Government Planning and Land Act of 1980 (Middleton 1991, c.3), which have found most favour with Government in respect of urban re-development at local level over the last fourteen years. Manchester has two; the Trafford Park Development Corporation, a so-called "second generation" UDC, established in 1987; and the Central Manchester Development Corporation, established in 1988 as a third generation initiative. At the same time as one was established in Sheffield (and two others, in Bristol and Leeds). The UDCs have the power to acquire, assemble and redevelop land, and they also have the power to exercise planning control over its use by others. But they have no responsibility for education, public health, policing and other matters for which the local authority retains full responsibility. Trafford Park UDC has a mandate for an area of 3,100 acres, some one and half miles from the city centre, surrounding the old Manchester Ship Canal and the Trafford Park industrial estate. The largest such estate outside London. Its main current focus of activity is the creation, on a phased basis, of a leisure and residential area on what used to be the Manchester docks, now referred to as Wharfside. In city centre Manchester, the Central Manchester Development Corporation has been closely involved, not only with the City Council's successful bid to become English City of Drama in 1994, with the renovation of the Whitworth Street corridor (creating new uses for Victorian buildings as offices, apartment blocks and a variety of private clubs) and with the Olympic Bid, but also with the revitalisation of the Manchester Festival, sponsored by Boddington's, the largest brewery in Manchester. CMDC's activities are centred around the Castlefield area, which, in part because of it being the site of a Roman fort (recently re-built as an "Urban Heritage Park") has been given the descriptor as "the Birthplace of Manchester". The objective of the Central Manchester Development Corporation is to create, in what used, only twenty years ago, to be an area known for its prostitution and an abattoir, a mixed area for "leisure and tourism", and specialist retail outlets. They aim to increase the use of

180

the central area under their jurisdiction by attracting both new-build housing units and also encouraging the renovation of existing warehouses built around the old canals for residential use. A squad of "rangers" has been appointed by the CMDC to police the Castlefield area, in particular with a view to the reduction of litter and what they term "anti-social behaviour". Another aspect of the CMDC strategy involves the pedestrianisation of streets, which, coupled with the relaxation of the licensing laws, it hopes will encourage greater public use of the area.

A similar strategy in nearby Salford, which includes the construction of a dozen gleaming new benches on a pedestrianised gentrified Georgian street (Acton Square), has been markedly unsuccessful in its own terms (creating, simply, a renovated space entirely empty of people). However, the Castlefield development has attracted office workers on summer evenings, and other populations at weekends, especially on the occasion of festivals and special events. This strategy seems typical of development corporation activities in other parts of England, harnessing the idea of architectural redevelopment to a notion of artistic revival in the centre of the city. This version of urban redevelopment has been encouraged on the grounds of its democratic and aesthetic potential, by the Comedia consultancy in London, in a large range of publications arguing for the opening up of English city centres to the artistic imagination (Worpole 1988, 1992; Comedia 1991), as well as by the Labour Party's then Shadow Minister for Arts and Media and a number of his collaborators in a recent popular text (Fisher and Owen 1991). James Donald wonders, as we do, whether planners and utopians who have been adopting this approach may be guilty of working with what he calls a "Concept City" as distinct from a grounded idea of the city as it is actually used (Donald 1992). What is clear in the Manchester case is that the attention which is paid to the renewal of the older, disused industrial areas, or to the continual remarketing of the already renovated areas of privatised consumption (in Manchester, the up-market shopping locations of St Anne's Square and King Street) does not, of itself, **generate a programme of action for the locations in the city that are most heavily used by the greater part of the city's population**. Our evidence suggests that many of **these** places continue to evoke anxiety, particularly (though not exclusively) amongst elderly residents and some unaccompanied women and which have become for many the main example, in their own cities, of what Yi-Fu Tuan has named "a landscape of fear" (Tuan 1979).

The task of urban renewal and redevelopment in Sheffield, in the absence of any development corporation with specific responsibility for the city centre, has fallen on the shoulders of the City Council itself. The only development corporation in the city, the Sheffield Development Corporation, established in 1988, has a mandate for the redevelopment of what is called by them the Lower Don Valley in Sheffield's East End, known to locals as Attercliffe - the erstwhile site of the city's massive steelworks, the vast bulk of which were razed to the ground in the mid-1980s - and does not extend into the city centre proper at all. The Development Corporation points to several hundred small companies which have been supported in the Valley during the few years of its existence, employing about 23,500 people. However the fundamental development in the Valley has been the opening of the Meadowhall Shopping Centre in September 1990. At the time of opening, this was the most expensive privately-funded business project ever to be completed outside London, at £400 million: it has 223 stores on two levels, occupying 1.5 million square feet and is equal in size, therefore, to twenty football pitches. It was visited in its first year of operation by 20 million shoppers. Its attraction appears to be the range of shops available undercover: however it is also true that eating-out in the restaurants at Meadowhall, window-shopping, and "hanging-out" are increasingly popular activities for some of these visitors, although "hanging-out" by the young is discouraged by Meadowhall's security staff. The forthcoming addition to Meadowhall of a cinema complex and a "pleasure park" ("Tivoli Gardens"), and the routing of Sheffield's "Supertram" transit system (due to open in 1994) past the shopping centre is likely to underwrite the increasing importance of Meadowhall.

Conversely the decline of Sheffield city centre is now a major topic of discussion in that city, most often referenced in terms of the number of city centre shops that are closing down or in difficulties. It is also discussed by Sheffield residents in terms of the extraordinary level of congestion on the roads[7] and the resulting dangerously high levels of carbon monoxide in the city's air. This is thought, locally, to have been a product of the de-regulation of local bus services in 1986, and to have been worsened as a result of the re-routing of traffic around the city centre during the construction of the Supertram route into the city.

Sheffield City Council has responded to the accelerating decline of the City Centre during the late 1980s by attempting to provide a framework through which new jobs would be created for Sheffielders, and, in particular, for the thousands thrown out of work by the closure of the steelworks. It was clearly recognised that the prosperity of the city centre, and of the city as a whole, was severely threatened by unemployment rates which had increased, very suddenly, from below the national average, to just over twice the new national averages of the 1980s). The World Student

Games (or Universiade) was one, potentially imaginative but ultimately unsuccessful, attempt to bring employment to Sheffield. It led to the building of six new sports facilities (including the Ponds Forge Swimming Pool, at a cost of £52 million, and the 40,000 seat Don Valley Stadium, costing £27 million), but culminated in a loss of £10.4 million, which has rebounded almost entirely on the Council and Council Tax-payers, with a resulting further twist in the financial crisis of the local authority. Severe cuts in council services have followed; the council workforce being cut from 27,000 in 1992 to 24,405 by September 1993, despite Sheffield council employees' voting in March 1993 to take a wage cut rather than face further job losses.[8] Sheffield's bid to national Government under the City Challenge scheme in 1992 for the release of monies to support particular programmes of redevelopment in respect of housing or commercial activity subsequently came to little, rejected as it was in favour of schemes advanced in other urban areas.

The Council is eager to promote "a new vision for the city centre" as a way of arresting the ongoing process of decline. The most public expression of this is a report produced by local academics in Sheffield in close collaboration with the urban planners working out of various different agencies in the city. This Report, *The Sheffield Central Area Study 2010: A Vision of Quality* (Foley and Lawless 1992), given full page coverage in the local evening newspaper, *The Star* on its release, argues that the best strategy for regenerating the central area is by a policy of zoning, identifying particular areas of the city according to their most appropriate use.[9] The report has received a generally favourable response by the local press and the current Council, and future developments in the city may be framed very much along these lines. CMDC, by contrast, has adopted a different approach to city zoning, attempting to create **new** uses of central areas. Both approaches to zoning of the city are open to the criticism, voiced earlier, that too much attention is focused on the development of limited segments of the urban territory (usually with a purely commercial vision) and that simultaneously areas with minimal or declining use-value (industrial areas with no waterfront properties or views, and areas of the central core which are heavily used, on a routine basis, by the mass of the city's population) are "residualised".[10]

The landscape of public space in Manchester and Sheffield

In August and October of 1992 we conducted a street survey in six sites in Manchester and five in Sheffield (including the Meadowhall complex) designed to discover the use(s) made at different times of the day and night of each survey site, feelings elicited by that particular site and attitudes to the city in general, including reactions to its physical structure and to less tangible considerations (which nevertheless shape the experience of life in an urban conurbation) - for example, its atmosphere, warmth or friendliness. The sites were major pedestrian thoroughfares, chosen to capture diversity in the city in terms of the differing reasons for which it is used and "the publics" who might use it. Our aim was to construct what we have called a **taxonomy** of use i.e. a framework for identifying the different publics using each space. In Greater Manchester 1,032 people were interviewed - 666 in Manchester city centre sites, 181 in an area to the north of the city, but within the City of Manchester's local authority boundaries, and 185 in Stockport, a town to the south of the city, also within the Greater Manchester conurbation. In Sheffield 801 people were interviewed, 489 respondents in the central core, 128 in an area approximately one mile to the north of this area and 184 within Meadowhall.

For the bulk of our respondents use of the centres of Manchester and Sheffield for purposes of work, shopping and leisure **routinely** involved the regular negotiation of a relatively small number of buildings and streets. In Manchester, these were the Arndale Centre, Market Street, Piccadilly Gardens, St Anne's Square, Deansgate, and the city centre bus and rail stations; in Sheffield, Fargate and High Street, the Moor, the Markets, the "Hole in the Road" and the new Transport Interchange on Pond Street (still uniformally referred to as "the bus station" by nearly all respondents). These streets and buildings constitute a key element in what the American social geographer, Kevin Lynch, called the "image of the city", and are also important markers in the "mental maps" which, Lynch insisted, the residents of all cities develop for practical and indicative purposes (Lynch 1960,1972). They can also be referred to as *locales*, as theorised by Tony Giddens, places which:

> provide the settings of interaction (which) in turn (are) essential to specifying its contextuality. (Giddens 1984, p.118)

He observes, further, that:

> The constitution of locales certainly depends upon the phenomena given pride of place by Hagerstrand: the body, its media of mobility and communication, in relation to physical properties of the surrounding world. Locales provide for a good deal of the "fixity"

184

underlying institutions, although there is no clear sense in which they "determine" such "fixity".(Giddens 1984, p.118)

Giddens' point is made more clear when he outlines his reason for his use of the term "locale" in preference to that of "space": his concern being to emphasise how "properties of settings are employed in a chronic way by agents in the constitution of encounters of space and time" (Giddens, p.119). Hagerstrand refers to the "station" - a "stopping place" at which actors curtail their movement for the purpose of a social encounter or a gathering, a social occasion. A key interest in this research is to understand the ways in which a variety of publics in Manchester and Sheffield do exactly this in a variety of different locales that constitute the centres of those two cities.[11]

The sample: The city users with whom we made contact consisted, predominantly, of 18-35 year olds. This age range made up 53.1 per cent of the Manchester sample and 53.2 per cent of the Sheffield. 27.5 per cent of the Manchester sample and 27.1 per cent of the Sheffield sample were aged 36-55. This left 14.7 per cent of our Manchester respondents and 17.2 per cent of our Sheffield respondents at age 55 or over. The 1991 census figures for these cities are not produced in a form which is directly comparable to our survey data, but it is apparent that the above age ranges do not represent those found in the population usually resident in both cities. Our sample exhibits a marked bias towards the under 35's, suggesting that younger people make more use of the public spaces of our cities. The sample also included a high proportion of male respondents, the number of female respondents reaching only 75 per cent in the case of Manchester and 74.6 per cent in the case of Sheffield, of the male total. Perhaps unsurprisingly women outnumbered men as shoppers in both cities whilst, as leisure users, men predominated; the number of women using Manchester for leisure purposes only reached 44.2 per cent of the male total and in Sheffield the number of women reached 61 per cent of the male total. Our figures are striking in that they show a greater proportion of male respondents at every site with the sole exception of High Street in Sheffield. It seems valid to conclude that these public spaces are dominated by male rather than female users.

We also we found, in both cities, that the percentage of non-white ethnic groups in our sample, was greater than the percentage shown in census returns for "the usually resident population" of the city. For Manchester 12.7 per cent of our sample were from non-white ethnic groups as opposed to 8.9 per cent in census returns and in Sheffield 13.9 as opposed to 5.1 per cent in the census returns. These figures may reflect the fact that at least one site in each city was in an ethnically mixed area. However even taking account of this possible bias the figures still show higher than expected percentages of all non-white groups.

The different uses made of the city

For the purpose of this section we have concentrated on the central core of the city, those areas of our cities which include its main shopping areas and transport interchanges, commonly referred to as the "city centre". In the words of a Manchester promotional campaign the city centre is "right at the heart of things", a phrase intended to evoke the centrality of the place, the attraction to a city's residents of its core, the warmth of its crowded streets and a place of social as well as economic activity. It is a place that contains both "public concourses" (St Ann's Square) and markets (the Arndale, King Street) in both their Medieval and Enlightenment form (we should be minded here too of the notions of the market and "the marked place", as discussed by Sennett 1990). Four of our Manchester sites and three of Sheffield are therefore included in this preliminary description.

Respondents were invited to define for themselves their reason for being in that site at the time of interview, the advantage being that they could choose which, out of several possible activities which they might carry out that day, was the primary motivator. We wish to underline here the mundane nature of the use of these sites which our enquiries revealed - in Manchester the majority use was to work, 36.5 per cent and a further 21.7 per cent were there to shop. Once in the city the workforce routinely makes use of available commercial and social facilities, including restaurants and shops, however the main reason for being in that space, travelling on public transport or the publicly provided road systems that are also a part of the space with which we are concerned was to earn a wage. Shopping itself seems to be an activity often entered into "out of necessity" rather than as a casual search for pleasure or diversion. It is true that **in the more exclusive and expensive** shopping areas of **both** cities a higher percentage of shoppers were "window shopping or browsing" rather than intending to make any purchase (up to 36.4 per cent of the shoppers interviewed in Albert Square, Manchester) but the shopping activity in the cheaper shopping areas was clearly utilitarian - often involving a long search through shops and market places to find the best value for their money. The use of all our sites for purposes of leisure was small, 13.6 per cent for Manchester and 14.7 per cent for Sheffield - a higher percentage of our respondents categorised themselves as "Passing Through" the area (19.1 per cent and 22.3 per cent for Manchester and Sheffield respectively). Again this shows presence in the area as being a matter of necessity rather than choice.

Practical considerations involving ease of access to an area, the price of goods, whether shops catered for an individual's taste and possible crowding of the streets governed use of an area for shopping. Concerns over personal safety and crime were more prominent for those people who were making use of the city for purposes of leisure; in Manchester fear of crime was cited by 7.8 per cent, the reputation of an area by the same percentage and the general safety of an area by 13.4 per cent as reasons why they would avoid certain areas during their leisure activity. Similarly in Sheffield, 21 per cent of people using the city centre for leisure purposes avoided certain places due to concerns over safety or the reputation of an area. As leisure use of a space tends to occur after office or shopping hours, hours of darkness or at least times when the streets are less populated, this finding is unsurprising. So also are the frequent mentions of areas like Moss-Side and Hulme which were often cited by respondents very much as the "other" Manchester which they would not think of using for leisure purposes (and probably had not been visited by many at any time). However considerations concerning access to a place or individual preferences outweighed issues connected with fear or anxiety in governing the use of an area. In neither Manchester nor Sheffield did the crowds in an area feature as a consideration in respect of the use of an area for leisure.

The questionnaire also invited respondents to tell us which areas of the city they preferred and why. This was a chance for respondents to move away from their use of the city for different activities and to explore issues such as the aesthetics of the city and the nature of the urban environment. In this way different concerns emerged: familiarity with an area, the link between attachment to an area or building and childhood memories or family ties, the grand nature of a building or section of the city centre which increased a sense of civic pride or served to raise the spirit (individual or corporate). Those physical spaces most often cited by Manchester respondents were St Ann's Square, the Arndale Centre, Deansgate and Albert Square - all situated in the central core of the city. Areas preferred by Sheffield city centre users were by no means all in the city centre. The suburbs to the South West of the city, from Hunter's Bar and Ecclesall and out as far as Totley and Dore, were the preferred places cited by all respondents questioned in the three city centre sites. The second most popular place was Fargate/Orchard Square, then parks and gardens generally, followed by The Moor (a main street in the city centre which doubles as a street market).

When asked what generally attracted people to the cities, issues concerned with the general warmth and friendliness of the city emerged as most important to our respondents. Opportunities for a range of social activities in the city, the facilities on offer and the atmosphere of the city were also important to a wide range of the sample. The built environment and the size of the city were frequently mentioned in Manchester but less so for the Sheffield sample. The proximity of Sheffield to the countryside and the parks and gardens within the city itself were seen as positive attributes to living in Sheffield.

Those aspects of the city generally disliked were also explored. For Manchester and Sheffield the general custodianship by public authority of public spaces in the city was the main problem. A great many respondents were concerned about the level of litter and general dirt in their cities. For our Manchester sample the next most voiced areas of concern referred to the amount of begging and visible homelessness apparent on the streets. There was also concern about the built environment - much of which related to the Arndale Centre's imposition on the central landscape, but which also included the rundown area around Piccadilly, close as it is to well-used areas of the city centre. Next came concern over the general atmosphere of the city, the natural environment and lack of facilities. Concern over high levels of crime registered fewer spontaneous comments. Our Sheffield sample were concerned that facilities and shopping areas in the centre of town were of poor quality - often Meadowhall was used as a comparison. The political life of this city was also heavily criticised, particularly the way in which the council was thought to be (mis)managing the city's affairs. A high number considered redevelopment of the built environment to be necessary or found the architecture and design of parts of the city to be lacking. A number of white, and two Asian respondents, who had moved to Sheffield from other parts of the UK, considered the city's people to be less friendly than they had expected. A few respondents considered the city's people to be racist whereas others took the opportunity to express racist opinions themselves.

Our research strongly suggests that the "sense of well-being" of different publics in central urban areas is not straightforwardly related to the physical environment of these particular locales. Very frequently, the levels of anxiety evoked by particular locales seemed to have been a product of the types of people (**other** people) whom our respondents felt would be encountered in such spaces. However, this issue is little discussed in the current literature and planning practice, where the emphasis remains on physical aspects of the environment as a source of reassurance or of fear. National campaigns to improve the physical environment of car parks and to promote the redesign of residential and commercial areas have been in progress throughout the late 1980s and early 1990s.[12] The core assumption in such approaches is that there is some kind of direct relationship between the condition or appearance of these physical environments and the levels of crime, or fear of crime, obtaining in such locales (Wilson and Kelling 1982, Skogan 1987). The implication remains that those areas which are perceived as neglected by their custodians and therefore fearful, are not used by "ordinary citizens", ignoring the fact that there are inescapable and valid reasons why people continue to use them. Our own research demonstrates that the areas in our two cities which are the most neglected and aesthetically unappealing are by no means avoided by all or the least used. We want to offer some examples from Sheffield and Manchester, where factors other than the more general concerns outlined above come into play and shape the feelings surrounding a space, affecting its actual use.

Study 1: Manchester - Portland Street

Portland Street in Manchester was chosen as one of our survey sites because of the mixed use of the area. It is well-known as bordering on the red-light area of the city, it is close by Chorlton Street bus station, the entrance point by coach into the city and a station which was identified as a source of concern for residents in the pilot stage of this research. It is a short distance from Manchester's Chinatown and also the main path to the city's Gay Village. This consists of a small area dominated by gay clubs and bars, with a gay-run cafe and shops. It is off the beaten track for many, though adjacent to areas used by students. It was characterised in our sample by its use as an area for leisure and as an access point to other areas of the city or other cities served by the coach companies. Few of the respondents we interviewed were visiting Chinatown but the gay population of the city were in evidence throughout the weekend and early evening shifts. In contrast to our experience in Sheffield some men and women were confident enough to identify themselves as lesbian or gay when discussing why they used particular areas of the city. During weekdays the main users of the area were office and bank workers, a high proportion in management positions.

The descriptions of the area offered by these respondents confirmed that they saw the area as a dirty one, the second dirtiest in the city centre, not

189

particularly crowded but one of the most depressing and unattractive sites. It scored as the least friendly but was also seen as the most lively by far (it was the busiest site for our interviewers), fairly easy to negotiate, in terms of finding one's way around the area, and more surprisingly - given the area's reputation for prostitution and the more negative comments recorded above - was seen as the safest. Clearly there is an element in this perception of the area which is a result of a section of the population (in this example lesbian and gay men), unable to relax in other areas of the city due to discrimination, developing its own, more secure, space within the city. However this was not responsible in and of itself for the general definitions accorded the area as numbers of the lesbian and gay people interviewed were small in terms of the overall sample at that site. It seems this perception of the area, as being safe and secure, is shared by users as a whole.

This perception was reinforced in our examination of patterns of avoidance. Although Portland Street was the busiest site during the period of the survey, people were less likely to treat the crowded nature of the area as a reason for avoidance than they were at other sites in the city centre. Indeed, four respondents had actually experienced some "trouble" or crime in that area, **as opposed to one in all other Manchester city sites combined.** Nonetheless it was not seen as a more fearful place than elsewhere in the city. Although the "type of people" expected to be found in the area did lead to its being avoided by six men and four women respondents interviewed in the city centre - higher than for any other areas throughout Manchester - it was not clear whether these comments were attributable to the "gayness" of the area, to its reputation as an area for prostitution, or to any other factor.

The accounts collected during this street survey from the users of this area seem to point to the existence of an area which although originally developed by its users to cater for a minority "scene", and thereby populating the area because of this identity, has become generally well used and liked. A potentially fearful and unsafe area has been made more attractive to others for whom the area was not primarily intended.

Study 2: Sheffield - Flat Street, High Street and Orchard Square

We received many strongly worded comments highlighting the unaesthetic, dirty and graffiti covered environment of Flat Street, a well known area of Sheffield city centre adjacent to the transport interchange, yet this site was the second busiest of our four sites and heavily used for shopping. The key to its continued and heavy use lies in the fact that it has a number of cheap shops including a butchers, a "Lo-Cost" supermarket, a fish and chip shop and a cafe. The shoppers at this site do not have any affinity with it aesthetically, neither are they impervious or immune to its aesthetic and environmental failings. They have developed a **routine accommodation** to the physical space out of necessity.

Sheffield city centre provides another example which further underlines our view that although many people find certain places unsavoury or "fearful" and would, if possible, avoid being in them, these feelings do not necessarily **govern** their everyday use of these places in practice. Sheffield's High Street, is a part of the city centre that is showing many archetypal signs of neglect and urban decay: many of the shops are boarded up and covered with graffiti and the streets and pavements are dirty. On one side of High Street the buildings overhang the pavement, forming a gloomy covered walkway and both sides of the street decant down two escalators which descend below ground level into a large subway built in 1967 and known then as the "Civic Circle" but now universally referred to by Sheffielders as the "Hole in the Road"; the object of much critical attention during the period of our research. However, High Street was also the busiest of our four Sheffield sites and the only one at which the total number of women respondents outnumbered men. Fargate, by contrast, only 100-150 yards south, and the city centre location most liked by our respondents, is mainly used for shopping, has been pedestrianised since the 1960s, is relatively clean and spacious, and features a fountain with flower beds and "Orchard Square", a recently gentrified stable yard design, open air shopping forum with two tiers, completed in December 1987. It was the joint second busiest of our four sites. However we should note that, even here, male respondents out numbered female.

These two "different" sites are particularly interesting for comparison given that they were, in the 1960s, a single continuous shopping street. The aura of Fargate used to extend to High Street, at the bottom of High Street a "respectable" department store, Walsh's (now owned by the House of Fraser) was opened in 1953. The separation of Fargate and High Street is a function of the pedestrianisation of Fargate in the 1960s and also the intensification of bus traffic on High Street consequent on deregulation of bus services in 1986.

It is apparent then, that High Street has a number of features which are believed to increase fear of crime, to lead to avoidance and to create a "landscape of fear", but our survey found it had the highest percentage of evening use out of any of our four sites. Fargate, in contrast, a site featuring several of the supposed antidotes to avoidance and fear had the

191

lowest percentage of evening use. Women use this area as a matter of necessity or for very practical purposes, although they would choose to avoid it if possible. Fargate on the other hand is a place where women feel more confident but it is nevertheless the least populated in the evenings. The speculation must be offered out that if Fargate, which currently shuts down at 5.30pm, were to be more creatively exploited in the evening, it could become a place which women (and many others) would use and feel relatively safe and happy.

Concluding remarks

In this first presentation on the research we are undertaking into the physical environment, the patterns of urban redevelopment, the state of the local economy, local folklore, and the sense of public well-being in these two North of England cities, we would like to highlight three closely connected conclusions.

First "going to town" must be seen as an essentially **mundane** occupation. Primarily, the city centres are places where people work - many in rather monotonous and unrewarding jobs, poorly paid, and usually on a "9 to 5" basis. These are not cities which are dominated in everyday practice by the ostensibly exciting job challenges of the 1980s Enterprise Culture (although there is some sense of that around Manchester's financial district and, albeit unknown to most Mancunians, the Exchange Quay development near Salford Quays). Travel to and from the city centre for the bulk of the commuting population is by bus, by British Rail (either one of which may be in very dilapidated condition) or by car. The much celebrated, speedy and reliable Metrolink light transit system in Manchester (highly successful though it has been in meeting its targets in respect of usership) will still only be responsible for about 15 per cent of the commuting journeys to be made in and out of Manchester over the four years to 1997 (Greater Manchester PTE, personal communication). The opening of the Supertram in Sheffield in 1994, will again not resolve the pressing problems of traffic congestion caused by bus deregulation "at a stroke". Travel to and from these city centres, for most commuters, will continue to be a problematic rather than a pleasurable aspect of daily use of the city.

Use of the city centre for purposes of shopping or leisure does create more options for some users, but we wish to emphasise the ways in which shopping in city centre Manchester has now devolved into a choice between the expensive "locales" of King Street and Kendals, on the one hand, and Piccadilly and Oldham Street, on the other: the chronic, creative solution for many shoppers and families is avoidance of such a brute choice via the exploration of alternative shopping centres in suburban areas. However the exercise of that choice is not equally available to all Mancunians and Sheffielders, especially in the aftermath of fourteen years of free market driven recomposition of the local labour market. In a situation where fully one third of a city's population is below the national "poverty line", as in Manchester, the image we need in order to make sense of shopping visits in town - so far from being the classic image of the casual *flaneur* inspecting the windows of fashionable arcades in nineteenth century Paris - needs reconstruction. There are shoppers on King Street in Manchester whose behaviour and use of that locale would approximate the descriptions offered out by Baudelaire but a much larger proportion of the window shopping in city centre Manchester involves the calculated search for bargains in the product name chain stores, on market stalls or in the increasing range of shops which, true to the logic of the free market, have grown up to provide affordable clothes and food for the urban poor. Our city centres will continue to be visited in the evenings by people visiting the theatres, or concert halls and also the night clubs and bars in the centre. For the moment, however, the future of Sheffield city centre, at least during the daylight hours, appears to be bound up with its use by office workers and by those members of the urban poor continuing to look for bargains in the covered Markets or on the open street market on the Moor, and the cheap stores nearby.

The second observation, provoked by our work on these two cities, is that patterns of use and well being in city centres cannot be analyzed by reference to a simple minded distinction between locales of private consumption and public spaces (spaces which are publicly owned, or specifically targeted at a general public by a local authority or other agency). Even a municipally owned "public park" is put to a variety of uses, from "public" use, for example the playing of more or less organized sports games, to "private" use, which could even include sexual liaisons. So also are privately owned places, nominally targeted at particular groups of private consumers, frequently reappropriated: one thinks of the ways in which the forecourt of shopping malls in Los Angeles and other major North American cities have become an alternative, after hours playground for the urban poor.[13] But we do want to emphasise the miserable character of much public, i.e. municipal or national State, provision in England, as one element in any explanation of why citizens in England might be drawn to the spheres of private provision and private consumption (the shopping mall) in preference to the publicly provided alternative. How do we explain the extraordinarily widespread use of cold, blank concrete blocks, as the architects and urban planners' first preference, during the 1960s, except in terms of its cheapness and ease of manufacture? We are interested here in identifying the political, economic and cultural processes that gave rise to a physical, material environment (for example, in parks, around urban underpasses, on public housing estates) that now appears ugly, unattended and unfriendly to all but a small percentage of users of urban space, and seeing those processes as a problem for any political or social discourse that points to "public provision" as an answer to the strains of contemporary urban experience. Our suspicion is that the low level of provision for the public **by private and public agencies alike** is a peculiarly and continuing cultural problem in England and one which requires sociological explanation. In terms of the locales we have described in this paper as routine places of public resort, the pavements and buildings around Piccadilly Railway Station in Manchester and "The Hole in the Road" in Sheffield should then be understood as absolute archetypes, on the streets of our two cities, of this meanness of public architecture and public provision.

Thirdly, we have been insistent in our discussion of these dispiriting, and sometimes ominous and threatening places, in the truth that people do actually continue to use these places, often in very great numbers. We are also interested in how they use them, the practical strategies they adopt and the neutralisation that accompany this use, although we have not had the space in this paper to discuss the different strategies adopted by our different publics in any detail. We have been struck, however, by the low expectations held by the bulk of our respondents with respect to the quality or the condition of the urban locales they routinely have to negotiate, and the level of public provision in them. The litter around the railways stations in Manchester and Sheffield seems to be seen, in some sense, and disliked, but it does not intrude into consciousness as a form of squalor that could effectively be rectified through consistent custodianship of public space by a local authority.

We want to finish with two theoretical queries, which we will want to follow up later in this research, and which are included here for discussion and response from our readers. This is a report on research in which an attempt is being made to explore the "sense of well being" in two cities, in which there are many common features born of their nineteenth century industrial heritage, and many discontinuities - of size, or local politics and local culture, and, most obviously of all in present circumstances, of economic potential in the free market reconfiguration that is affecting Britain as a whole, as well as the rest of the developed world. We need to move forward from the present survey and ethnographic work to try and identify the dimensions through which different publics will, or will not be able, to find a sense of well being in these two cities. What is clear is that the major issue affecting the sense of well being for the majority will be the availability of work, and that is an urgent matter of **public policy** for the nineties. The question of local provision of "public goods" is more complicated: we have argued that reliance on the urban regenerative efforts of the Urban Development Corporations leave behind too extensive a range of unattended, residualised areas in urban space (emblematic symbols of neglect), which contribute to a devaluation of public territories as a whole. Public authorities, on the other hand, strapped for finance and sometimes for imagination, have not shown that they can avoid the disasters of building for the public interest that took place in the 1960s. Does the crisis of the city centre in Sheffield signal the arrival of a new moment in which Sheffield no longer is the livable city it always believed itself to be? Does the fact of Manchester being able to claim some qualities of Molotch and Logan's "headquarter city" signal a prospect for Manchester in the late 1990s that is unavailable in Sheffield, and does this sense of possibility communicate itself in Manchester for every public in that city?

In the meantime, the residualised areas, territories and spaces continue to dominate many parts of the central areas of English cities, whilst also being necessary routes for publics walking through town. On the evidence gathered in this research so far, they still are entered by large sections of the urban population (except at night) on the grounds, often, of necessity, on their routine, everyday "trips into town".

Notes

1. The current research is a development of a pilot project into "public sense of well-being" in shopping centres and bus stations in Manchester, carried out in 1990 and funded by the University of Salford Research Committee and the Greater Manchester Passenger Transport Executive. This research is reported in Taylor 1991a, 1991b and 1992. The current project was made possible through an Economic and Social Research Council grant (R-000-23-3048) awarded in December 1991.

2. We have in mind here, *inter alia*, theoretical commentaries on the city constructed from within the perspective of Marxist political

economy by David Harvey (Harvey 1985;1989 Part III), the contemplation of "the city" from a particular kind of feminist perspective by Elizabeth Wilson (1991), the phenomenology of urban experience offered out by Michel de Certeau (1984) and, not least, the philosophical and historical reflexions on urban design and social life of Richard Sennett (1990).

3. Manchester and Sheffield were identified for comparative examination on the grounds of their interest to the primary grant-holder (as the city of his current residence and his city of origin, respectively), but also, on the grounds of the markedly different levels of reported crime in these cities. According to the figures in Chief Constables' annual reports for 1991, the crime rates per head of population were 1:7.3 in Greater Manchester and 1.13.7 in Sheffield. An initial hypothesis informing this enquiry was that these different levels of reported crime might be a measure, in some important sense, of the difference in size and population of these two, otherwise comparable, old ex-industrial cities, situated a mere 38 miles apart in the heart of the North of England.

4. For further discussion of the responses of the Greater Manchester population to the de-regulation of local bus service provision, see Taylor 1991a.

5. For discussion of the issue of litter as a measure of the neglect of public custodial roles by the State, see Taylor 1990.

6. Throughout the 1980s and into the early 1990s, the British press became increasingly aware of disastrous under financing of the railway system in Britain, by comparison with other member states in the European Community. Few commentators went further to investigate the ways in which the resourcing of national and local transport systems has been connected up, for example in France, to the issue of citizenship rights, in respect of personal safety (on the one hand, from accidents, and, on the other, from personal assaults and criminal theft). In Paris, for example, the initiation in 1989 by the **Regie Autonome des Transport Parisene** (the RATP) of a dedicated "Network and Intervention" strategy on the Metro, involving the redesign of stations, effective police public relations and a variety of other measures, resulted in a 27 per cent decline in the number of assaults on passengers by the end of 1991 (Kozar 1992).

7.   It is worth observing that the level of road congestion in Sheffield is probably no greater than that which obtains on the main arterial roads leading in and out of the city centre of Manchester on the average weekday morning and evening. But where Manchester, built around four major motorways, has been dealing with major road delays for years, especially during rush hours, Sheffield was experiencing this aspect of big city life for the first time. Attuned during the 1970s to the most reliable and cheapest bus service in England, and widely experiencing itself in travel and other terms as "the largest village in England", it was doing so without an equivalent sized network of major roads and motorways.

8.   Figures from Sheffield City Council's Employment Unit.

9.   The particular example used of zoning in the *Sheffield Area Study* is the area of Sheffield now referred to as "the Cultural Industries Quarter". This area, around the old tram sheds at the junction of Shoreham Street and Queens Road, is the area built up by the Council, at the high point of its activities within the "Socialist Republic of South Yorkshire" in the mid 1970s (see Clarke 1987). The Quarter contains a multi-purpose night club-cum-social centre, the Leadmill, and a film production and recording facility, the *Red Tape Studies*, both originally established via grants and subsidies from the local council.

10.   For example, an editorial in *City Life*, December 1992, Manchester's entertainment guide, bemoans the cult of "Civic Boosterism" as an expression merely of the kind of "trickle down" economics which has just been politically defeated in the US, and proclaims that such an approach to urban redevelopment has been shown to do little for indigenous residents "who only visit the malls and office blocks to clean them". The activities of the Central Manchester Development Corporation may prosper and the Council may proclaim the success of particular initiatives in respect of city centre shopping areas, *City Life* argues, but, in the meantime "Greater Manchester will have leaked more people out of the inner city to the suburbs, unemployment will have gone up, poverty will have increased, crime will have risen, inner city schools will be worse, the dispossessed, disenfranchised underclass will have grown" (*City Life* 218, editorial, 18 December 1992-7 January 1993).

11.   The layout and "feel" of Greater Manchester has been the subject of a very considerable literature, perhaps most famously of all in Engels' detailed account of the ways in which the city had organised what he called the segregation of the social classes (cf. Engels 1844, and the commentaries in Marcus 1973 and Donald 1992). Other "readings" of Manchester have been attempted by Chadwick and also by the American anthropologist, E.V.Walter, during the course of an academic attachment at the University of Manchester (1988). There is as yet no dedicated study of the reconfigurations of buildings and space that have occurred during the 1980s (for example, in respect of the Salford Quays developments, the renovations in Castlefield and Whitworth Street, and the introduction of Metrolink), and it is not our purpose here to offer out any such overall account. Sheffield by contrast, has not attracted either a scholarly literature, or a literature of social commentary, with respect to its layout or "feel", although a great deal of local history has been produced (cf. for example, Vickers 1972,1978, Walton 1968) and has also been the subject of significant criminological research investigation during the 1970s and 1980s, focusing on the relationship between crime rates and housing type in particular areas (Baldwin, Bottoms and Walker 1976; Mawby 1979; and Pepinsky 1987).

12.   One such initiative is the *Secured by Design* scheme, developed by the Association of Chief Police Officers, which was launched in September 1992. Aimed at developers of new car parks as well as operators of existing facilities, this can grant two levels of award - gold and silver -to car parks which meet certain security requirements, for example in respect of lighting and surveillance (Webb, Brown and Bennett 1992).

13.   The forecourts of supermarkets in England have also performed a vital role in the construction of excitement and alternative entertainment for working class youngsters in England. See Taylor and Walton (1971) for a brief ethnographic account of the alternative uses of supermarket trolleys and car parks in Bradford in the early 1970s.

12 Men in public domains

Jeff Hearn

This paper theorizes the public domains by an explicit and critical focus on men and masculinities. Following the introduction, the first part reviews malestream conceptualisations of the relationship of the public and private domains that do not explicitly address the gendering of that relationship. These include patriarchalism, liberalism, marxism, rationalisation theory, pessimistic progressivism, discourse/postmodernist theory. The second part considers implicit critique of men that are contained within feminist accounts of the public and the private, including those drawing on culture, reproduction and law, theories of patriarchy and public patriarchy. The third and major part considers the implication of theories of public patriarchy for the explicit analysis of men and masculinities. These are extended through a discussion of the relationship of profeminism, materialism and postmodernism, including issues of plural perspectives, difference, interrelations of oppressions, and the re-emphasis on private domains for understanding the public.

Introduction

Writing and talking are different. This short piece of writing on the public/private, itself a kind of public document, interrelates and is in tension with talking in the future and now in the past. While this writing is being done in private, the product, the writing, becomes public. In contrast, the talking (on the public/private) will be and now has been in a public arena, yet it is likely to be experienced as involving more of my person, and in this sense a potentially more private activity. This writing is an activity **now**, a preparation for and a reference back to talking. Though different, writing and talking refer and defer to each other. What began as an "unfortunate" necessity now becomes a personal/private privilege, only to be reincorporated into the public. To put some of this another and much simpler way: writing and talking have diverse meanings in relation to each other - the other of each.

Thus to write on the public/private is already complicated by the public, or more accurately publicized or publicizable feature of writing. Furthermore, writing on the public/private is contextualized in at least two other ways: first, that I am a man writing; and second, that this writing is within, or in relation to, or even in contradiction with, academic and political traditions that have been and are dominant in different respects in the public domain(s). Accordingly, there are innumerable ways in which the power(s) of men, public men, dominant forms of writing, and dominant academic and political traditions, have mutually reinforced each other. In particular, it is truly amazing how theorizations of the public domains have managed to avoid theorizing men.

Men's domination in and of the public domain(s) includes material, social practices, such as the avoidance of caring labour, and discourses, such as discourses on care and work. Indeed material, social practices are themselves discursive - hence the concept of material, discursive practices. Men's domination in and of the public is material/discursive. An important aspect of (dominant, public) discourse is the construction of the valuing of the public over the private. Discursive constructions are both material and have material effects, such as "state intervention" into "family life" in the removal of children.

This **double** domination - of the public over the private, and of men within the public - is itself historical. Men's domination of the public domain(s) has been ancient, contested and culturally variable. In medieval European society there were definite separate spheres for women and men, for example, in religious, court and military arenas. By the fifteenth century women's participation in the public domains was increasing. In Restoration England of the late seventeenth and early eighteenth century, political and economic changes in urbanization, industrialization, and capital accumulation, were intimately connected with change in families, households and gender relations. Thus, Kimmel (1987) argues that not only were constructions of "women" and "femininity" undergoing relatively rapid change at this time, but so were constructions of "men" and "masculinity".

Eighteenth and nineteenth century industrialization in Europe and elsewhere clearly transformed the relationship of the public and private domains, most obviously through the large scale organization of paid work for children, women and men outside and away from the home. However, the assertion that the public/private dichotomy is a product simply of capitalism and capitalist development does not accord with historical evidence. Late nineteenth and early twentieth century transformations of economy and society included the growth of multi-organizations, the modern state, civil service and military, and the mass media, meant that not only were the institutions and organizations of the public domain much larger, more complex and more powerful, but that they were also much more able to dominate public domain discourse(s). Late twentieth century transformations of the public domain brings us to the words and debates of postmodernism, including the relation of globalization and fracturing of reality - the possibility that just as we are told there is an increasing resort to the private, so there is the possibility that everything may be public.

All these historical changes can be re-read as commentaries on men. The increasing power and dominance of public domain organizations and institutions has generally entailed greater power for men. In particular, such changes can be reconstructed in relation to men's power as a collectivity, different kinds of men (for example, of different economic classes, ages, "races"), particular individual men, and diverse forms of masculinity/ies (Carrigan, Connell and Lee 1985).

Despite all of this, men in academia continue to manage to avoid theorizing men in general, and men in the public domains in particular. It is extraordinary how studies can be conducted of the state, capitalism, imperialism, organizations, management, factories, bureaucracies, streets, the media, pubs, clubs, and other public domain institutions without addressing the basic sociological question of men's dominance there and associated dominance of private domains. The "disciplines" of sociology, economics, political science and other social sciences need to be transformed to analyse these issues, not least because these disciplines themselves represent a further example of men's public domain domination.

The contribution of the malestream

Part of the way public domain domination has been maintained by men is through the domination of public discourse. An important aspect of such public discourse is the construction of the public/private, particularly as a dichotomy. In most malestream theories and accounts, "men" are theoretically absent, theoretically avoided, theoretically implicit and/or theoretically explicit yet unproblematic. Within the malestream (men's domination of public discourse) (O'Brien 1981), the various dominant ways of making sense of the relationship of the private and the public may be summarized in a number of ways.

"Natural" divisions

First, and still most dominantly, is a flagrant reference to the "naturalness" of the public/private division. "Men" and "women", "public" and "private" are seen as they are because of a supposed balanced complementarity. The private between them as given. This approach comes in many guises: philosophical, economic, political, sociobiological, and so on. The classical legacy has provided elaborate, and sometimes contradictory, rationales for keeping women out of public life. In the *The Politics* Aristotle (1962) placed women alongside children and slaves. Women were assumed to need a certain amount of coercion to maintain their inherent goodness and purity within the private domain. Meanwhile men were the social norm through their domination of the public domain of "politics". While ridiculous in its conception, this patriarchalism persists, whether in its classical or modern forms.[1]

While patriarchalism and liberalism may be easily contrasted, Pateman (1983) demonstrates, drawing in particular on the work of Locke (1966) and his *Second Treatise*, that liberalism is dominantly based in the separation of paternal (private) and political (public) power, and women's "natural" difference and subordination as against men's individualism. Thus liberalism is characteristically patriarchal-liberalism. It is upon such naturalistic assumptions that the public liberal state is founded as a further "umpire" of/by men.

The progressive power of public domains and public men

A second major tradition may be understood as part of the view of "man"/humanity coming out of "Nature": similarly, the public comes out of the private, and progressively takes over the private. This strand is therefore structured in change rather than in the stability of the first approach. This second approach is particularly dominant in the social sciences, particularly economics and sociology. Its two most well known exponents within the sociological malestream are Marx/Marxists (in their explicitly progressive and optimistic view of the socialization of production and reproduction) and Weber/Weberians (in their implicitly progressive and generally optimistic view of rationalization). "Men" are typically presented as the explicit or implicit "motor" of social change.

The progressive reduction of public men by the public domains

Another and contrasting group of malestream theorists who have stressed the importance, indeed the growing importance of the public domain have done so in the terms of its impact on people's personal and domestic lives. Those pessimistic progressives, such as Sennett, Lasch and Jacoby, in different ways emphasise the negative consequences of modernization for citizens, for which we can usually read "public men". Hence, Sennett (1977) writes of *The Fall of Public Man* and the collapse into the private, narcissism and the "tyrannies of intimacy" - hence the "diminished" individual man.

The transcendence of the public domains and public men by public discourse

A fourth contribution of malestream thought is in terms of transcendence of the public and the private through discourse. In this sense the public/private division cannot just be pre-conceived as a shifting boundary that moves back and forth; rather it is a political discursive reality in itself. The most influential malestream social theorist in this respect is Foucault (1981). Significantly, while his work deals with the history of sexuality in great detail, much of his writing is curiously genderless, failing to recognize the interplay of sexuality, violence, material, pain and sexual domination. Even so his work is very important in raising questions on the construction of the public, the private, and their interrelations **in/as discourse**.

There are a number of issues that are not dealt with satisfactorily in all these malestream accounts. They include most obviously the question of gender domination by men, that is itself the focus of feminist theory and practice. There follows from this the neglect of the determination of the public by the private, the attachment to dichotomy, the neglect of the complex interrelations of the public and private, and avoidance and issues of differences and diversity.

Feminist critiques of the public and the private

There are several reasons for feminist concern with the issues of the relationship of the private and public domains. One is summed up in the phrase, "the personal is political". There are all sorts of ways in which the personal or private is potentially public or political. Historical change around the public/private division or relation is especially important in gender terms as both evidence of change and inspiration of further change. Historically, many of the tasks formerly performed by women in the home and community, such as health care, education, agriculture, production of goods, have been transferred from the home to organizations, with their frequent re-closure, usually by men.

Then there are the various ideological critiques of the private and the public. One example is the view that what counts as "private", and what counts as "public", is largely ideological. Warfare and the military may be seen as "public", yet they entail the take-over, and sometimes the destruction, of people's homes, the barracking of soldiers, the private worlds of army camps, and all manner of private experiences, some distressing and damaging beyond belief. "Family life" or "home life" may be considered private, yet may entail interrelations and negotiations with all manner of other institutions and organizations. Then there is the question of the fundamental gendering of the public and private domains, and their relations. Public/private "divisions" or differences are made problematic by seeing them as **gendered**. For example, Joan Kelly (1979) has argued that the public/private "division" is false in the sense that women's experience, personal and social, is shaped by the simultaneous operation of the relations of work and sex.

Some theorists argue that the public/private relation is fundamentally gendered in terms of the structuring of **reproduction**, patriarchy or a patriarchal society (O'Brien 1981). Others focus on the institution of **law**, as the stipulation of meaning in regulation in and by the public, as against non-regulation in the private (O'Donovan 1985). In some analyses law in general is fundamental to patriarchy. Feminist anthropological approaches have often emphasised the variety of cultural links between "women", "private" and "nature" and "men", "public" and "culture".[2] In short the public/private division is cultural.

Work/care

One of the most important contributions of such theorizing is the attention to the social bases of patriarchy, other than those that arise from capitalism. In particular this involves the recognition (rather than undervaluing) of activities other than paid work, and their conceptualization as work. These include biology (Firestone 1970), sexuality (MacKinnon 1982), the domestic mode of production (Delphy 1977, 1984), kinship pattern (Weinbaum 1978), biological reproduction and the care of dependent children (O'Brien 1981), reproduction more generally (Vogel 1983, Hearn 1987), sex-affective production (the production of sexuality, bonding, and affection as the core processes of society) (Ferguson and Folbre 1981, Ferguson 1989). In turn these approaches emphasise forms of labour other than narrowly defined productive labour including reproductive labour (O'Brien 1981), sexual labour (Hearn and Parkin 1987), people work (Goffman 1961, Stacey 1981, 1982), emotion labour (Hochschild 1983), childwork (Hearn 1983), and solidarity labour (Lynch 1989). Accordingly care is seen as work.

Thus such care/work might include unpaid work in private, childcare, care of the elderly, care of those with illness and disability; it also includes emotion labour, in both public and private. Indeed productive labour and management can be reconceptualized as emotion/care work.

Patriarchy, patriarchies and public patriarchies

At about the same time (in the late 1970s) that some feminists were dismissing or severely criticizing the **concept** of patriarchy, others were working on these difficulties by making clearer distinctions between **types of patriarchy**. If patriarchy refers to a monolithic structure, then it is as limited as any monolithic concept, say, a monolithic concept of capitalism. Similarly, some theorists have been at pains to attend to the complexities of patriarchy in terms of different sites and structures of patriarchal relations (Walby 1986), types of specifically patriarchal relations (Hearn 1987), and the contradictions of patriarchal and other relations (Ramazanoglu 1988). Some of these distinctions between types of patriarchy have been drawn in relation to capitalism - hence the term "capitalist patriarchy"; others have been focused on the private and the public domains - hence the terms "private patriarchy" and "public patriarchy". These are powerful concepts for examining the problem of public men and public masculinities explicitly in terms of gender. They also give a rationale for the need to talk of patriarchies rather than just patriarchy; rather than seeing patriarchy as a social monolith, there are many different patriarchies - of different shapes and sizes.

The concept of public patriarchy, or, as I prefer, public patriarchies, is clearly a development of the generic concept of patriarchy - the former presupposes the latter (Hearn 1992). Whereas the concept "capitalist patriarchy" attempts to relate capitalism and patriarchy, or more precisely capitalist and patriarchal social relations, the concept of public patriarchy focuses on the way in which patriarchy is formed with respect to the public domain. Although different writers provide different descriptions and explanations of public patriarchy, all in some way refer to historical change in the power of men in the public domain vis-a-vis the power of the father and men in the private domain. Public patriarchy is thus usually contrasted with private patriarchy. It is often linked to the recognition of the state as gendered (Connell 1990).

The concept of public patriarchy represents, on the one hand, a gendered, usually feminist, reworking of the long-established malestream tradition of the development and extension of the public domains over the private domains, the shift from traditional to modern society, from mechanical to organic solidarity; on another, it represents a reworking of the concept of patriarchy to take account of both differentiations between different types of patriarchy, and the power and dominance of the public domains. Thus the concept of public patriarchy is both a development of a particular malestream tradition, and an expression of the restructuring rather than the end of patriarchy. It also brings together feminist debates on patriarchy and feminist debates on the public and private domains.

Just as the word "patriarchy" means different things within different frameworks and politics, so the words "public patriarchy" have a variety of meanings. They are, however, brought together in giving some kind of prominence to the power and dominance of the public domains in patriarchy. Usually this is contrasted with the prominence of the private domains under private patriarchy; and usually too there is an assumption of an historical shift from private patriarchy to public patriarchy.

Theorizing public patriarchy has involved a number of debates and disagreements. First, there are substantive differences on the basis or bases of public patriarchy. Alternative formulations include those that emphasize particular elements in gender relations (e.g. sexuality), institutional developments (e.g. state law), or the growth of the public domain itself more generally. Men's private and public appropriation of women includes not only women's labour, but also other aspects of women from sexuality to psychological and emotional care. Andrea Dworkin (1983) has argued that there are two major forms of patriarchy, a private and a public type, in which women's sexuality is controlled by men within the private domain and the public domain respectively. The weakening of private patriarchy is in turn accompanied by the massive growth in pornography and other public forms of men's control of women's sexuality, in both material practice and imaging. Secondly, there are variations around the historical movement from private patriarchy towards public patriarchy, and whether it is the introduction of waged labour, monopoly capitalism, the post-war state, or the modern welfare state that is seen as the crucial social, and "genderic", shift. Thus, if private patriarchy has indeed changed towards public patriarchy, we need to specify the form of that change. Different description accounts of this change are in effect different explanations - in terms of capitalism, the State, men, certain categories of men, and so on. Thirdly, and linked to the previous point, there are differences in cultural and national context. Fourthly, the nature of the relationship of private patriarchy and public patriarchy is contested. Fifthly, there are differences in the interpretation of these changes, as welcome or unwelcome, as actually or potentially liberating or oppressive. The earliest use of the term that I know of is by Carol Brown in "Mothers, fathers, and children: from private to public patriarchy", published in 1981 in the *Women and Revolution* collection edited by Lydia Sargent on the theme of Heidi Hartmann's (1979) classic famous article "The unhappy marriage of Marxism and Feminism ...". In the same year, Zillah Eisenstein elaborated the rather similar notions of family patriarchy (or the patriarchal family), and social patriarchy. Several other feminist commentators have developed similar notions contrasting public and private forms of patriarchy, through slightly different conceptual frameworks (see Table 12.1), along a variety of historical timescales (see Figure 12.1).

This last theme noted is developed particularly by Scandinavian feminists emphasising the relation between women as clients, citizens and employees of the State. Related themes have been developed in Australian feminist debates on women in the State, as femocrats and others.

These various interpretations of public patriarchy analyse the restructuring of patriarchy not the end of patriarchy. The shift is generally seen as integrally related to ever reproducing private patriarchy. In these accounts the focus is usually on one of these two major institutional blocks of the public domains - the state or the capitalist/market sector - and rather less so on the public domain institutions of opinion formation, including **culture and media**. Indeed **cultural accounts** and explanations of public patriarchy or accounts of **cultural change** in public patriarchy are rare.

Table 12.1

Private patriarchy, public patriarchy, and related concepts

Private patriarchy	Public patriarchy	Brown 1981 Dworkin 1983 Walby 1990a, 1990b
Family patriarchy	Social patriarchy	Eisenstein 1981
Familial patriarchy		Ursel 1986
Private domain	Public domain	Laurin-Frenette 1982 Guillaumin 1980
Private appropriation	Collective appropriation	Stacey and Davies 1983
Personal forms of dominance	"Structural" dominance	Holter 1984
"Patriarchy"	Reorganized patriarchy	
Direct, personally exercised and legitimated dominance	Impersonal dominance	
Private dependence	Public dependence	Hernes 1984, 1987a, 1987b, 1988a, 1988b Borchorst & Siim 1987 Siim 1987, 1988

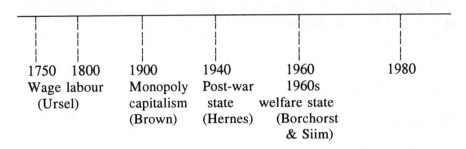

Figure 12.1 Historical timescales in conceptualising public patriarchy

Among several possible ways forward in the face of this variety, one important approach to public patriarchy is that of Sylvia Walby (1986, 1990a) who has argued that patriarchy cannot be reduced to the economic. Instead she has identified six structures of patriarchy: the patriarchal (household) mode of production, patriarchal relations in paid work, the patriarchal state, male violence, patriarchal relations in sexuality, and patriarchal culture. She has further developed this account to argue the change from private patriarchy to public patriarchy "involves a change both in the relation between the structures and within the structures" (Walby 1990a, p.24). Thus, she criticizes accounts that are limited to one or two structures, and suggests that "[w]hen all six patriarchal structures are included the account is more satisfactory" (1989, p.228). She has also argued that first-wave feminism, from around 1850 to 1930, is "a significantly under-rated political movement" (1990b, p.150), and that in Britain "a move towards a public patriarchy ... was a result of the successes of first-wave feminism in the context of an expanding capitalist economy" (1990b, p.157).

Implications for men and masculinities/deconstructing public patriarchies

In the final section, I would like to focus on two sets of closely interrelated questions. First, there are questions around the implications of theories of public patriarchy for men; and second, there are questions around the formulation of a different approach to public patriarchy, an approach of difference? These two sets of questions interrelate as they both facilitate a rethinking of theories of public patriarchy, by making socially problematic that which is taken for granted. The social analysis and deconstruction of dominant and superordinate groups, such as men, is frequently avoided, especially by the members of those groups. Rethinking theory in that way, including theories of public domains and public patriarchy, may turn theories upside down, and may produce new theory. It alerts us not just to the social mechanisms that maintain domination of the dominated, but the social mechanisms that maintain domination by the dominating.

Initial implications for men

Accounts of public patriarchy have usually been developed by feminist analysts in developing an account of the oppression of women. Less usual has been the attempt to consider the implications of public patriarchies for men. Yet public patriarchies are clearly about men and men's power. So what **initial** implications follow for men from feminist theories of public patriarchy?

First, if men's power over women shifts to men in the public domain, then at least some men in public domain institutions will be involved in those relative increases of power, and perhaps authority. This entails attention to different kinds of men, such as state managers, "mascorats", professionals. Second, there are the impacts of feminism and women more generally upon men, both individually and collectively. Third, the growth of (some) men's power in the public domains is closely linked with differentiation of power between men - the power of some men over other men. Fourth, there are the impacts of men's public domain power over men in private, both directly and indirectly, as, for example, in greater state intervention in childcare. Fifth, the increasing dominance of the public domains has potentially increased importance in the construction of masculinities, socially and psychologically. Sixth, there is the possibility of the distinction, perhaps increasing distinction, between private masculinities and public masculinities.

Problematizing public patriarchies

Feminist theories of public patriarchy are to my mind the most important set of theories for considering the relationship of the public domains and the private domains. I have already noted some of their implications for men and masculinities. Additionally, there is a need to develop these theories in relation to issues of diversity, difference, and de-differentiation.

While deconstructive projects have been viewed with some suspicion by some feminists, others have seen a strong compatibility between feminism and deconstruction in its various poststructuralist and postmodernist forms. I do not want to engage with a general debate on the relationship of feminism and deconstructions, except to say that some deconstructive approaches have been rightly criticized for neglecting or diluting power relations, and for ignoring feminism and feminist theory and practice. Some postmodernist writing appears to have been written by men as if feminism never existed. Rather I would like to argue that profeminist deconstruction has a particular use in undermining "men" and "men's power". This applies in at least two ways.

1   The deconstruction of the supposed monolith of men as "white, heterosexual, able-bodied men" (WHAM's).

2   The deconstruction of men's power as the practices, processes and justifications of men's power are shown to be contradictory, flawed, even empty.

These approaches emphasise the fragmentation of different types of men and of different bases of men's power; and the fracturing of men's experience (Hearn 1992). To do so, however, does not necessarily reduce attention to power and specifically men's power as a gender class; indeed the analysis of fragmentation and fracturing merely adds to the complexities of men's power both individually and collectively. In these ways, deconstructive approaches, like those that are psychoanalytic, have quite different implications and potentials for the analysis of women and other dominated groups. Furthermore, this approach to men in public patriarchies involves elaborating, not diluting, materialism. Through such a critical, power-directed profeminist poststructuralism and postmodernism, attention may be directed towards materialist deconstruction: problematizing, pluralizing, exploring differences, without diluting power. The intersection of profeminism, materialism and postmodernism appears to be particularly promising for the further analysis of the power of men in public patriarchies in its full capacity.

Deconstructing grand narratives

In considering public patriarchy, there is a danger of constructing a false grand narrative in to which the power of all men is fitted. It is important not to take gendered change as part of some inevitable historical or geographical evolution or progression framed by "turning points" or natural development. "Public patriarchy" is very much a shorthand for a set of historical and geographical circumstances rather than a "stage" in history or geography. It is partly for this reason that it is more accurate to speak of public patriarchies rather than public patriarchy. There are many different patriarchies of different scale and location, not a single form or a single concept. Such a pluralizing of patriarchies suggests a pluralizing of powers not a pluralizing of countervailing influences, as in some notions of pluralism.

Diversity, difference and fragmentation

Table 12.2
Comparison of public and private "zones"

Walby (1986, 1990a) (Sites, arenas and social structures)	Hearn (1987) (Social relations and social processes)	Habermas (1984,1987) (System and life world)	Fraser (1989) (Societal zones)
Capitalist Work	Reproduction of Labour Power	Private Sector	Official Economy
State	Regeneration/ Degeneration/ Professions	Public Administration System	State
Family	Procreation/ Fatherhood	Private Intimacy and Family	Family
Culture	Ideology	Public Opinion Formation	Public Political Discourse
Violence	Violence/State		
Sexuality	Sexuality/ Hierarchic Heterosexuality		

Following on from this plural perspective, we may consider the existence of public domains rather than the public domain, multiple and fragmented material bases of patriarchies, and multiple zones in the public domains (see Table 12.2).

In each case attention may be directed to men's relationship not just to the economy and the state, but to sexuality, violence, culture and procreation (Walby 1986, 1990a; Hearn 1987). Fragmentation may thus develop in relation to different bases of men's power, different kinds of men, and different parts of men's lives and actions.

Further diversities exist both between the public and the private, and between different meanings of the public. These include variations in time and space, for example, the public as in the street and as in organisations; in the extent of resource accumulation; in the forms of interpersonal interactions and interpersonal processes; and in the construction of the self/selves.

Interrelations of oppressions

This complexity also leads to concern with multiple oppressions and the intersection of men's power as men with other powers or lack of powers. These other realms of power include age, (dis)ability, economic class, "race"/ethnicity and sexuality. These interrelations of oppressions both enhance the power of particular men, for example, men who are capitalists, and complicate or undermine the power of others, for example, black men (Hearn and Collinson 1990, 1994). Such powers are themselves formed partly in the public domains. Thus the intersection of public domain processes and multiple oppressions is especially important, as is the metatheoretical relationship of postmodernism and the materiality of multiple oppressions (Hearn and Parkin 1993).

Fracturings of experience

Not surprisingly, men's experiences of the public domains are frequently, and perhaps characteristically contradictory and fractured, including ambiguities, paradoxes, disjunctions, and resonances and parallels with other meanings; they may defy pre-ordered meanings.

Against dichotomies: back to the private

An emphasis on difference may apply not only to the operation of the public domains but to the very idea of the public domains. Thus to understand men in the public domains it is necessary also to deconstruct the very idea of the public. Specifically, the division of men's lives into public and private may be seen as a world of difference: as a division that is either arbitrary or itself based on a public domain construction or based in the labour of the private. In particular, men in the public domains have to be understood in terms of men's relationship to different forms of private labour and nurture in private, including avoidance, performance, control and management.

To challenge the public/private dichotomy means not accepting pre-given definitions of the public (as visible, organizational, production) and the private (as invisible, domestic, reproduction) definitions that have usually been defined dominantly by men. As such, one of the repercussions of challenging that dichotomy is to open up new ways of working and theorizing, that may provide possibilities for change for women, and in a different way for men. Just as women's lives are not neatly divided in this way, nor are men's, or at least some men's. It means fundamentally questioning dichotomous thinking, including the division between objective and subjective.

Reconceptualizing the public/private

This leads on to the question of how we conceptualize the public/private relationship. There are a number of different ways in which the relationship of the public and the private can be conceptualized. First, the public and the private can be understood as (relatively) **given**, separate, fixed, unchanging, and complementary. Second, the relationship may be understood as historically changing, whereby the **boundary** between the two realms shifts progressively, often seen as determined by an external force, for example, capitalism. Third, it may be more accurate to see the public/private as matters of contradictory **interrelations**:

i   through individual biographical experience of the public and private

ii   through the life of a particular group, family or other primary collectivity

iii   through the social relations of a particular social structure or structured category, from example, a particular gendered or sexually structured collectivity.

Thus rather than seeing the public and the private as zones or fixed

214

domains, one might consider how parts of the public and the private **co-exist** for individuals, social groups, or socially structured collectivities in their material lives. Accordingly, one might consider how aspects of the public interdignate in private spaces and vice versa.

A fourth possibility is to focus on the **space between** the public and the private. Just as Stacey and Davies (1983) have talked about "intermediate zones" and Meyrowitz (1986) has talked of "middle regions", so one might think of social experiences that have the quality of not just being **between** the public and private, but being **both** public and private - hence the term the public/private or public privacy.

For all these reasons, it is more accurate to conceptualize the public/private as **differences** not a divide or dichotomy. This is partly to overcome the idea of distinct separation, and partly to involve the multiple meanings of difference - as separation, diversity, constant deferral, self-reference, unity divided from itself, and anti-foundationalism.

Beyond the public/private

This brings me to the question of how can we go beyond the conceptualization of the public and the private. And in turn, how am I and are we to make some sense of all this? Well, I think in several ways.

First, it is possible to construct more and **more complex models of the relationship of the public and the private** - by different material bases (procreation, sexuality, nurture, violence, paid labour, state development, culture and so on) that are differentially organized and differentially experienced (in time/space, in resource accumulation, in interaction, and in some sense of selves). Such complex matrices themselves change in time and space.

A second possible conclusion is not in terms of increasingly detailed relations of public and private, but in terms of **the transcendence of the actual concepts of public and private**. This might involve attending to alternative conceptualizations, for example, the distribution of nurture or of sexual processes or of violence regardless of its apparent location in the "public" or "private". Alternatively, it might involve conceptualizing different activities as **both between** the public and private and **both** public and private. Reconceptualizing might entail both using the notions of public and private, and transcending them, and as such is characteristic of debates and tensions between modernism and postmodernism (Hearn 1992).

A third possibility is to return to where I began and to consider **the**

public/private in terms of men. The growth of the power of the public domains, and especially the state involves processes of **publicization** of activities and **consolidation** of men's power. It also involves **fragmentation** of men's power as different realms (of state, capitalism, opinion-formation, culture) develop relatively autonomously, and **fracturing** of men's experiences. The relations of those four elements seem to be especially important, for both women and men.

The ways these relations are experienced are also particularly complex and variable. For myself what is called the public is often intensely private; and what is called the private is similarly public. Increasingly, the words do not make experiential sense. This may be a product of my particular interests, activities, style of life, politics, job; or it may be the result of more general social processes, for example, globalization, state policies, media and cultural developments. Perhaps most important is the need to differentiate how these experiences are for different kinds of people in relation to different activities, such as sexuality, nurture, paid labour, violence. It is necessary not to underestimate the power of public domains, and of certain men there, in defining power, objectivity, persons, signs and senses. The intensity of such definitions become clearer if one thinks of particular examples of activities, such as on the one hand, the dominant sexual regimes in many public domain organizations, and on the other, the ways that such organizations may still intervene tentatively against the violence and abuse in private, and yet be places of different violence and abuse themselves. It is perhaps only through a focus on particular examples that the detailed operation of the public/private can be understood, reconceptualized and changed.

Men, violence and the public domains

How do these kinds of approaches operate within substantive analyses. In *Men in the Public Eye* (Hearn 1992), I have examined men at the turn of the century through the examination of "public men" as social relations, through organizational structures, in organizational processes, and as "persons". These are not four levels but rather four realms of analysis, that interconnect and reproduce each other. As a way of focusing on a substantive area, I shall briefly address the men in the public domains through the lens of violence, including men's interpersonal violence and men's institutional violence, for example, through the military. Having said that, adopting a particular focus does not mean that the construction of public men as social relations occurs in segmented realms or arenas.

216

Public men are produced in the **intersection** of several arenas, for example, the simultaneous operation of (hetero)sexuality, private violence and the state. For example, nineteenth century state legislation on husband's violence to wives is "constitutive" of men in public as the formulators of legislation and of women and men in private. The 1853 Criminal Procedure Amendment Act made communication between husbands and wives beyond the jurisdiction of the courts, and made spouses not competent to give evidence for or against each other; accordingly, the public domains constructed the private. The 1878 Matrimonial Causes Act allowed women to use cruelty as grounds for divorce, thus recognizing a division between sexuality and violence. We are currently seeing the beginnings of changes in legal practice on men's rape of women in marriage, again constituting public men and private men in a reciprocal relationship.

Public men are constituted more specifically through the structures of organization, for example, in the growth of oganizational technologies, such as the capacity of military violence, and in the rise of management. The development of such a specific occupational group is premised not only on organizational separation from private labours, but also on further separations within organizations. This applies not only to the management of commercial organizations, but to state management and the management of military, paramilitary and police organizations. The 1854 Trevelyan-Northcote Report laid the basis of the modern Civil Service and recommended appointment (of men) on "merit". From the 1860s to 1890 the so-called "open competitive examinations" were developed - for men. Managerial development also included more specialist innovations. For example, the General Staff of the British Army was instituted in 1904 and revived in December 1915. Contemporary state management includes men's domination of the management of powers of policing and surveillance; military and paramilitary violence; violence in the restraint of prisoners, suspected criminals and others. This constitutes a significant occupational grouping that is defined as management, entails managerial careers, that controls the violence of other workers (police, prison officers etc.) and of others in private, and formulates a particular version of public men and public masculinities. Moreover such managerial men both often controlled the private lives of others and had their own private lives.

Public men in the public domains are of course not simply formed through organizational structures; equally important are organizational processes. Sometimes these appear to reproduce the public and the private within the public. This appears to be the case in the practice of sexuality within organizations. The late nineteenth century saw particular concern over what would now be called sexual harassment. Cindy Sondik Aron (1987) has described the fears of immorality with the employment of women in U.S. Federal Government Offices from the 1860s. This included both the corrupting influences of "immoral women" and the corruption of "moral women" by men. Similar dynamics were described with the employment of women in the Post Office in Britain in the 1870's, and fears of their sexualizing influences on men. Practical difficulties included the installation of toilets and the serving of meals. Aron reports that by the 1890s "(t)he line between good natured, "innocent" flirtation and impropriety had become muddled and difficult to determine" (p.174). In 1891-2 a strike took place at Evans and Berry Weavers, Nelson, Lancashire, over the "immoral language and conduct" of one of the men overlookers towards the women weavers. This was followed by an "independent inquiry" by a Committee of three local clergymen. Their report found that "the offences ... are not uncommon among men who have the oversight of the female operatives" (Fowler 1985): public intervention into sexual harassment was legitimate; men were being named.

Campaigns against sexual harassment from the 1870s have made it a widely recognized phenomenon, as are organizational policies against it. Current developments included the development of policies against personal harassment and against (physical) violence in and around organizations (Hearn 1994). Public men are increasingly being constituted in terms of what was formerly considered (by men) to be private, i.e. actions of sexuality and violence.

Finally, public men are specifically constituted as "persons". This has much to do with the recognition of individual men as "unique individuals" (rather than members of gender class), as people with "masculinity", "masculine characters/personalities", and even "male subjectivity". One version of these has been developed through psychoanalysis. The psychoanalytic constitution of public men is a complex bringing of the private into the public. Partly it offers various "Achilles Heels" for men, showing vulnerability, contradictions and possible rationalizations; it creates space for the public(iz)ation of the sufferings of those violated by men. It also facilitates even more oppressive means of men dominating women. Of special interest, psychoanalysis has contradictory implications for men who have been violent in private to women. It may provide explanations and rationalizations; it may also uncover deep motivations; it may offer both oppressive and emancipatory potential for women violated; and most recently in anti-violence counselling groups for men, it reconfirms the subjectivity of the man, and his redemption through the group - the transfer of violent acts against women to inter-psychic and intra-psychic processes in the group.

These are just some examples of the possible way of connecting the theorizing of public domains and the theorizing of public men. It is equally necessary to theorize the public domains by attention to gender relations, and specifically the domination of men, as it is to theorize men, and specifically public men, through attention to the public domains. What is remarkable is how these fundamental questions have been avoided in academic analyses, particularly by men - itself an instance of a further particular kind of domination by men, that itself deserves theorizing and critique.

Notes

1.   See Elshtain 1981, Pateman 1983, and Schochet 1975.

2.   See for example, Rosaldo 1974, Ortner 1974, and Moore 1987.

13 What happened to the sociology of the street?

Joel Richman

Street pavements represent the low-mark of the urban environment -
square miles of patched asphalt of no discernible texture and colour,
erratically perforated by metal grilles through which escape the
stenches of the sewers, carried aloft on clouds of tepid steam.
Street pavements are the giant recipients of the city's offal.... but
most of the time the street acres are parched: soot drifting before
the wind like black powder snow, miniature tornadoes swirling
scrap. And this is not the last of its unedifying aspects; to remind
us how transient are men's achievements, streets are torn up in an
eternal ritual, baring a netherworld of pipes and strands of cables,
as ugly and mysterious as the great Cretan labyrinth. (Rudofsky
1969, p.265)

The entrée into this chapter via Rudofsky's vivid metaphors remains apt.
Together with other lone voices, Jacobs (1960) and Anderson (1986), who
have promoted the social significance of the street, the promise of a
consistent sociology of the street remains a mirage. Streets, often
subsumed under the organizing category of public space/place, have been
the intellectual domain of others: for example environmental designers like
Brill (1989) demythologizing our nostalgic loss of the public - much
remains, colonized by special interests, not only gangs with claims to
turfs; the new genre of phenomenological architecture espoused by
Norberg-Schulz (1980) with concepts of "being" drawn from Heidegger;

the older investments of ecological psychologists like Barker (1968) onwards; not least the host of human geographers and transport planners.

However, sociologists have produced texts with inviting street titles, but neglecting their significance. This was typical of those writing after World War II on working class life. The earliest, Paneth's *Branch Street* (1944), was more concerned with the area as a zone of transition for the Irish; poverty-diseases (only three children from 400 achieved full nutrition); "erraticism" of child development lacking adult supervision (conveyed within a Freudian model) and personality formation. Snippets about the street merely confirmed children's bad habits of greediness and the use of aggression for excitement. Kerr's *Ship Street* (1958), a Liverpool slum with a residual working class, focused on dock work and group-solidarity morality: thieving from bosses was acceptable, but not from one's own group. Again, developmental stages and becoming a "mum" were to the fore. The street only a minor addendum when noted that, for example "toss" (gambling) in your own local street was not permitted, but taking money from the bookie was.

Similar forays into working class life, Mogey (1956) in Oxford, had the aside that adolescents hang around street corners talking about girls. In Mays (1954 and 1959) the street was a similar omission. Young and Willmott (1957) listed street activities in Bethnal Green; homage at war memorials, street parties and gambling. There was no linking between street activities and community; dense survey data on households had no street counterpart. Street life could not be accommodated within the research agenda, emphasising the impact of economic change and concerned whether the new working class was becoming **home centred**. Streets had little analytical import, assumed to disappear with the old order. Later class interests, for example Gill's (1977) *Luke Street*, centred on housing policies and delinquency. The chapter, the boys on Casey's corner, is significant only for the site of story telling of thieving strategies, without the sophistication of street observations found in a US counterpart, Liebow's (1967) *Tally's Corner*.

The expectation that the multiplying studies on public order would give more analytical interest to streets has not been fulfilled. Surprisingly, because law enforcement agencies have developed tactics based on street knowledge. Northam's (1988) study of riot police does not index "streets". Waddington (1992) has a cover depicting street scenes of a burn-baby type, but neglects to index streets. Streets have to be teased out of the core theme: manifestations of state power; the symbolic boundary of Railton Road, the front line in the Brixton riot 1981, proceeded by Operation Swamp when 943 people were "sussed" on the street; road blocks and anti

222

picketing tactics in the coal dispute, 1983. In Fine and Millar's (1985) more personalized accounts of coal disputes streets also have little elevation, although street collections - tokens of public support are indexed.

Aims

The substance of the paper has three primary aims:

1. To emphasize the sociological significance of streets.

2. Posit reasons for their sociological neglect.

3. Briefly suggest tacks for accessing their theoretical importance; for example via the rise of homelessness in the developed world.

Background

Streets are one of the few undisputed universals whose evolutionary development from tracks has mirrored human progress. Streets are the supreme conduits between institutional forms of our life cycles, especially the status giving identity of work and home. For a minority, street people, the street is emblematic. Because the street lacks precise definition, dependent as it is on cultural variants, there should be no disbarring of a sociological focus. The gestation of urban sociology was not terminated because of the vagueness of the parameters of urban/city - still not reconciled. When Mumford (1961) posed: what is a city? - he emphasized that there was no embracing definition. Hellenic and Roman thought never made an urban and rural differentiation, unlike modern writers.

A sociology of the street would encompass social behaviour embedded primarily in public places along transit networks culturally designated as roads/streets and their counterparts. Streets also include pavements (sidewalks), although Jacobs (1960) differentiated the two. During the Middle Ages European cities abandoned pavements; to reappear in seventeenth century London. Leon Battista Alberti, the fifteenth century philosopher/architect, accepted the bridge as a street component. Streets also have their own furniture - Japanese power lines are rarely hidden; the former Eastern bloc had sloganized hoardings glaring economic targets. The historian Bedarida (1980) has also commented that historical studies

223

of streets remain underdeveloped, but then wildly asserts that because streets are shared space they must therefore be "neutral space" with a code of behaviour hinged to the lowest common denominator, disqualifying them from a creative part in social life. This downgrading culturally is common, thus the street becomes unworthy of serious study.

Significance of streets

Streets are a large proportion of urban territory. The major experience of cities is through streets. City imagery is variegated. To the Manchester busman streets become routes, ranked according to types of time harassment. One estate with many elderly becomes "cripple canyon": slow moving passengers means "delays". A route with bus multi competition becomes the "wall of death". Women have a greater sense of dangerousness and plan their circuit accordingly. Jacobs (1960, p.29) asserts: "Think of the city and what comes to mind? Its streets. If a city's streets look interesting, the city looks interesting; if they look dull, the city looks dull".

Kostoff (1991), an architectural historian, has distinguished five cultural designs of cities. They have been planned as grids, others transforming into organic patterns; the symbolic and diagrammatic layout; the Baroque plan; and urban skyline. Their skeletal template being streets, but less so for the urban skyline. The Baroque, which supplanted the organic medieval city, relied on long axial streets. Grids transcended the ancient Greeks, eighth century Heijokyo, Japan, eighteenth century Philadelphia and English new towns. Street layouts inform us cross-culturally. American streets are generally unreflective of topographical, botanical, historical or mythological interests. Their utilitarian grid-iron impersonality, conveyed rather by number exudes a rational business ethic. The Italians have long honoured their streets with a complex taxonomy indicating whether the street is crooked, tree lined, descending and water flanked, etc.

Lynch's (1960) pioneering study of how Bostonians developed cognitive maps via streets (and other paths and nodes) has generated a wealth of other urban legibilities. The planning of the new city of Ciudad Guayana, Venezuela, was sponsored by Lynch's principles. Evans et al. (1982) emphasized the significance of urban markers for the elderly-major street walkers. The elderly in Orange[1] were asked to recall "significant" buildings. They had the same recall as the young, but relied more on markers of symbolic meanings of street frontages, especially if sited with high pedestrian/vehicle activity. Visual preferences of street scenes have also fallen within the orbit of cross cultural psychologists. Nasar (1984)[2] showed how foreign street scenes were rated more favourably. This preference was explained by "novelty".

Streets are important means of signalling continuity and change, especially of ideological import. Street names are the first refurbishing of social transformation. The collapse of the USSR, for example, has led to semiotic shuffles. The Ukrainian city of Lvov has changed over half its street titles. "Peace Street" (formerly Stalin Street, formerly Hitler Strasse...) to "Stephan Bandera Street": the Ukrainian nationalist with German support opposed the Red Army, 1944. To Jews, the resurgence of Ukrainian nationalism has been fused with anti-Semitism. Again, Harare hailed its freedom from colonialism with renamings from its liberation pantheon: Samora Machel Avenue, Julius Nyere Way.... Rhodes Avenue became Herbert Chitepo Avenue.

Mayor Dinkin's courting of the New York Irish vote was symbolised by his presence at the ceremonial naming of "Joseph Doherty Corner", a site outside his cell in the Manhattan Correctional Centre - having been detained for seven years as an alleged IRA suspect. National concerns have street displays. New York has a "death clock" in Times Square (cost, $200,000), now registering nationally a hundred firearm killings per day. Los Angeles and other cities have "debt clocks": the national debt is $4 trillion.

Children's street games are major conveyors of historical remembrances. Roberts (1978) noted that Salford children during his childhood played "bobber and kibs", a game illustrated on ancient Greek vases. Street games are very receptive to wider public interest. The Opies (1987, p.116) recorded seven year olds in Fife 1954, singing: "Marilyn Munroe fell in the snow, her skirt blew up and the boy said "Oh"'.

The street still remains central to political processes; as fonts of freedom of expression, extensions of institutional power and as challenges to established order. Global imagery has "resanctified" streets. The rise of Khomeini, the breaching of the Berlin wall, Yeltsin's attack on the White House etc., were global street theatre. Dubcek's riposte is apt: "The government (Communist) is telling us that the street is not the place for things to be resolved, but I say the street was the place. The voice of the people must be heard". Freedom marches, as with USA civil rights of the 1960s, are street marches.

Streets have long been a crucial appendage of religion. Streets are capable of accommodating full memberships (buildings are not) and mass displays of collective symbols. Pilgrimages, pledges of faith, are as old as streets. Streets have always oscillated between the secular everyday and sacredness, not only religiously. Victory parades, national anniversaries, inaugurations and so on are street centred, albeit today in more technically controlled ways. The walkabout and glad handing are obligatory rituals for those in "high places". As in Greek drama modern gods, with media formulated persona, descend and mingle to proclaim they are representative of the people. With industrial disputes the street also becomes the public gallery for the revealing Durkheimian totemic banners, emphasising the virtues of solidarity and the progression of rights through collective struggle. Thus the street is an important adjunct to organisations like trade unions whose everyday administration is normally hierarchial, impersonal and mechanistic.

Absence of street sociology

This neglect can be attributed, partly, to the nineteenth century agenda set by the sociological founders. Streets, *per se* did not fit into their numerous enterprises. Their theorising about the direction of industrial society was arm chair based. Field work was generally alien. (Marx got a nil return on the one survey he sent, not bothering to ask a question on alienation, because it was "self-evident".) Although each provided their own version of social order involving discussion on rules, will, principles and accountabilities, there was general agreement that the switch from traditional to industrial society involved a displacement of the public to institutional and complex organizations. Street life as part of the old order found no analytical niche within the newly constituted models of industrial society of gesellschaft, legal rationality or organic solidarity. For example, Tonnies heavily influenced by Hobbes, was concerned with deriving sociology from the philosophy of history and law, using social structure without content. The street assumed to be devoid of structure fell out of the sociological imagination. Although Tonnies did some empirical research (e.g., on poverty using social statistics) his political support for the Kiel strike 1896-7, was not accompanied by any street commentary.

Weber's tome, the *City* (first published in *Economy and Society*) was really a contribution to political sociology, littered with ideal types of market, fortress, rentier and merchant cities, etc. Durkheim's urban interest was largely confined to regarding it as a site of a new division of labour. Weber and Durkheim, together with Marx, were ambiguous in how they argued for the city - it being both an independent entity and simultaneously a product of change, as well as having no street agenda.

226

Explicit in their analyses was spatial separation of different institutions, but, the obvious linkages were never translated into streets. Yet major European cities were being reshaped then: Haussman replanned Paris with wide streets to inhibit barricades.

Simmel's sharper eye for detail and capacity for popular, social commentary occasionally remarked on streets. Arguing that the metropolis produced a more intense, sensory bombardment especially when crossing the road, which could not be reduced by the same strategies used to screen other aspects of cosmopolitan life with institutional formatting. Marx eliminated the possibility of a street sociology by disenfranchizing the lumpen proletariat from an historical role. Engels (1969, p.58) had a few street jottings. In London for the first time in 1843 found: "something repulsive about the turmoil of the streets.... brutal indifference in capitalism". Yet noticed some orderliness: "only agreement is a tacit one; that each keep to his own side of the pavement, so as not to delay the opposing stream of the crowd".

Mayhew could be acclaimed as the forgotten founder of a sociology of the street. It is exceptional in texts of general sociology to find him. Like Simmel and Marx he published in the press, that being insufficient for detracting from academic recognition. He did become an anti-establishment figure with an idiosyncratic life style forcing him to retreat to Germany 1860-70. His attacks on Chartism and strikes also provided no radical support. Humphreys (1977) showed how Mayhew used statistical frames to calculate the diet of the poor from food sold in streets (herrings and sprats the key source of protein); evaluated status hierarchies of street sellers; used open-ended interviews for narrative reconstruction of life histories (even asked a cripple if he was a cripple when dreaming); produced elaborate classifications of streets, their goods and people (even the material which dirtied them); elaborated how matrilocality was not a social pathology but a response to street poverty (negating the conventional wisdom that street *habitués*, dangerous classes, were a mass of depravity despoiling the Empire's great capital); avoided locking his analyses into an evolutionary framework; perceptively charted the impact of state regulations on streets (especially new laws on obstruction affecting fixed site barrows); made pictorial presentation of his subjects.[3] Despite Humphreys' criticism of his "'classifying mania", Mayhew's achievements were considerable.

Booth's studies of poverty (influenced more by Leplay's analysis of household budgets than Mayhew) supplemented the 1881 census details with some street observations, having sojourned with the poor. His innovatory coloured maps showed that the extreme poor congregated in certain streets. Booth's poverty focus outweighed any street interest, intellectually.

Urban sociology, a logical home for street studies, did little. Its ecological/spatial phase was geared elsewhere. Neighbourhood studies were interested in whether it was declining or gaining significance. It was a myth that the Chicago school/s produced many vibrant street studies: Faris's (1970) list confirmed that studies akin to street on tramps, skidrow and street-characters were the exception. The hobo was considered atavistic, a frontier relic, to be integrated via education into mainstream society - the school's policy matched the European anti-street movements. Cressey (1932) welcomed the cinema (palace of dreams), to empty street corners. The fifty year follow up of the *Jack Roller* (1982) a mugger, contained more on his short stay in a hydrotherapy ward (related to psychiatric treatment) than street interest.

The street fared much better in ghetto studies, a mixture of interests, more recently urban ethnography. Hapgood's (1965, 1979) recollections, a gentile observer of New York's Jewish ghetto in the early 1900s[4] is vibrant with street minutiae of theoretical relevance. "You can write a social history of our country by **walking** through a neighbourhood". (p.XI). The impact of time, the festival calendar, meant that "on the first night of the High Holy Days the streets were silent, dark and deserted". (p.XII) "Because tenements were crowded and dirty the real life of the ghetto was in the street" (p.244) could be written of the black ghetto today. Hapgood's street existentialism: "in the crowded street that my love and my imagination call me" (p.249) is echoed by Brown (1965, p.69) on Harlem: "...If home was so miserable the street was the place to be. I wonder if mine was really miserable, or if there was so much happening out in the street that it made home dull".

Street features like the crowd have attracted numerous disciplines. Whyte's (1955) analysis of the street festa, as a microcosm of community interests, produced no lineage. Cohen's (1982) longitudinal, ritual analysis of the Notting Hill carnival did sign post the anthropological potential of ceremonial drama. Historians like Rudé[5] argued strongly of the crowd's strategic part in European history and that most street participants were mainstreamers with just causes, but excluded from the state political process. Sociologists rarely tapped into this historical thrust. Rather, these street interests fell within the provision of collective behaviour - a rag bag of topical interests. Proxemics (mainly popular psychology with sociological overtones) picked up some street matters, concerned with the use of space generally, including office layouts, etc.

Street down-grading was also associated with the lingering ideas of nineteenth century contagion theories; crowds driven by lower instincts which Le Bon (1920) attributed to "inferiors" - savages, women and children! He worried lest the crowd mentality shifted into institutional forms, like juries. It is noteworthy that *The Guardian* (1st May 1992) had the heading; "When the jury takes to the street": explaining the triggering of the Los Angeles riot after the mainly white jury refused to convict police of brutality towards motorist Rodney King: the video of the police assault was shown world wide. Since the 1960s rioters have been "normalized" by those supporting the "bottom dog". Street protests defined as means of rectifying historical injustices. "Looting reflected anger and desire for reparation" (*International Herald Tribune,* 8th May 1992). However, law enforcement agencies on the side of the "top dog" usually disagree. Chief of Police Parker after the Los Angeles Watts Riot 1965, declared that rioters behaved like monkeys in a zoo. Over five days loss of property amounted to over $200 million and thirty five people died (28 black), but reconstruction of events showed violence was not indiscriminate; schools, churches and libraries were not torched, only those white stores which "overcharged" were attacked. Looters in cars obeyed the traffic lights.

Reicher (1984) demonstrated the research possibilities from constructing a real time analysis of crowd action, offering the opportunity for testing a range of socio-psychological theories of riot origin and progression, thereby confirming regularity for an event formerly considered spontaneous and irrational. Reicher utilizes the Bristol riot of Saint Pauls, on 2nd April 1980, precipitated by a police raid on the Black and White cafe, Grosvenor Road; suspecting the illicit sale of drugs and alcohol. The use of media tapes, insurance and police reports together with interviews with rioters etc, exemplified the value of mixed sources for investigating episodic phenomena as riots. Real time construction (used successfully in the study of disasters) facilitated the testing of a gamut of crowd theories: "agitator", "collective mind", "games model", "referent and information influence", and "J-curve" etc. Reicher (p.1) opines that "crowd behaviour is more sophisticated and creative than hitherto allowed and the neglect of this field should be remedied". Briefly summating, like the Watts riot definition of community limited rioting behaviour; intra group identification of a "gemeinschaft warmthness" - against the "alien" intrusion of police and media who subscribed to views represented in the McCone report [6] that rioters were an amorphous mass, with anti social instincts releasing an irrational, destructive orgy against authority.

Methodological "difficulties" have been suggested as a barrier against a street sociology: the street ostensibly devoid of "convenient" benchmarks for structural analyses. Much depends, of course, on the subject of street interest. The complexities of walking behaviour, for example, can be interpreted from film - but few sociologists today are interested in or competent to handle visual data. Again, depending on the street theme danger to the researcher(s) must be considered. Williams et al. (1992) are among the first sociologists to raise systematically this issue and offer a range of strategies to minimise risks.[7] Williams (p.351) studied crack dealers and argued that "street people act on their intuitions and are experts in reading behaviour". If ethnographers displayed fear they risked becoming victims. Street ethnographers negotiating entrance to deviant groups have always run the risk of being suspected of being an informer. The etiquette of the street necessitates that the researcher never approached directly upper level dealers, but through the validation of their screening personae - steerers, touts, runners and lookouts. Women ethnographers are especially at risk from sexual attack by crack aroused respondents and have been forced to terminate their research.

Forward the sociology of the street

Sociology and social problems have had a long coupling, albeit that the conventional wisdom of "problem" would be challenged. State research funding today encourages the "relevant". A current problem entwined with street is homelessness. Shlay and Rossi pointedly began their comprehensive review:

> Research on homelessness in the 1980s has been prompted by the increased numbers and visibility of homeless persons including men, women and families, as well as young people without families'. (Shlay and Rossi 1992, p.129)

Tessler and Dennis (1992) concurred in opening their symposium of research funded by the National Institute of Mental Health.

The street has always provided the setting for variations in visibility for different groupings, evoking differential moral responses indicative of the wider value system and change processes. In the Middle Ages there was the idealization of men of poverty, beggars in the Franciscan tradition of denial. Industrialization reversed the piety image. Vagrancy, especially linked to mental disorder invoked harsh sanctions; "randomness" of thought threatened a world succumbing to the Protestant ethic governed by the time cult of precision.

The depression of the 1930s to some extent destigmatized street vagrancy, because of its generality and the collapse of work. In 1930 the US recorded over 200,000 homeless children. In the 1960s vagrancy was narrowly defined as a skidrow (or Hobohemia) issue; alcoholism and "moral defect" the cause; social work would eradicate it. In the 1980s homelessness has undergone dramatic redefinition. The street is now the barometer of critical change. Homelessness is complex; urban renewal, gentrification of cheap property, rapid unemployment, changing dynamics of family and the deinstitutionalization of the mentally disordered are factors - the latter constitute only a minority of homelessness. Third World homeless is primarily the product of recent mass migration from the countryside. US homeless are long term residents. Shlay and Rossi (1992) show seventy five per cent of homeless to be also unemployed. In the US mentally disordered homeless tend to be homeless longest; twenty seven per cent of all homeless people are women.

Snow and Anderson (1993), with a triangulation of methods, have signposted the way of generating a sociology of the street linked to a homeless genre. They overcame the limitations of surveys, summarized by Tessler, Shlay and others; ascribing homeless status (most don't sleep on the street) has methodological difficulties when relying only on interviews. Putting the homeless of Austin, Texas under the microscope Snow and Anderson used narrative reconstruction accounts, network analysis, participant observation - as well as surveys to tap into street life (for most it is routinized), street talk, making-out strategies: begging, selling plasma, panhandling rubbish, cultivating the "Sally Army" and intermittent jobs. Each survival strategy is a probe into the local and national political economy. A grounded typology of homelessness was produced: recently dislocated, straddlers, tramps and bums. Each further refined - for example "bums" into traditional and rednecks; "tramps" into traditional and hippie. Each typification had a given cluster of characteristics in terms of time on the street, income for selling plasma and type of shelter used, etc. The status categories of homeless were distinctive and hierarchically ordered as those found within status conscious organizations. Relevantly the study concludes: "In our attempts to understand the homeless we have been struck more by their normalcy than by their pathology". (p.314)

A second pathway to the study of the street can be via concepts of time. Temporal frameworks and of analysis have had no consistent direction within sociology: philosophy and psychology have aggrandized themselves with temporal concerns. All events are time linked. All cultures can be portrayed as temporal expressions. Gurvitch (1964) wanted to reconstitute sociology around the "problem" of time and by his endeavours made less opaque the temporal imperatives in Marx's theory of change. Aveni's (1990) larger enterprise has illuminated further ancient cultures by showing, for example, the impact on public life of the Maya 260 day cycle and others. Zerubavel (1979) produced new insights into the social processes of the hospital (the latter rested uneasy within organizational orthodoxies) by tracing the generation and meshing of different time interests; ultimately the patient (case/bed) becoming a unit of time. Young's (1988) *Metronomic Society*, offers other possibilities for a street sociology, with his developmental model of time consciousness and self.

The street is the overflow of the dominant times of institutional interests and more diverse personal ones. The clock and traffic signal are the foundation of urban order noted Wirth (1938); echoing Simmel's comments on the chaos that would befall Berlin if public clocks were to deviate by an hour. Snow and Anderson's (1993) homeless are mainly powerless disenfranchised by the industrial time cult but still regulated by other time interests (for example, law enforcement), left to secure their own temporary, time-niches. They know the temporal hazards of street existence - congregation during "work-time" in the central business zone and being "busted" by the police. Space and time are intimately linked.

A third intellectual investment into street sociology is possible by means of phenomenology. Inner experience and private discourse can be linked to "doing walking". Phenomenological architecture has "stolen" this march on sociology. Simmel hinted at this possibility, but his concern with the "mind of metropolis" pointed elsewhere. Street phenomenology would have the consequence of liberating the street from its taken for granted mundaneness and lack of focused study. The street is awaiting, for example, a Buber (1992) mode "I and thou" type of analysis: hearing and listening are the main activities for Buber. The street produces its own rhapsodies and cadences, as well as its own silence.

Conclusion

The limitations of this truncated, partisan laudation (more a pastiche) for the sociology of the street is recognized. There are many omissions. Nothing has been said on the pre-industrial city with its sophisticated appearential ordering, not only public life. Third world cities also did not get a nod. Possibilities from the anthropological tradition did not figure. Street "tracings" from Malinowski's (1982) nascent research in Mexico on the changing use of Ocotlan streets (and market) under increasing commercialization, could be raised.

There could be those who would argue that a sociology of the street was unnecessary - there being already a surfeit of sociological specialisms, or that its substance could be accredited elsewhere - for example under intellectual elasticity of the "public". They have yet to speak out on this matter. Sociology's virtue has been the production of "insights" into the intricacies of society, from numerous starting positions. The sociology of the street would provide another valuable *entrée* into this endless but exciting task.

Notes

1. A Californian town of 85,000 population with a square, grid planned, interposed by a traffic circle containing a park.

2. The research was undertaken with problematical samples of USA and Japanese graduates shown slides and videos of four cities in each country - e.g., Osaka and San Francisco.

3. His wood cuts were made by Richard Beard, one of London's earliest photographers.

4. He received half a million letters of recollections after his first publication.

5. See also Perkins 1981, and Kay 1988.

6. See Cohen 1970.

7. Danger can be present in other research fields; family contexts are laced with potential violence, as social workers know.

14 Men of steel: Gay men and the management of public harassment

Carol Brookes Gardner

Who does it? Stupid, ignorant people. I've done my share of arguing with idiots, and it doesn't help. They get more dense. I get tight in my throat. I wish for great physical strength to defend myself. I wish for the ability not to harbor great hatred - because I do, and it doesn't help anything, it doesn't help them or me. I wish to be able to help others who are put upon or those in trouble. I wish to have the courage of my convictions, and I don't. I wish for the Man of Steel to come out of the Man of Silk.

Chuck, ballet dancer, aged 39

The great problems are to be encountered in the streets.

Friedrich Nietzsche

There are few legitimate instances of talk and interaction in public places between strangers, but many abuses and many target groups that receive, more than their share, these abuses. We feel we have a right to expect talk to occur only in a certain narrow set of contacts and attentions, such as stereotyped greetings, sometimes appended to discussions of weather or sports, or service encounter transactions; we can give help when needed, as when a stranger asks directions or the time; we many watch over unwatched children in a supervisory way; or we may give the small amount of notice legitimated by civil inattention. In thos abuses that can be termed **public harassment**, however, talk and nonverbal communication are used to evaluate, threaten, or physically injure another person. Among common targets of public harassment in the United States are those citizens perceived as gay, lesbian, and bisexual. In this study, I discuss the situation of gany and bisexual men, concentrate on verbal harassment, and emphasize the strategies that men reported to manage this harassment. As a result of this analysis of 56 indepth interviews, I concluded that gay men ono only received various forms of nonviolent harassement in public places that are distinctive and eloquent as to the way in which society sees them, but also that men spent time evaluating, choosing, and sometimes perfecting their strategies.

These cases of lapsed civility were often **street remarks**: street remarks are evaluative comments received from strangers that effectively define the situation, attempt labeling of the recipient, and may express the giver's displeasure or contempt for the recipient (see Gardner 1980 for the specific case of women who receive street remarks from men). As such, namecalling, vulgar comments, and innuendo constituted involuntary "outings" over which gay men had no control. Added to these were instances of silent miming or mimicking, hands on physical harassment like shoving or trailing a person, and other incivilities. Men's strategizing to manage these difficulties must also be seen in the light of the suspicion of and undeniable violence from the general public that condition gay men's experience of public places.

Men judged gay are often felt to be dangerous by the heterosexual public, and men strangers judged gay have traditionally been considered a particular threat to boys. An etiquette book of as recently as 1972 advises readers that boys especially should be warned against

> the male stranger who may seek him out or sit next to him on any
> public transportation and try to stike up a conversation. While such
> an overture may be perfectly innocent, the boy should be told gently
> the necessary facts concerning deviates. If any action or
> conversation seems to be of a suspicious nature, such a boy should
> find another seat. (Vanderbilt 1972, p.723)

Thus, homophobic suspicion, often in the guise of concern about the youth of America, is one contingency of public places for gay men. The possibility of violence is another. Gay men in public have special reason to fear bashing, hate crimes, rape, and other forms of public assault (Anderson 1982; Miller and Humphreys 1980)[1] and police harassment and brutality (Karmen 1983; Rubinstein 1973). In addition, gay men are still subject to some crimes and threats of crime that ultimately depend on discovery of their homosexuality; this discovery can often occur when a gay man frequents a merkedly gay establishment or haunt and becomes, for example, subject to extortion (Harry 1982).

When considered against these truly momentous events that can cost a man his health, his job, or his life, verbal and nonverbal **gaybaiting**, as I have called it (Gardner forthcoming) can seem trivial. Yet gaybaiting can, for example, hold up a humiliating picture of gay men and, as it does so, can creat, reinstate, or perpetuate feelings of shame, anger, and despair. Acts of gaybaiting can be witnessed by unsympathetic bystanders and in fact often seem produced for a temprary theater of appreciative observers. Thus, gaybaiting makes publicly available with what little compuction strangers can scorn gay men. For sympathetic observers, gaybaiting incidents are lessons in the practical power politics of the street. Gay and bisexual men informants reported a variety of stategies they used to manage gaybaiting and counted many instances of management satisfactory. These strategies are sometimes part of a well thought out plan of action, sometimes born of the moment. Some elements of these stategies are shared with other publicly harassed groups, notably women's strategies for handling harassment in public (Gardner 1980) and workplace or school situations (Backhouse and Cohen 1979; Benson and Thompson 1982).[2]

I concentrate on the most frequently reported gaybaiting incidents and on the management strategies informants reported. Most often reported were namecalling, taunting, and verbal and nonverbal ridicule on city streets. I also incude occurrances typical of the semipublic situations, such as places of business and eating establishments. To trace the path of this generalized suspicion and these intrusions is to begin to account for the ways in which this sense of vulnerability is constructed, experienced, and managed, as well as ways in which public treatment contributed to an individual's private sense of self.

First, I note the empirical materials on which this study is based. Then, after characterizing the public harassment of gay and bisexual men in particular, I discuss their management strategies.

Empirical materials

This paper is based on 56 in depth interviews with men who resided in

Indianapolis, Indiana, and the surrounding area. To assure as diverse a sample as possible, I gathered informants by posting or distributing notices of the project at a local university, in stores, in gay bars, at the Damien Center (which supports people who are HIV+ and their partners and families), and at the local Gay Pride Day gathering. An article about Gay Pride day in a mass circulation newspaper announced that I would be at the site and was interested in recruiting informants; another, in a local gay publication, reported that I sought interviewees. Notices and articles noted I would donate $10 to the local Damien Centre for each completed interview with gay, bisexual, or lesbian individuals about their experiences in public places.[3] One local and one regional gay newpaper contained articles on the project that encouraged readers to contact me. Because of the method of obtaining informants for this project, they were likely to have had some contact and identification with the gay community.

Most informants (32) had read about the project in one of the newspaper articles. Ten responded to flyers. Eight were word of mouth referrals from previous informants.

In interviews, I asked informants about both positive and negative experiences in public places. Throughout, I was careful to stress that interviews would be confidential. The notice had said that I wanted to talk with gay, bisexual, and lesbian citizens about their distinctive experiences in public places: 4 men of the 56 identified as bisexual, the rest as gay. Interviews took from a half hour to five hours; the average was 90 minutes. I asked informants their personal experience of nonviolent harassment in public places, either expressing or receiving these contacts; how they handled this harassment; and the effect, if any, of this harassemnt on their lives. I also asked about "good" experiences from strangers. Throughout, I asked informants to distinguish between strangers they judged gay and strangers they judged straight.

For the most part, interviewees were young men: 21 were between 20 and 35, 21 were between 36 and 45, and 8 were between 50 and 70 years old. All interviewees were white. Thirty four were in permanent relationships at the time of the interview; 16 others had been so. Their occupations and socioeconomic standing covered a wide range of professions and socioeconimic strata, as well as the welfare dependent or unemployed: thus, I included business executives, engineers, health professionals, police officers, waiters, secretaries, entertainers, clerks, librarians, and colledge students.

In repeating my informants' descriptions of nonviolent harassment, I have occasionallly omitted the exact name of a site. In some cases, an informant requested that I do this; in others, I have resisted identifying a gay owned establishment.

Various factors conditioned informants' experiences of nonviolent harassment. First, 19 of the 56 informants had also received violent harassment from strangers. This ranged from being hit or beaten up, to having a limb or jaw broken, to homosexual rape, to being assaulted by a volley of rocks, broken bottles, or other missiles. Of the 31 remaining informants, 20 had experienced some smaller violent incident that they did not consider as serious, such as rocks thrown at them by small children, or had been threatened with violence. Only 11 informants had no direct experience of violence or threats of violence from strangers in public places. However, all mentioned violent experiences that friends had had.

Second, informants had all either lived in Indiana for most of their lives or visited Indiana often. Thus, they were subject to the laws of Indiana with regard to homosexuality and were knowledgable about local cases of presectution for, for example, Hand holding (*Indianapolis Star*, 1990), problems of police brutality (Mitchell 1991), harassment by straight neighbours (Sullivan 1990), and serial murders with a string of gay male victims (Ford 1990).

Though interviews centered on informants' experiences with nonvilent harassment, most informants had direct experience with stranger violence in public places. Moreover, their experiences in ublic, whether violent or nonviolent, took place in a social and political context that was unsympathetic at best, dangerous at worst, and in which their civil rights went unprotected. Some informants mentioned that, in contrast to the East or West Coasts or Chicago, Indianapolis or Indian were "not safe", or "less evolved", or simply "frightening". In speaking of his decision to "play the straight role no more" in presenting a public appearance, a young man said he knew, however, that "Politically, it's easier to be mainstream, especially in Indiana". Other men said that Indiana was simply consistent in its abuse with other cities, states, and countries.

Informants reported that nonvilent harassment was constant and lifelong, thus reinforcing, possibly from many strangers and many times a day, the negative view which much of society held of homsexuality and of men in particual. A few informants reprted nonvilent harassment that had started as young as 6 or 7 years of age. For most, it began (as did violent harassment) in their teenaged years, and simply continued.[4] Some 6 informants said that, because they themselves were "masculine", or "straight", appearing, they received little harassment because they escaped ready categorization as gay. They were well aware, however, that friends or lovers they felt were more "effeminate" were often harassed, as they might be in the company of such a friend or lover.[5]

The character of gaybaiting: what, where, and who

Types of public harassment: the constant call for management strategies.
Gay and bisexual informants mentioned abuses of all types. Though
interviews concentrated on relatievely "low level" incidents, informants
had a wide range of these to discuss: spitting, sniggering slyly or blatantly
laughing, throwing some small sissile, slurs, catcalls, the refusal of service
or markedly poor service at a business establishment, "mild" hitting or
poking, elbowing aside, mocking by miming, pointed and audicble talk
"meant" to be heard by the target, and outright staring as if a man was,
not a citizen, but "the evening's entertainment", as one man phrased it. In
short, a man could be abused at any aspect of his presence in public.

Though name calling was the most often reported type of harassment for
streets and open public spaces, it was unpredictable. For a librarian in his
forties, the canonical case was "two guys driving by downtown in a pickup
and they yell, 'Queer'!" He added: "but, unfortunately, [this type of name
calling] can happen in many other circusmstances, too". As well as "drive
bys", informants reported that name calling could come from other
pedestrians, either standing at a distance, commenting close by, or
muttering so that no one but the target could hear:

> An older black man walked by me on the street, and he just casually
> said "Fag" to me, without putting a lot into it, just as if that was
> what I was, and in case no one else knew it, he'd illuminate them.

In addition to the term of abuse itself, some informants noted the "tone"
or "way" anything was said to them. It might be "hateful", "scornful", or
"a malicious, hateful tone of contempt".

Some name calling abuse was broadcast to more than just the target.
Clearly, the sider the audience, the more potential for shaming. Yet more
quiet, even whispered slurs could also waken shame, too. Another
possibility was that name calling would turn didactic, as when it was
balbeling for the education of another person, as when a mother pointed
out two men to her samll child and elucidated, "**Those** are homosexuals"
(and see Fricke 1981, p.86).

More complexly, many informants described receiving the mocking
verbal evaluation similar to street remarks women receive, crafted to make
women feel out of role no matter what action they took (Gardner 1980).
Others could engage in **foolmaking** (Gardner forthcoming) by casting any
small action as offensive or ridiculous:

In spring, I was downtown by myself on a Saturday, going by a building with glass walls in which I could see myself. I happen to have a case of adult acne, and I stopped to look at myself. Two men in a truck went by, and one yelled, "Do you think you're pretty?" hatefully, it wasn't witty or joking. They were really close. Then he turned to his friend and said, "Damn faggots!" I felt like I shouldn't have been looking, then I thought, "I have the right to do that".

Most informants said that they had felt harassed by the scrutiny of others. Gaze, sometimes accompanied by an expression connoting wonder, scorn, or amusement and sometimes also accompanied by pointing and laughter, sent a powerful message. For example, a young secretary and his partner had stopped their car at a light when they looked over to notice a man, woman, and two children of 10 or 12:

in an old junk type car. They looked over at us and they all started laughing. There was nothing to laugh at except us. **My** car was in fine shape. And at Fall Creek and Delaware, late afternoon, there were two women in a car across from us at the light. My partner said, "Look, they're laughing at us". They were.

As significant as harassment in open places between those who shared no alignment to interaction, harassment in semipublic sites or situations could be equally insidious.

A variety of places: where public harassment occurred. Sites for gaybaiting encompassed virtually every site where a gay man might venture. Men experienced nonviolent harassment both on public streets and avenues and in public sites like malls, stores, parks, and spuares. In these cases, the men were not engaged in talk or encounters with the strangers who harassed them, but were passersby or rightful users of facilities like malls or parks. In the case of semipublic harassment, gay men were acting in the roles of customers or were momentarily engaged in ratified talk with strangers when greeting them or offering or seeking help.

Public harassment also took place in semipublic sites like stores and restaurants, and in situations of legitimate talk between strangers, such as when offering to help or simply greeting another person. Or when the individual was in a performer/expert role.

In stores and restaurants, 42 informants reported they themselves had received harassment, including rudeness, harassing comments overheard or delivered directly, slow service or no service, and refusal to seat or

241

serve.

Rudeness and hectoring comments could come during a service encounter or the server could let the individual overhear her or his estimate of the person afterwards. Thus, when one professional man and his lover attempted to check into a hotel and specified a single key and a single bed, they noted the clerk's manner changed, and he "slammed the key down. We were on vacation to relax. It spoiled [the vacation]". Service could be withheld or limited in a variety of ways: Informants noted that a waiter or clerk could manage to avoid noting their existence; orders or requests could be ignored, botched, or sluggishly carried out; men's complaints might be received complacently; service might be refused on various accounts, For example, that the restaurant was full (when it manifestly wasn't) or tickets refused on the shaky premise the movie theater was full on a weekday afternoon.

The naive and well meaning heterosxual might imagine that gay or gay friendly establishments offered a welcome shelter. Once inside, this was often ture. However, "known" gay bars or estaurants could require the entering or exiting man to run the gauntlet. A computer specialist reported:

> Across the street [from the gay bar], they [public harassers] would sit and watch us. [We were] wearing everything from business suits to female impersonators doing a **really** bad job. They would simply watch sometimes. We were one of their larger sources of entertainment.

For some men, staring in general or particular instances of staring could connote menace, promising that the incident would later turn violent. Both patently public and semi public situations yield harassment, then, with the "overhearable remark" constituting and intermediate case.

A wide range of offenders: who committed public harassment. As might be expected by now, men (collectively) reported that virtually any individual or group member might gaybait. Though a man could report different groups a likely to be offenders, even men who believed that "it's your racial minorities" or "redneck white crackers are the worst" invariably also reported being abused by others patently outside this category. Overall in public harassment, women and children are probably the least frequent offenders; thye were notably present, however, as verbal and sometimes nonverbal abusers of gay and bisexual men. This membership gave a very different cast to the work on women as victims

242

of public harassment (Gardner 1980; Stanko 1980). As well as victims, women are active participants in the public harassment of gay men and they, as primary caretakers, have the opportunity to socialize their offspring to so harass, too.

Management strategies for dealing with gaybaiting: men's solutions

Both explicit and unconsciously arrived at strategies combine to help the individaul cope with the many varieties of, sites for, and authors of public harassment. I would not suggest that, despite what some men said, even the most "empowering" of these strategies substitutes for the needed social changes that would make gaybaiting unthinkable.

General reactions to nonviolent harassment

Overwhelmingly, gay men attributed blame for nonviolent harassment to their harassers for the most part, though a few mentioned that some gay men brought about their own harassment by dress, manner, or behaviour.[6]

"Bringing it on ourselves": Of nearly sixty informants, only three believed that gay men themselves were responsible for stimulating nonviolent harassment, typically by "flaunting" or by "going where they had no business", as a secretary in his thirties remarked. Among traits designed to attract the attention of others and stimulate harassment, said a health professional in his forties were "faggy clothes, a swishy manner, and a lisp", as well as

> being indiscreet by kissing or holding hands, or being foolish by going where you don't belong, like to family night at a restaurant or to a redneck neighbourhood.

A journalist suggested that, though gay people experienced harassment in public, this was "by their own choice. Most of them have asked for it, and I'm talking about gay men now, not gay women. They flame, they flaunt, they dress flamboyantly because they want to stick out". When members of the gay community act in these "discernibly" gay ways, "we're bringing it on ourselves", he added. Considering the breadth of gaybaiting, however, one might suggest that even if gay men "bring it on themselves", there are a myriad sites, situations, and individuals more than prepared to help them do just that.

243

Strategizing: There are a number of techniques that are efforts to change the definition of the situation. Sometimes by hoping to deny the intruder the floor, sometimes by reeducating the intruder in the significance of her or his behaviour. These strategies, conscious and unconscious, planned and spur of the moment, responded to vastly different phenomena, were sometimes practiced with different motives, and informants felt the stategies met with different levels of success. In assembling a repertoire of strategies, men sometimes mentioned that they were helped by observing others and taking them as their models. As they managed public harassment, would the speaker, like this entertainer:

> I've been all over the world, and the world has in it a lot of frightened, ignorant people. But in Buenos Aires, walking down the street, it's difinitely macho heaven. Claudine and Christiane [two women in the ballet company] were wearing shorts, to whistling and catcalls, and I was watching how they dealt with it. They were serene: they just walked through it. I took that as my way, and from then on, in North Africa, Turkey, where ever, whatever happened, that was OK. If I met someone, fine. If they yelled something at and I could sense what it was, OK; I didn't let it bother me.

One man hoped to start a group himself, partly to promote the sort of self esteem that could tackle public harassment and help young gays, lesbians and bisexuals effectively deal with gaybaiting.

Avoidance: Informants mentioned several different **avoidance strategies**, ways of escaping nonviolent harassment that involved avoiding certain sites, situations, or companions that would increase the likelihood of being categorized as gay or being in range of those intolerent of gays. Most informants (47 in fact) said they had modified their behaviour by avoiding sites or avoiding public places in general. Most extreme were the 7 informants who reported they had avoided going into public places in general for periods of time such as "years" or "months" after a particular incidence of nonviolent or, in one case, violent harassment. For one professional man, the 27 years before he admitted to himself he was gay were the worst in terms of harassment:

> There have been very few [bad experiences], mainly because I was isolated for so long. Walls around me on all sides......I got some catcalls in public and at school. Mostly I avoided going out altogether, partly to avoid getting the catcalls.

244

Some men did not experience fear at the thought of harassment so much as anticipated relazation at the thought of staying home:

> Sometimes I'm sure that I'll avoid going out of the house. I don't want to go to a particular function because someone in the crowd is sure to be an asshole, a homophobe. You know what they say about us, one out of ten? Well, it's true for them: one out of ten is an asshole. So I'll stay home, maybe with a couple of gay friends, just lounge on the sofa where I can relax and dress the way I want, not worry about the impression I'm making.

But fear of harassment could lead men to appraise a site or situation for its potential, then accept or reject it: "My partner and I were going to go to Dairy Queen on the East Side. But from the car I saw that it was mostly young white girls and I wouldn't go in because of fear of being made fun of". Others regionally segmented the city into "safe" and "dangerous" parts: "I tend to stay in the north part of the city and away from downtown. I go to state parks. I haven't had any problems there".

Ignoring or denying: Ignoring and denying are the psychic equivalent of avoiding places or the public sphere altogether: The individual refuses to admit that gaybaiting is occuring (while being quite capable of informing me that they were unaware).

Although informants found particular incidents disturbing, frightening, or even menacing, some noted that less vivid instances especially could be handled by ignoring or dismissing them: "I've had people look at me questioningly, but I'm not intimidated. I disregard it and I don't let it affect me". Rarely, a man could project his "unawareness" convincingly on the aspiring harassers, as did one librarian, who counted himself straight appearing and said that he had discounted namecalling incidients easily as a teen: "I said, 'Me? No!' and I looked around puzzled. They drove by. It was over quickly. Just Texas teens. I didn't worry about it". Less pleasantly, an individual might retain some fugitive memory of an incident but "blank out", as a manual laborer said he did:

> At times it's so bad I've just gone blank. I stopped to get a paper downtown, and I guess I've got kind of feminine gestures, because two men standing at a bus stop were doing everything just as I did it, put the quarter in the machin, etc, but with flounces I guess you'd say. I got away, but I've no idea how. Then I threw the paper in a trash can. I have no idea why.

Thus, purposeful ignoring might be experienced positively or negatively.

Some informants said they purposely ignored nonviolent harassment. Some said they did not, in fact, "hear" or "see" harassment at all unless it was physical, or they knew it occurred but "blocked it" and made an immediate effort to forget it (see Gardner 1980; Feagin 1991). Others said, admiting hearing verbal, they didn't "let slurs get to the heart of me".

One reason for not answering back or for ignoring was that harassment often occurred in disadvantageous circumstances that effectively squelch or prevent reply or retaliation:

> So many of these incidents were not really "to my face", but behind my back. On the canal in Broad Ripple, a car went by and the occupants yelled 'Faggots!' to me and my straight friend walking by. How can one respond to that?

Finally, not answering back or reacting could be the basis for an "empowering incident". It could be reconstructed as self control, whereby the individual's restraint symbolically portrayed the strength of gays and the ineffectualness of straight harassment.

"I should've said....": Many men reported they had reactions in mind, though they thought it judicious not to. Sometimes they envisioned a smart rejoinder or riposte. These later reconstructions allowed the wisdom and wit of hindsight. A man who heard two men queuing for a foreign film loudly label it "faggy" said:

> I should've said, "At least it's not a Bergman film, you'd have to read the subtitles". But I only thought of it later, so I didn't.

> When they yelled "Damn faggots!" I was going to yell at them, "Yes, that's what I am, you've got it". I didn't.

A performer, who had had a woman namecall during his song, said he had confronted her, but in general:

> I'm happy with not retaliating. In my gut, I'd like to be abusive, to dismantle the person intellectually and physically. But I handle things maturely. I don't want there to be more violence in the world. I'm pretty pleased with this strategy.

Others too, refrain because of a nonviolent philosophy.

246

Still others believed that not answering back or otherwise retaliating cost in dignity what it gained in satisfaction:

> Four of us, not nelly, were walking down the street. But these collegiate types could tell and started yelling "Fag!" My friends wanted to beat them up, but I said no, it'd be more dignified to just walk away. So we did, but the guys just kept yelling at us.

Ignoring and denying is a strategy gay and bisexual men share with women who are publicly harassed (Gardner 1980). For women, courtship (or seemingly courtship) situations provide the protective cover of a man, so that accompaniment is often useful. For gay men, this is not always so.

Company: Unlike the publicly harassed woman, companionship does not always aid the gay man, especially if the companion is another gay man. In such cases, if both are discernibly gay, both become gaybaiting targets. At stake in gay male presence in public places is commonly said to be some ultimate threat to the family as a social institution: the harasser who sees a gay man can become insensed that the "family life" of America is being assailed (and this is sometimes the substance of verbal threats to gay men). Harassers presumed two gay men were lovers, and thus company seemed to make it clear that the traditional nuclear family was not a goal of the couple.

Answering back: Most informants said they longed to "answer back", but most prudently said they did not do so. First, because they were often outnumbered and to do so might be dangerous:

> I wouldn't try to stop, talk, and explain. They might have a gun or something, you never know.

> I don't believe this is an appropriate forum for a discussion of belief systems, and especially not so when you're outnumbered.

Second, answering back would implicitly display an involvement that would give harassers satisfaction. Harassers were "unmovable", said one man, that is, could not (or could not always) be debated with hope of change. Another echoes:

> I never respond to anything verbal. There's no sense in trying to change someone who's set in their ways. And they wanted me to

yell back. I knew the guys wanted me to get angry.

A third reason to adopt a judicious silence as strategy was a man's fear of being believed by anyone else who might later need to be told of the incident, such as police, official agents, or even friends. More threatening was retaliation from child harassers, who might, men suspected, claim child molesting. For example, in an incident where a secretary was surrounded by a group of young boys, he said:

> If I'd reacted, one of the boys could've said I tried to make a pass at him. I didn't worry about physical violence.

In fact, some men mentioned that to speak back and not fear retaliation was a right:

> I should be able to go up to someone and say, "Yes, we're gay, grow up! You should be ashamed of yourself". I should be able to do that without fear of getting hit.

Answering back, of course, might be angry, placating, or attempted reasoning. The latter two were rarely reported, perhaps since harassers are implicitly set in their ways. One man, who occasionally had tried to reason, reported of an incident where children and an adult surrounder him:

> I started to try to reason with them, then just tried to go by authoritatively. They ran, and one threw a rock at me.

Showing anger, though not fighting, often felt "good", "satisfying", or "fitting" to many men. One man, when namecalled, often replied, "Come over here! Want to fight? Right now? Here on the sidewalk?"
Or men might "choose their spots" and sites for angry or even, responses. Often those who felt threatened in public would not at work in semipublic situations. One man said:

> I **do** answer back at my work [as a waiter]. I have to tolerate enough crap from the general public: I'm not going to be slurred because I'm gay. "How I choose to live my life is my own business", or I'll say something less diplomatic.

But responses were not always effective, even for customers:

248

At a fast food restaurant with a friend, I heard the woman behind the counter say to another worker, "Look at those two fags". "Excuse me", I said, "I'm not sure I heard that insult". We complained to the manager, but nothing happened. We heard the manager laughing with the woman about it. We weren't taken seriously. ....Later a straight friend told me he admired me for taking it to the manager.

Even proponents of standing up of one's rights agreed that to do so constantly was enery consuming. Unlike citizens for whom walking down the street was "just walking down the street", mounting an armamentarium of strategies and trying to judge their best chance for using them was wearying for informants, "which sometimes leads to my 'agoraphobia', which is why I just want to stay home", said a health care professional.

Flaunting: acting up and putting on. Acting up or putting on are similar to making a "scene" (Goffman 1963). They are acts that catch, distill, focus, and interpret events and imply a larger significance. Though there seems little room for spontaneous and creative action when harassed, nevertheless potential victims take aim, take advantage of crevices of opportunity, and turn tables on oppressors.

Thus, men reported taking advantage of namecalling, as pure categorization and abuse turned into apparent discovery or compliment. Standing on the street waiting for a light to change, some yelled, "Faggot!" at me. I yelled "Thanky you!" Another informant said, "I heard someone mutter 'Queer', and I said [in an interested and helpful interrogative tone], 'Yes?'" One brave jokester said: "Some guys yelled, 'Fag!' at me and I said, 'And proud of it!'" Or potential acting up could be wishfully hypothesized or planned: "I've always wanted to sit outside a straight bar and yell 'Straight!'" or more ambitious scenes could be mounted:

I was in the mall with my lover. We were holding hands and French kissing and people in Kokomo [Indiana] were not ready to see two guys kissing in Target. Pretty soon we had a crowd of twenty or thirty people following us down the mall chanting "Fags should be killed!" So [what did we do] to end it? We went to the jewellers and looked at wedding rings. The crowd gathered outside, but the lady in the jewellers was calm and cool, and she said to them, "Why don't you all go away? I think they're beautiful". And my friend, Davy, who was very effeminate, said [with a "limpwristed"

249

gesture], "Yes, go **away!**"

Finally, some men noted that acting up, though satisfactory, could only be carried on in relatively safe circustances, since it might provoke or outrage others. Also, some men mentioned that "acting up require[d] energy", and thus was taxing and "pall[ed]" with age.

Humour, shock, and surprise are all more minor realizations of acting up. One example is the man accused of being a sissy who obligingly answers in a lisp (and, while his harasser guffaws, beats a judicious retreat).

Strategizing: summary. Strategizing can so occupy an individual's time in public places that he misses activities or opportunities that he might otherwise take up. One man, for example, remarked that avoiding certain areas of town has "destroyed his social life", since this is where many of his friends lived. Another noted that keeping his "eyes to [him]self" occasionally caused him to trip over a curb he had not seen.

Discussion

Management stategies reported were avoidance, ignoring or denying, varied types of answering back, and engineering scenes or displays of acting. An added effect was **the ironicization of public places**. Ironicization occurs when there is a disjucture in definitions of reality between persons; sometimes the disjucture is resolved when an individual defends one definition against another (Pollner 1987, pp.70-7). Such a disjucture might occur when an individual notes that she or he cannot respind to colours as most others can and hence chooses to self label as colour blind; or when an individual believes she or he is engaged in routine work tasks of a trustworthy employee but notes others are talking about her or him often and furtively, and thus is labelled paranoid. With regard to events in public places, an individual might, were he asked, define himself as engaged in the mundane task of walking from one public place to another, with no special agenda or task in mind. To others, observing him, he might be regarded as soliciting by his mere presence; perceiving their self righteous catcalls, he might decide to label his own treatment as harassment.

One element of the individual's behaviour in response to disjuctures is sometimes to reevaluate his own behaviour and to argue a deeper meaning for events engineered by others. Thus, to some men interviewed, nonverbal harassment in public sometimes retrospectively assumed a symbolic importance and possessed an alienating potential. It might, for example, lead them to weigh being gay against other traits that might lead to harassment.

In general, devising management strategies for public places is especially difficult, since rapidly varied circumstances and situations of public places create seemingly endless sets of emergent norms: thus, it is hard for an individual to take action, since she or he must have an active role in defining and imposing a dfinition of the situation on others. Again, nonviolent harassment is typically the first and defining move of the encounter, to which the target must respond: this response must then be a counter definition that may fail. Thus, when a young store clerk in his twenties anwsers back, "Keep your hands to yourself", to a man who has been mocking him nonverbally and silently manhandling him, the offended as likely as the offender will be perceived as breaching by individuals who see it.

Thus, the measures that gay men sometimes take in constucting a "passing" personal appearance (or carefully deconstucting one to shock or gibe) reminds hetersexual men of the care that they routinely take, certainly out of awareness much of the time, **not** to be taken as gay. As well, it reminds all citizens of the care they take when in public not to be taken as members of categories whose competence or morality is in question or can easily be thrown into question, as can that of not just gays and lesbians, but of women, people with disabilities, the aged, et al. (Or be considered a crime target, but this is seperate or too inaccessible, as can women, who routinely have tenuous accesibility tensely maintained). Part of heterosexuals' practical energy must be devoted to mounting a presentation that is not or cannot be confused woth "gay", and also to keep out of areas that connote gayness. Also, in private and occupational areas, both gays and straights sometimes avoid gay companions whose copresence may later embarrass them when they must do a public presence together, perhaps to avoid these individuals altogether in job hires or as neighbours so that they will not have to consider the range of public troubles they have. Nongays will (understandably must, to avoid bashing) devote some presentational energy and endeavor to seeming heterosexual, ensuring that they cannot be taken as gay and thus threatening.

I will now suggest what the significance of my findings are in terms of

1.   their contribution to the situated self indiviuals present in public

2.   their relationship to the informal social control of public places

3.   their effect on the complementary situated self those who wish to be taken as heterosexual must demonstrate in public.

In general, the situated self of public places requires individuals to suppress apparent homosexuality, shunning the behavioral, gestual, and material tokens of homosexuality. Thus, even some informants who had experienced undeniable harassment sometimes reported that their actions were themselves the lure for harassment; as members of the larger culture, they were correct, for the citizens whose public behaviour does not express submission to general social definitions, whatever her or his private behaviour may involve, is open to social control in public places. In terms of treatment, public places can supply expressive gay indiviuals, both women and men, with a self regularly profaned by street remarks, by distinctive treatment in shops and restaurants, and by vulnerability to and fear of physical violence. The individual's experience in public places, then, can underline other negative experience. At the same time, they make it more unlikely that gay men can chieve the egalitarian courtesy and trust that is, within limits, normative for public places in middle class society. Thish varioan status in public places in general carries an unpleasant connotation for the individual's place in the society as a whole, suggesting that social control of individuals both exists and is diffusely available for any heterosexual, of any age, in public places. Indeed, it is exercised by the apparently heterosexual, andy by gays who are not identified as homosexual, whether they intend to or not, by mere presence.

These harassments signal that gay citizens, along with other social categories, experience a **situational disadvantage** in public places: a social disadvantage that may be, but is not necessarily, experienced in other spheres o flife. Though the individual may have some opportunities to modify the impact of this disadvantage, for the moment escaping to regional refuges like restaurants, bars, or bookstores associated with her or his own subculture, it will nevertheless characterize part of her or his public life. Ordinarily too, this situational disadvantage goes unremarked; is considered unpleasant but something the individual should not dwell on; is trivial and thus should not constitute the heart of the individual's feelings about her or himself. But in as much as the individual has a situated self appropriate to public places, as Erving Goffman has told us she or he does (1963, p.112), being at an habitual disadvantage will corrode the character of this self.

The creation of this "situated self" of public places can itself have a deep effect on the other selves we feel free to select, adopt, display, and own. The nature of both perception and experience is importantly related to possibilities for communication inpublic places in US culture generally. This situated self appropriate to public places is supported, in addition to other elements, by various sets of strategies of presentation and impression management such as the reactive strategies gay citizens report with regard to exploitations of presence: in the end, then, what has been used to manage intrusion becomes a part of the superstructure that supports it. Among other things, I have used this article to contemplate the type of situated self that exploitations of presence foster and how the activities of that self can be played out given the general character of public places. Recently, gay men experiencing differential treatment in public places have begun to identify it clearly as form of hate crime or harassment.

Another result of the social control of gay men in public places is that, as for other situationally disadvantaged groups, it necessarily destroys whatever intragroup solidarity might be possible and that it complicates intergroup appeals in the face of hostility or incivility, both because of ergent norms and because of the difficulties of framing an appeal without verbal skill and intuition: one individual does not come to another's aid in part because she or he believes it will be ineffective to do so; and, if the cases reported here are representative the individual is right. The experience of various types of negative control in public yields a situated self delimited in a neatly symbolic way by geography and site, as well as by circumstance and concern. Thus, social control suggests that gay men are physically safer at home and that a symbolic closet has been extended to the street.

A further effect of these activities is the portrait they paint of each sexual preference to the other. For gay men especially, engaging in token activities like handholding with a lover or displaying token clothing will result in negative sanctions alienating them from the majority of nonoffending heterosexuals with whom they come into contact in public places. Likewise, heterosexuals conscious of gay citizens' fears in public (and their story would constitute a separate article of concerns and tactics) will take pains to moderate their own behaviour, yet can appear over solicitous, patronizing, or pointedly tolerant when they do so, in effect, confirming the stereotypes all the same. Conspicuously and benevolently smiling to communicate that, though other straights might be bigoted and intolerant, they themselves are not.

Notes

1. See also, National Gay and Lesbian Task Force 1986 and US Congress House Committee of Criminal Justice 1986.

2. See also, Farley 1978; Gruber 1989; Gruber and Bjorn 1990; Littler-Bishop, et al. 1982; Rowe 1981; and WWUI 1978.

3. Fewer than 20 lesbians responded, and I judged them too few for a seperate study.

4. In this it differs from age delimited harassment that can occur to children, for example. In addition, women feel that many forms of harassment, such as street remarks (Gardner 1980) and pinching and groping (Gardner 1994), occur mainly to young or attractive women. Gay men know nonviolent harassment to be lifelong.

5. I have ignored on crucial element in documenting the public harassment of gay and bisexual men, and that is simply the indices harassers use in judging men gay. Men were voluble on this point, and it constitutes another article (or two) that elucidates membership categorization devices, in Indiana, apparently anything from walking a small fluffy dog, to wearing a pair of glasses and an "unconfident" manner can mark a man as gay.

6. Again, much needs to be said about indices that ype a man as gay. Even informants who did not belive that they (or others) were responsible for "stimulating" harassment, reported modifying their own dress, manner, or behaviou in hopes of diminishing harassment of all types.

Part 4
POSTSCRIPT

15 Of matters public and civil

Christopher G. A. Bryant

The editors asked me at very short notice to offer some concluding remarks at the International Conference on the the Public Sphere in January 1993, and, once bitten, but apparently not twice shy, they have kindly asked me to do the same for the resultant book. It was not easy then because of the range and diversity of the papers presented, and it is not much easier now, despite longer notice, because a great deal of that range and diversity has here found its way into print. If I am expected to rise above the debates and offer some judicious or portentious summation, I can only apologise for failing. Instead my comments are no more than personal responses to some of what was offered and some of what was not. They are organised around four themes: the public sphere, civil society and citizenship, location and dislocation, and new political agendas.

The public sphere

The editors tell us that from the outset they "have eschewed abstract analysis in favour of grounded accounts" (p. xvii). These are not the only alternatives. There is much to be said for theoretical discourse which is sensitive to the circumstances of its own generation and subsequent development. The "public sphere", for example, means something distinctive for all those acquainted with the work of Jürgen Habermas and

257

his antecedents, especially Hannah Arendt (1958), even if Habermas's original German does not demand translation as public *sphere*. There is thus nothing to be gained by extending its referents, especially when other terms like public sector, public interest, public domain and public place are readily available.

Habermas's concept of the public sphere *(Offentlichkeit)* dates from his 1962 *Habilitationsschrift* which was known in English as *The Structural Transformation of the Public Sphere* long before the publication of a translation in 1989. It refers to a space between the private realm of the family and of civil society (narrowly conceived in terms of commodity exchange and social labour) and the public authority of state and court, which developed from the late 17th century onwards in different ways and at different times in England, France and Germany. It was a space in which individual members of the bourgeoisie manifested their different interests and views in public and sought to reconcile them. New institutions from newspapers to reading societies and literary salons provided opportunities for critical-rational discussion and the formation of public opinion. Citizens were able to demand of the state that it only impose such constraints on their action as had found favour in public discussion. *"Public debate was supposed to transform* voluntas *into a* ratio *that in the public competition of private arguments came into being as the consensus about what was practically necessary in the interest of all"* (p. 83; original italics).

Habermas gives the bourgeois or liberal public sphere a precise historical location. From the 1870s onwards it changed in character; "with the further development of capitalism", in Thomas McCarthy's summary: "the public body expanded beyond the bourgeoisie to include groups that were systematically disadvantaged by the workings of the free market and sought state regulation and compensation" (McCarthy, 1989, p. xii). This led in the late 19th and 20th centuries to the interpenetration of state and society, and the demise of the liberal public sphere. The successor public sphere of the social welfare state bureaucracies has consistently presented obstacles to critical-rational discussion; these have included corporatist interest representation from which the public is excluded, and media management of consensus and promotion of consumer culture. Nevertheless a kernal of emancipatory potential has remained, as Habermas (1992) himself now acknowledges. We are left with the fundamental question, as framed by Craig Calhoun, "What are the social conditions ... for a rational-critical debate about the public issues conducted by private persons willing to let arguments and not statuses determine decisions" (Calhoun, 1992, p. 1).

Subsequent writers have treated the public sphere as a feature of *modern* societies. Nancy Fraser, for example, describes it as follows.

> It designates a theater in modern societies in which political participation is enacted through the medium of talk. It is the space in which citizens deliberate about their common affairs, and hence an institutionalized arena of discursive interaction. This arena is conceptually distinct from the state; it is a site for the production and circulation of discourses that can in principle be critical of the state. The public sphere in Habermas's sense is also conceptually distinct from the official economy [i.e. the economy beyond the household economy]; it is not an arena of market relations but rather of discursive relations, a theater for debating and deliberating rather than buying and selling. Thus, this concept of the public sphere permits us to keep in view the distinction among state apparatuses, economic markets, and democratic associations, distinctions that are essential to democratic theory (Fraser, 1992, pp. 110-11).

Peter Golding has reminded us that Habermas's account of the origins of the public sphere is contestable, and that he lauds what was largely a male, as well as a bourgeois, phenomenon. But the idea of a public sphere in which critical-rational discussion prevails has escaped the origins claimed for it and is now conceivable as both a political project and a critical standard. Fraser, for example, does not dismiss the notion of a public sphere because historically it has been male dominated, but rather seeks female inclusion.

Having acknowledged the criticisms of Habermas's pessimistic view of the contemporary public sphere, Golding concludes that there is much to be pessimistic about (in Britain at least).

> In particular the deepening threat to public service broadcasting, the severe partisanship of the national press, the public relations character of the centripetal state, and the widening inequalities of the communication marketplace, all support a view which diagnoses the public sphere as a domain inhabited by those comfortably ensconced within Galbraith's "culture of contentment" (1992), while excluding significant and populous sections of the community (p.39).

As Golding says, the very notion of a public sphere presupposes that citizens have the means to participate in it. That assumption is denied by the "substitution of consumption gradients linked to market forces for citizenship based on communication rights" (p. 39).

I would add two points to Golding's excellent analysis, one critical of it and the other in support. First, Golding does not include among the criticisms of Habermas's pessimistic view of the contemporary public sphere the point that more people are better educated than ever before. I recognise that the *Sun*'s circulation figures tempt one to think otherwise, but that this is so does give the supporters of democracy more to work on than the pessimists sometimes suppose. It is, as John Thompson (1993) contends, all too easy to exaggerate the passivity and manipulability of media consumers in a structurally transformed public sphere.

Second, Golding's analysis largely treats Britain as a self contained unit immune from the effects of media globalisation. Yet in one respect, at least, media globalisation gives further grounds for pessimism. In the run up to the renewal of the BBC's charter, the future of public service broadcasting is much debated. It is not easy, however, for ordinary citizens to have their say, and to "talk back" to the BBC - but nor is it impossible. Citizens can write to the BBC, to MPs, to newspapers; they can talk about it in homes and workplaces, with friends and neighbours, workmates and colleagues, and a little of this formation of opinion, no doubt filtered selectively and slantedly by journalists, pollsters and politicans, will reach those who make decisions about the BBC. It may be imperfect but it is not to be dismissed. Now imagine, instead, that an impoverished BBC could not maintain news services of the standard to which we have become accustomed (and that ITN was insufficiently funded to fill the gap); suppose, too, that CNN or some equivalent increasingly displaced the BBC - remembering that CNN is a commercial satellite news service run from Atlanta, responsible only to its owners, but aimed at a world audience. How could citizens talk back to CNN? Any difficulties they now have with the BBC would be as nothing by comparison. Of course this scenario may not happen, but given continued undermining of both the BBC and public service broadcasting by the New Right and by newspaper magnates, and given developments in satellite broadcasting technology, it could happen and the consequences for the public sphere and for democracy would be grave.

Richard Sparks raises the issue of the limits to the public sphere, to what citizens can and should deliberate without hindrance. It is easier to appreciate his point if one bears in mind the Concise Oxford Dictionary definition of "privacy", viz. "Being withdrawn from society or public

260

interest". Who can properly withdraw, what can properly be withdrawn, from society and public interest? (cf. Bryant 1978, p.59). There can be few more fundamental matters of public interest than what happens to those whom the state has deprived of their liberty, and yet, as Sparks comments, prisons have always been "sequestered, apart and in these senses 'private' places" (p. 79). Whilst in principle democratic politicians and public officials have had to answer for what goes on in them, in practice a great deal has escaped public scrutiny.

It is against this background that Sparks questions the legitimacy of the private prisons already established in the United States and Canada and now favoured by the British Home Office. The issue is this: "On what grounds can the internal order of the prison claim justified authority?" (p. 81). Advocates of private prisons point to the terms of the formal contracts concluded with the state; but contracts, like Weberian bureaucracies, do not necessarily anticipate all eventualities, and prisoners, in particular, have often resisted prison authorities. More generally "neither the government nor the private sector has been much minded to discuss those features of the distribution of power in prison which escape ... contractual definition" (p. 92-3). And those who do ask questions about private prisons have additionally to contend with management interest in the maintenance of commercial secrets and labour commitment, however prudential, to a private employer. In short, the internal order of the prison and its justification are hard enough to debate when prisons are the preserve of the state. When prisons are the profit opportunity of private firms they could elude the public sphere altogether.

Golding and Sparks say important things about the media and prisons in connection with a Habermasian notion of the public sphere. I would also like to alert readers to a fine paper given at the conference by Nicholas Stevenson (1993) which critically reassessed the Habermasian public sphere and confirmed that there remains much about communication, culture and citizenship in the contemporary world that can profitably be discussed in relation to it.

Civil society and citizenship

Though Habermas did not intend it, the public sphere has become a constituent of the sociological version of civil society as Alvin Gouldner (1980) was perhaps the first to recognise. By the sociological version of civil society, I mean all the ways in which citizens relate and associate outside the household without recourse to the market and independently of the state.[1] Alexis de Tocqueville's art of association is crucial to civil society, as is civility. Civility has to do with a common standard within which a multiplicity of ways of living, working and associating are tolerated. It demands that in all life outside the home we afford each other certain decencies and comforts as fellow citizens whatever else divides us. It cannot be stressed too strongly that it is a cool concept. It does not require us to like those whom we treat civilly, and as such it contrasts strongly with the warmth of communal, religious and national enthusiasms. On the other hand, it is about contact - not the situation in American cities, as described to the conference by Richard Sennett, in which the juxtaposition of differences is accompanied not by contact and exchange but indifference, hostility or even fear.

The relationship between civil society and nation differs between civic and ethnic nations as I have tried to show more fully elsewhere (Bryant, forthcoming). All nations imagine their past, connect it to their present and lay claim to a homeland. Civic nations may attribute a leading role in their formation to one or more particular ethnies but they also extend citizenship to all who permanently and lawfully reside within their territory and who join in the national imagining or at least refrain from contesting it. By definition they are pluralist and/or assimilationist. Ethnic nations, by contrast, relate citizenship and full participation in society to ethnicity and descent. They can and do develop civil societies but these are exclusive; residents of other ethnic origins, even of longstanding, are denied citizenship. There is a suspicion of difference and a rejection of pluralism. As a society of citizens, civil society can thus be inclusive and tolerant of pluralism (as in the Netherlands) or inclusive and assimilationist (as in France), or it can be exclusive and suspicious of pluralism (as in Germany) (cf. Brubaker 1992).

Civil society, then, is about the accommodation of difference; what varies are who count as citizens, the differences among them to be accommodated and the manner and degree to which accommodation is achieved. It is thus appropriate that Carol Brooks Gardner should analyse gaybaiting as instances of "lapsed civility" (p.236). Sennett also provided the conference with food for thought with his comments on the place of ritual in the negotiation of differences within the city and the regeneration of the city as a *theatrum mundi* (cf. Sennett 1977).

There are many convergences between what I have called the sociological version of civil society and Maurice Roche's thinking about citizenship. Roche's rational humanism requires that citizens wherever possible realise their potential as autonomous beings. That realisation involves state action from guaranteeing the rule of law to providing welfare in some circumstances. But his discussion of citizenship shifts the emphasis from rights to obligations, from making claims on the state to taking responsibility for oneself. This would seem consistent with one of the great lessons of the Thatcherite and Reaganite 1980s: no one can be indifferent to state dependency because those who are dependent on the state cannot depend on it. Entitlements to benefit are redefined more narrowly, the real value of benefits is reduced; some services are withdrawn, others are privatised and doubtfully regulated. Is it any wonder, then, that on the left as well as on the right there are misgivings about relying on the state, and an interest in reconstituting the discourse and practice of citizenship?

Citizens who take responsibility for themselves do not necessarily do so individually. As Roche notes, both the women's movement and the ecology movement operate significantly within civil society irrespective of any demands they may also make on the state and any impacts they may have on party politics. They aim to change the way we live not primarily by law but by changing our values, our norms and our selves. They also, of course, challenge the distinction between the private household and civil society (or, in Habermasian terms, the intimate sphere and the public sphere) insofar as their objects of concern - patriarchy, divisions of labour and responsibility, lifestyles and consumption, etc. - concern both. It is thus not surprising that Peter Simmons' excellent account of the green consumer should emphasise the blurring of the boundaries between public and private, or that Jeff Hearn's astute reflections on men and gender should repeatedly question the public/private distinction.

Location and dislocation

One feature of post-modernity is dedifferentiation, the dissolution of old principles of ordering and the division of labour in society that went with them. In the old order, or at least in its simplified representation, everything had its place, and everyone knew where they were. Now, by equally simplified contrast, there are no longer any sure principles of ordering for things, activities or people. From the disorganised capitalism described by Claus Offe (1985) and Scott Lash and John Urry (1987), to the public/private distinction and the gender roles at home and work just mentioned, to single items like the January 1994 decision of Marks and Spencer's to sell life insurance in their shops, nothing seems to fit a clear pattern any more.

Like Anthony Giddens (1990) I think this contrast is overdone, but I accept that it does highlight one kind of dislocation. Another has to do with geographical place. Visitors to Europort might suppose that all those oil tanks are artefacts of the oft cited Rotterdam spot market in oil. They are not. The market is now an electronic one, a network of computer links; most spot oil is traded on the high seas and the tankers are rerouted accordingly. Neither the dealing, nor the transfer of oil, takes place in Rotterdam. The London Stock Exchange, too, is an electronic market and no longer has a trading floor. And who, ten years ago, had heard of virtual reality?

Dislocation can be disorienting and a factor in the anomie of which Roche writes, but there would seem two reasons why this disorientation can easily be exaggerated. First, the commoner experience for most people is still that of place, of locale (Giddens, 1984), and of located activity. In other words for most people there may well still be a connection between their sense of place and their feeling of security. Karen Evans, Penny Fraser and Ian Taylor explore one small aspect of this in their account of the lived experience of places in Manchester and Sheffield and what they call well-being. Their concerns are often practical: how do people of different kinds experience streets, shopping centres, rail and bus stations and other public places at different times? Does the experience impinge on their consciousness. Is it agreeable? Does it generate anxiety? Councillors, planners, property developers, retailers, police, etc., would dearly like to know. The phenomenology of place which they are opening up, however, extends beyond matters of immediate practical significance to issues of ontological security and existential anxiety. Because public places are indeed public they lend themselves to shared experience. Evans, Fraser and Taylor's integration of focus groups in their research methodology has facilitated identification of that shared experience. How important to individual well-being is it that experience of place be shared, that our own experience be confirmed by others? There is scope here for a lot more research, including contributions to the sociology of the street for which Joel Richman has appealed so vividly.

My second reason for supposing that most people can cope with a good deal of geographical dislocation is that it often amounts to further instances of what Giddens calls "disembedding" - "the 'lifting out' of social relations from local contexts of interaction and their restructuring across indefinite spans of time-space" (Giddens 1990, p.21) - and this is an integral feature of the all modernity, and thus something within the experience of all of us, even if its incidence is increasing in late modernity. Disembedding mechanisms include "symbolic tokens", like money, and experts systems, like medecine. For both to work, there has to be trust, and for our ontological security to survive, that trust must not be misplaced too often. The issues this raises are too many and too ramifying for even a brief mention here except to say that it is very much in the public interest that trust be not misplaced too often.[2]

New political agendas

The neo-liberal ascendancy in Britain and America in the 1980s has come to an end. In America this was signalled by the election of President Clinton in November 1992. If Reaganism had delivered all it promised, Clinton would not have been elected. In Britain it was signalled by "Black Wednesday", the day in September 1992 when sterling was forced out of the European exchange rate mechanism by the money markets. If Thatcherism had positively transformed the British economy in the way its partisans claimed, it would never have happened. The question is: what could succeed neo-liberalism? In America the answer will partly be given by the Clinton administration, and I am unqualified to judge how it might turn out. In Britain the government of John Major, discredited within six months of its election with a parliamentary majority large enough to ensure that it will not fall, lurches on grotesquely to the ridicule of a mainly Conservative press which, as Golding has reminded us, backed it so strongly at the election. What are the alternatives, or, more accurately, what are the alternative programmes which would enable a different government to give a more convincing impression that it knew what it was doing?

Frances Fox Piven gave the conference an eloquent defence of the achievements of the public sector, but she also acknowledged the irreversible globalisation of capitalism. Indeed she believed we are suffering the transition to a new international economic order, and that in time new institutions, structures of governance, forms of mobilisation and popular leverage will emerge. But what structures, and how they will emerge, she was not able to say. In the interim she urged us to save and revivify as much of our public sector and welfare state inheritance as possible. The revision of Fox Piven's presentation published here omits much of the larger picture and settles for a spirited defence of the welfare state, including the virtues of *centralised* welfare provision. Either way, the mixture of fierce pride in past achievements and uncertainty about the future will be familiar to many supporters of the British Labour Party, but it is unlikely to win converts because it does not address the economy and society of the short and medium term future. That citizens feel insecure in

265

their jobs (if they have them) or about their old age, or that they fear for their children's prospects, does not necessarily mean that they also believe that what Jessop *et al.* (1988) called the Keynesian welfare state is recoverable.

Elliott Currie comes nearer to articulation of an alternative programme to neo-liberalism. Currie begins by demanding that we confront the accumulating evidence for jobless, or even job reducing, economic growth as the likely future course of development in advanced economies. This is a disturbing prospect because the British Government and Opposition, having swallowed what few ecological doubts they ever had, are not alone in assuming that if recession could give way to steady growth significant reductions in unemployment would surely follow. It is questionable, however, whether enough new small businesses can survive, and enough old small businesses grow, to compensate for the unending shake out of labour by large private sector firms in both the industrial and service sectors. As Currie puts it with provocative directness, "markets for most goods and services in the advanced societies are simply not growing nearly fast enough to match the growth in worldwide capacity to produce them" (p. 70). Chronic overcapacity threatens. In America even in the so-called knowledge economy jobs are being shed.

So how should we respond to this dismal prospect? Currie offers a number of responses, three of which I want to comment on. The first, work sharing, has found little favour with those in work. It has also seemed like an admission of defeat to all the major British parties and continues to be only of marginal interest to them. In Germany and France, however, governments, firms and unions are beginning to wonder whether a four day working week, for example, might not be an essential element in an industrial policy for the late 1990s and I think they are right to do so (Cohen 1993). The government could use the public sector to advance work sharing, but there are also public ways of inducing the private sector to do so. Introduction of a large premium on employers' National Insurance rates in Britain, or their equivalents elsewhere, for employees who work five days a week, as compared with those who work up to four, would be one.

The second, expansion of the public and non-profit sectors of the economy, is a very complex proposition. In the liberal context of the European Single Market and the GATT Uruguay Round, the production of all internationally traded goods and services has to be competitive and that repeatedly means capital intensive. What we need to do, I suggest, is to identify where labour intensive production does not put us at a competitive disadavantage, and preferably, too, does not lead to an inferior

266

product, and then work out how it can be paid for. There is, as Currie says, no shortage of work that needs doing in areas like education, health and care of the elderly and it is often done better with more labour rather than less. Much of this work is in the public sector but the principle I am promoting could apply to providers in a properly regulated private sector.

A third point Currie makes is that the intensification of work for many of those who remain in jobs denies them the time, the opportunities, and the physical and mental health necessary to enjoy what their earnings can buy, and all this whilst others are denied paid work at all. Too many people have too much or too little work, and the process of material enrichment too often impoverishes spiritually those who endure it. Currie celebrates the example of William Morris and there is much to be said for greater valuation of arts and crafts. But it must also be possible to construct an appeal to self interested individuals which persuades them that their lives often turn out to be less gratifying than they had anticipated. To secure electoral support for measures to promote work sharing will require construction of a coalition far broader than those for whom Morris strikes a chord.

In the space remaining to me, I would like to mention one other approach to redefinition of the political agenda - the reassertion of an older conservatism in a succession of publications by John Gray. These include a book published by the Institute of Economic Affairs (IEA), the think-tank more usually associated with the New Right, and frequent articles for *The Guardian* (Gray 1992,1993). In one of the latter, Gray recently complained that:

> There has always been, especially in America, a school of market fundamentalism, or capitalist utopianism, which sees communities and distinctive cultures as barbarous relics not worth preserving when they come into conflict with the imperatives of the market. The surprising and ironical development in the eighties was the conquest of British conservatism by this libertarian view, with its explicit denial, or repudiation, of the human need for rootedness in a common environment (Gray 1994a).

Gray seeks, among other things, to recover and regenerate notions of national self-determination (in the face of economic globalisation and the European Union), the integrity of national and other cultures, public service, moral community, social market, human welfare, and common responsibility for the environment - to which Green (1993) in another IEA book has added civil society. Gray is a conservative for whom Mrs

Thatcher's claim that there is no such thing as society is as absurd as it is for any social scientist. His formulations are often contestable - I reject, for example, his idea of nation - but they do constitute a long overdue conservative determination to go beyond the New Right, and they do offer enough points of contact with the concerns of the left to make a concerted attack on neo-liberalism possible. Indeed Gray himself now looks to the Labour Party both to espouse "the decent conservative values that the Tories have turned their backs on" (1994b) and to find radical and forward looking ways of dismantling the neo-liberal inheritance of the quango-state and the unfettered market.[3]

Notes

1. For different versions of civil society, see Bryant (1992 & 1993) and Kumar (1993). I value (the sociological version of) civil society, as do Jean Cohen and Andrew Arato (1992) whose reconstruction incorporates the public sphere. Krishan Kumar, Adam Seligman (1992) and Keith Tester (1992) (like Francis Fox Piven) do not.

2. One way into the tangle of issues is through Ulrich Beck (1986) and Anthony Giddens (1990 & 1991) on trust, risk and identity. Another is via Zygmunt Bauman (1992) on postmodernity.

3. I have paid particular attention to Gray because of his association with the Institute of Economic Affairs, a think-tank of the New Right in the 1980s. He is, however, but one source for a new political sociology which would emphasise the third term in the triumvirate of state, market and something else. Different writers would variously make that something else civil society, community, associations and networks. They include Amitai Etzioni (1988 and 1993), Alan Wolfe (1989), Paul Hirst (1994) and Ian Gough (1994). Whatever their differences, all these writers, in effect, recognise the absurdity of expecting the state to enforce the non-contractual elements in contract, to use a Durkheimian formulation, which is precisely what neo-liberals, in their haplessness, end up doing.

Bibliography

Abercrombie, N. (1992), "The Privilege of the Producer" in Keat, R. and Abercrombie, N. (eds.), *Enterprise Culture*, Routledge, London.

Adams, R. (1992), *Prison Riots in Britain and the USA*, Macmillan, London.

Alderson, J. (1979), *Policing Freedom*, McDonald and Evans, Plymouth.

Anderson, C.L. (1982), "Males as Sexual Assault Victims" *Journal of Homosexuality*, Vol. 7. pp. 145-62.

Anderson, S. (1986), *On Streets*, MIT Press, Cambridge, Mass.

Andrews, G. (ed.), (1991), *Citizenship*, Lawrence and Wishart, London.

Arendt, H. (1958), *The Human Condition*, Chicago University Press.

Aristotle, (1962), *The Politics*, Penguin, Harmondsworth, trans. Sinclair, T.A. Rev. trans. Saunders, T.J. 1981.

Aron, C.S. (1987), *Ladies and Gentlemen of the Civil Service: Middle Class Workers in Victorian America*, Oxford University Press, New York and Oxford.

Ashworth, A. (1993) "Sentencing By Numbers", *Criminal Justice Matters*, No. 14 (Winter 1993-4), pp. 6-7.

Atkins, P. (1987), *Guide Across Manchester*, Swinton: North West Civic Trust (first published 1976; Revised edition by Philip Atkins and Paul Daniels).

Attfield, R. (1983), *The Ethics of Environmental Concern*, Blackwell, Oxford.

Aveni, A. (1990), *Empires of Time: Calendars, Clocks and Culture*, I.B.

269

Tauris and C/o Ltd, London.

Backhouse, C. and Cohen. L. (1979), *Secret Oppression: Sexual Harassment,* Macmillan, Toronto.

Bailey, C. (1984), *Beyond the Present and the Particular: A Theory of Liberal Education,* Routledge and Kegan Paul, London.

Baldwin J. and Bottoms A.E. (1976), *The Urban Criminal,* Tavistock, London.

Ball, S.J. (1990), *Politics and Policy Making in Education,* Routledge, London.

Balls, E. (1993), "Danger: Men Not at Work", in Balls, E. and Gregg, P. (ed.), *Work and Welfare: Tackling the Jobs Deficit,* The Commission on Social Justice, Institute for Public Policy Research, London.

Barker, R. (1986), *Ecological Psychology,* Stanford University Press.

Bauman, Z. (1992), "Moral Space", *Lecture to Department of Social Anthropology,* University of Manchester, 5 December.

Bauman, Z. (1992), *Intimations of Postmodernity,* Routledge, London

Baumgartner, M.P. (1988), *The Moral Order of a Suburb,* Oxford University Press.

Beatt, A. (1992), "Market Forces", *Police Review,* 4th September.

Beck, U. (German 1986), *Risk Society: Towards a New Modernity,* Sage, London 1992.

Bedarida, F. (1980), "Street in the Structure and Life of the City: Reflections on Nineteenth Century London and Paris", *Journal of Urban History,* Vol. 6, pp. 17-28.

Bell, D. (1993), *Communitarianism and its Critics,* Clarendon Press, Oxford.

Benson, D.J. and Thomson, G.E. (1982), "Sexual Harassment On A University Campus: The Confluence of Authority Relations, Sexual Interest and Gender Stratification", *Social Problems,* Vol. 29, pp. 236-51.

Billig, M. et. al. (1993), "In the Hands of the Spin Doctors: Television, Politics and the 1992 General Election", in Miller, N. and Allen, R. (eds.), *It's Live But is it Real?,* John Libbey, pp. 111-121.

Bittner, E. (1980), *The Function of the Police in Modern Society,* Oelgeschlager, Gunn & Hain, Cambridge, Mass.

Borchorst, A. and Siim, B. (1987), "Women and the Advanced Welfare State: A New Kind of Patriarchal Power?' in Sassoon, A.S. (ed.) *Women and the State: The Shifting Boundaries of Public and Private,* Hutchinson, London, pp. 128-57.

Bourdieu, P. (1977), *Outline of a Theory of Practice,* Cambridge University Press.

Bourdieu, P. (1984), *Distinction: A Social Critique of the Judgement of Taste*, Routledge & and Kegan Paul, London.

Bowden, T. (1978), *Beyond the Limits of the Law*, Penguin, Harmondsworth.

Box, S. and Hale, C. (1985), "Unemployment, Imprisonment and Prison Overcrowding", *Contemporary Crises*, 9, pp. 208-29.

Brand New Product Development. (1988), *The Green Consumer?*, Brand New Product Development Ltd, London.

Brill, M. (1989), "Transformation, Nostalgia and Illusion in Public Life and Public Space", in Altman, I. and Zube, E.H. (eds.), *Public Places and Spaces*, Plenum Press, New York.

Broadcasting Standards Council, (1992), *The Future of Children's Television in Britain*, HMSO, London.

Broadfoot, P. (1985), "Changing Patterns of Educational Accountability in England and France", *Comparative Education*, Vol. 21, pp. 273-86.

Brody, D. (1992), "The Breakdown of Labour's Social Contract", *Dissent*, Winter, Vol. 39, pp. 32-41.

Brown, C. (1965), *Manchild in the Promised Lane*, Signet, New York.

Brown, C. (1981), "Mothers, Fathers and Children: From Private to Public Patriarchy", in Sargent, L. (ed.), *Women and Revolution: The Unhappy Marriage of Marxism and Feminism*, Pluto, London, pp. 239-67.

Brubaker, R. (1992), *Citizenship and Nationhood in France and Germany*, Blackwell, London.

Brundtland, G. et al. (1987), *Our Common Future (The Brundtland Report)*, Oxford University Press.

Bryant, C.G.A. (1978), "Privacy, Privatisation and Self-Determination", in Young, J.B. (ed) *Privacy*, Wiley, Chichester, pp. 59-83.

Bryant, C.A.G. (1992), "Civil Society and Pluralism: A Conceptual Analysis", *Sisyphus: Social Studies*, Vol. 1 (VIII), pp. 103-19.

Bryant, C.A.G. (1993), "Social Self-Organisation, Civility and Sociology: A Comment on Kumar's "Civil Society"", *British Journal of Sociology*, Vol. 44, pp. 397-401.

Bryant, C.A.G. (forthcoming) "Civic Nation, Civil Society, Civil Religion", in Hall, J.A. (ed.), *Civil Society: Theory, History and Comparison*, Polity Press, Cambridge.

Buber, M. (ed. S.N. Eisenstadt), (1992) *On Intersubjectivity and Cultural Creativity*, University of Chicago.

Butler, S. and Kondratas, A.(1987), *Out of the Poverty Trap: A Conservative Strategy for Welfare Reform*, Free Press, London.

Cairncross, F. (1991), *Costing the Earth*, Economist Books/Business

Books, London.

Calhoun, C. (1992a) "Introduction: Habermas and the Public Sphere" to Calhoun (1992b), pp. 1-48

Calhoun, C. (ed.), (1992b), *Habermas and the Public Sphere*, MIT Press, Cambridge, Mass.

Carlen, P. (1983), *Women's Imprisonment*, Routledge, London.

Carrigan, T. Connell, B. and Lee, J. (1985), "Toward A New Sociology of Masculinity", *Theory and Society*, Vol. 14, pp. 551-604.

Cavadino, M. and Dignan, J. (1992), *The Penal System: An Introduction*, Sage, London.

Centre for Social Welfare Policy and Law.(1994), *Jobless, Penniless, Often Homeless: State General Assistance Cuts Leave "Employables" Struggling for Survival*, Centre for Social Welfare Policy and Law, New York City.

Chadwick, G.F. (1973), "The Face of the Victorian City" in Dyos, H.J. and Wolff, M. (eds.), *The Victorian City: Images and Realities*, Routledge & Kegan Paul, London.

Christie, N. (1993), *Crime Control as Industry*, Routledge, London.

Clarke, A. (1987), *The Rise and Fall of the Socialist Republic: A History of the South Yorkshire County Council*, Sheaf Publishing, Sheffield.

Cohen, A. (1982),"Drama and Politics in the Development of a London Carvival", in Frankenberg, R. (ed.), *Custom and Conflict in British Society*, Manchester University Press.

Cohen, N. (ed.), (1970), *The Los Angeles Riot. A Socio-Psychological Study,* Praeger, New York.

Cohen, R. (1993), "Europe Weighs Four-Day Week to Tackle Jobs Crisis", *The Guardian*, 24 November, p. 12.

Cohen, S. (1985), *Visions of Social Control*, Polity Press, Cambridge.

Comedia. (1991), *Out of Hours: A Summary Report*, Comedia/Gulbenkian, London.

Committee of Public Accounts. (1990), *Publicity Services for Government Departments*, HMSO, London.

Connell, R.W. (1990), "Gender, The State and Sexual Politics: Theory and Appraisal", *Theory and Society*, Vol. 19, pp. 507-44.

Conservative Research Department. (1985), "Education", *Politics Today*, No. 14.

Conway, P. (1993), "The Informal Justice System in Northern Ireland", A paper presented to the *British Criminology Conference*, University of Cardiff, 29-31 July.

Cooke, P. (ed.), (1989), *Localities: The Changing Face of Urban Britain*, Unwin Hyman, London.

Corrado, M. (1989), *The Greening Consumer in Britain*, WAPOR 1989 Conference, Stockholm, September 1989.

Corrado, M. and Ross, M. (1990), *Green issues in Britain and the Value of Green Research Data*, ESOMAR Congress, Monte Carlo, September 1990.

Cressey, P. (1932), "The Role of Motion Pictures in an Institutional Area", *Journal of Educational Sociology*, Vol. 6, pp. 238-44.

Crewe, I. (1987), "Tories Prosper From A Paradox", *The Guardian*, 16 June.

Crewe, I. (1992), "Why Did Labour Lose (Yet Again)?", *Politics Review*, Vol. 2, No. 1.

Cunningham, W.C. and Taylor, T. (1985), *Private Security and Police in America*, Chancellor Press, Portland, Oregon.

Curran, C. (1979), *A Seamless Robe: Broadcasting Philosophy and Practice*, Collins, London.

Curran, J. (1988) "Rethinking the Media as a Public Sphere", in Downes, D. (ed.), *Contrasts in Tolerance*, Macmillan, London.

Curran, J. (1990), "The New Revisionism in Mass Communication: A Reappraisal", *European Journal of Communication*, Vol.5, pp. 135 -164.

Curran, J. (1991), "Rethinking the Media as a Public Sphere", in Dahlgren, P. and Sparks, C. (eds.), *Communication and Citizenship*, Routledge, London.

Curtice, J. (1992), "On the Record", *The Guardian*, 13 April.

Cutright, P. (1965), "Political Structure, Economic Development and National Social Security Programmes", *American Journal of Sociology* Vol. 70.

Cutright, P. (1967), "Income Distribution: A Cross National Analysis", *Social Forces*, Vol. 46.

Cutright, P. (1974), "Components of Change in the Number of Female Family Heads Aged 15-44", *Journal of Marriage and the Family*, Vol. 36, pp. 714-21.

Cutright, P. and Madras, P.(1974), "AFDC and the Marital and Family Status of Ever Married Women Aged 15-44: United States, 1950-70", *Sociology and Social Research*, No. 60.

Dahlgren, P. and Sparks, C. (eds.), (1991), *Communication and Citizenship*, Routledge, London.

Dahlgren, P. (1991), "Introduction", in Dahlgren, P. and Sparks, C. (eds.), *Communication and Citizenship*, Routledge, London.

Dahrendorf, R. (1988), *The Modern Social Conflict*, Weidenfeld and Nicolson, London.

Davies, S. (1989), "Streets ahead", *Police Review*, 10 November.

de Certeau, M. (1984), *The Practice of Everyday Life*, the University of California Press, Berkeley.

Delphy, C. (1977), *The Main Enemy: A Materialist Analysis of Women's Oppression*, WRRC, London.

Delphy, C. (1984), *Close to Home: A Materialist Analysis of Women's Oppression*, Hutchinson, London.

Department of the Environment. (1992), *The UK Environment*, HMSO, London.

Dietz, M. (1992), "Context is All: Feminism and Theories of Citizenship", in Mouffe, C. (ed.), *Dimensions of Radical Democracy*, Verso, London.

Donald, J. and Grealy, J. (1983), "The Unpleasant Fact of Inequality: Standards, Literacy and Culture", in Wolpe, A.M. and Donald, J. (eds.), *Is There Anyone Here From Education?*, Pluto Press.

Donald, J. (1992), "Metropolis: The City as Text", in Bocock, R. and Thompson, K. (eds.), *Social and Cultural Forms of Modernity*, The Open University Press, Buckingham.

Donzelot, J. (1979), *The Policing of Families*, Hutchinson, London.

Downes, D. (1988), *Contrasts in Tolerance*, Macmillan, London.

Doyal, L. and Gough, I. (1984), "A Theory of Human Need", *Critical Social Policy*, Vol. 4.

Doyal, L. and Gough, I. (1991), *A Theory of Human Need*, Macmillan, Basingstoke.

Durkheim, E. (1964), *The Division of Labour*, (original 1893), Free Press, New York.

Durkheim, E. (1970), *Suicide: A Study in Sociology* (original 1897), Routledge, London.

Durning, A. (1992), *How Much is Enough? The Consumer Society and the Future of the Earth*, Earthscan, London.

Dworkin, A. 1983. *Right Wing Women: The Politics of Domesticated Females*, Women's Press, London.

Economic Report of the President. (1994), Government Printing Office, Washington, US.

Edgell, S. and Duke, V. (1981), *The Social and Political Effect of the Public Expenditure Cuts*, SSRC Report HR7415.

Edgell, S. and Duke, V. (1985), *Changes in the Social and Political Effects of the Public Expenditure Cuts*, ESRC Report G0023107

Edgell, S. and Duke, V. (1991), *A Measure of Thatcherism*, Harper Collins, London.

EEC (1992), "Council Regulation (EEC) No 880/92 of 23 March 1992 on a Community Eco-label Award Scheme", *Official Journal of the European Communities*, No. L 99, 11 April 92, pp. 1-6.

Eisenstein, Z. (1981), *The Radical Future of Liberal Feminism*, Longman, New York.

Eisenstein, Z. (1983), "The State, the Patriarchal Family, and Working Mothers", in Diamond, I. (ed), *Families, Politics, and Public Policy*, Longman Green, New York.

Ekins, P. and Max-Neef, M. (eds.), (1992), *Real-Life Economics: Understanding Wealth Creation*, Routledge, London.

Elkington, J. and Hailes, J. (1989a), *The Green Consumer Guide: From Shampoo to Champagne, High Street Shopping for a Better Environment*, Victor Gollancz, London.

Elkington, J. and Hailes, J. (1989b), *The Green Consumer's Supermarket Shopping Guide*, Victor Gollancz, London.

Elliott, P. (1982), "Intellectuals, the Information Society, and the Disappearance of the Public Sphere", *Media, Culture and Society*, Vol. 4, pp. 243-53.

Ellwood, D.T. and Bane, M.J. (1986), "The Impact of AFDC on Family Structure and Living Arrangements", *Research in Labour Economics*, No. 7.

Elshtain, J.B. (1981), *Public Man, Private Woman*, Martin Robertson, Oxford.

Elshtain, J.B. (1993), *Public Man, Private Woman*, 2nd ed. Princeton University Press.

Engels, F. (1969), *Condition of the English Working Class*, Panther Books, London. (First published in 1844).

Esping-Anderson, G. (1985), *Politics Against Markets*, Princeton University Press.

Esping-Anderson, G. (1990), *The Three Worlds of Welfare Capitalism*, Princeton University Press, Princeton; Polity Press, Cambridge.

Etzioni, Amitai (1988) *The Moral Dimension: Towards a New Economics*, Free Press, New York.

Etzioni, A. (1993), *The Spirit of Community*, Free Press, New York.

EUROBAROMETER (1992), *Europeans and the Environment in 1992: Survey Conducted in the Context of the EUROBAROMETER 37.0*, Commission of the European Communities, Brussels.

Evans, G.W. Smith, C. and Pezdek, K. (1982), "Cognitive Maps and Urban Forms", *Journal of American Planning Association*, Vol. 48, pp. 232-44.

Ewald, F. (1992), "L'expertise, une illusion nécessaire", in Theys, J. and Kalaora, B. (eds.), *La Terre outragée: Les experts sont formels!*,

Editions Autrement, Paris.

Faris, R.E.L. (1970), *Chicago Sociology 1920-32*, University of Chicago Press.

Farley, L.(1978), *Sexual Shakedown: The Sexual Harassment of Women on the Job*, McGraw Hill, New York.

Feagin, J.(1991), "The Continuing Significance Of Race: Anti-black Discrimination in Public Places", *American Sociological Review*, Vol 56, pp.101-16.

Ferguson, A. (1989), *Blood At The Root*, Pandora, London.

Ferguson, A. and Folbre, N. (1981) "The Unhappy Marriage of Patriarchy and Capitalism" in Sargent, L. (ed.), *Women and Revolution*, South End Press, Boston, pp. 313-18.

Finch, J. (1989), *Family Obligations and Social Change*, Polity Press, Cambridge.

Fine, B. and Millar, R. (1985), *Policing the Miner's Strike*, Lawrence and Wishart Ltd, London.

Firestone, S. (1970), *The Dialectic of Sex*, Jonathan Cape, London.

Fisher, M. and Owen, U. (eds.),(1991), *Whose City?*, Penguin, London.

Fiske, J. (1987), *Television Culture*, Methuen, London.

Flavel, W.R.H. (1973), "Research Into Security Organizations", paper presented to the *Second Bristol Seminar on the Sociology of the Police*, (unpublished).

Flax, J. (1990), *Thinking Fragments: Psychoanalysis, Feminism, and Post Modernism in the Contemporary West*, University of California Press, Berkeley.

Fleischaker, T.(1991), "IUPUI Seeks Gays/Lesbians For Study On Subtle Slurs", *The Word*, (Indianapolis), July, p.5.

Foley, P. and Lawless, P. (1992), *The Sheffield Central Area Study: 2010 a Vision of Quality*, Sheffield Chamber of Commerce, Sheffield City Council, Sheffield Development Corporation, Sheffield Hallam University, University of Sheffield.

Ford, D.A.(1990), "Investigating Serial Murder: The Case of Indiana's 'Gay Murders'", in Egger,S. (ed.), *Serial Murder: An Elusive Phenomenon*, Praeger, New York, pp. 113-33.

Foucault, M. (1981), *The History of Sexuality. Volume One: An Introduction*, Penguin, Harmondsworth.

Fowler, L. (1985). "Women and Work: Sexual Harassment, Patriarchy and the Labour Process", unpub. M.Sc. Dissertation, University of Bradford.

Fraser, N. (1987), "Women, Welfare, and the Politics of Need Interpretation" *Thesis Eleven*, p. 17.

Fraser, N. (1989), *Unruly Practices: Power, Discourse and Gender in Contemporary Social Theory*, Polity Press, Cambridge.

Fraser, N. (1990), "Rethinking the Public Sphere", *Social Text*, Vol. 25/26, pp. 56-80.

Fraser, N. (1992) "Rethinking the Public Sphere: A Contribution to the Critique of Actually Existing Democracy", in Calhoun, C. (ed), (1992b), pp. 109-42.

Freud, S. (1961), *Beyond the Pleasure Principle*, W. W. Norton, New York.

Fricke, A. (1981), *Reflections of a Rock Lobster: A Story about Growing Up Gay*, Alyson, Boston.

Fulton, R. (1989), "Private Sector Involvement in the Remand System" in Farrell, M. (ed.), *Punishment for Profit?*, ISTD, London.

Galbraith, J.K. (1992), *The Culture of Contentment*, Houghton Mifflin, Boston.

Gamble, A. (1988), *The Free Economy and the Strong State*, Macmillan London.

Gardiner, E. (1989), "Prisons: An Alternative Approach", in Farrell, M. (ed), *Punishment for Profit?*, ISTD, London.

Gardner, C.B. (1980), "Passing By", *Sociological Inquiry*, Vol 50, pp. 328-56.

Gardner, C. and Sheppard, J. (1989), *Consuming Passion: the Rise of Retail Culture*, Unwin Hyman, London.

Garland, D (1990), *Punishment and Modern Society*, Oxford University Press.

Garnham, N. (1986), "The Media and the Public Sphere" in Golding, P. et. al. (eds.), *Communicating Politics: Mass Communications and the Political Process*, Leicester University Press.

Garreau, J. (1991), *Edge City: Life on the New Frontier*, Doubleday, New York.

Geertz, C. (1983), *Local Knowledge: Essays in Interpretative Anthropology*, Basic Books, New York.

Giddens, A. (1984), *The Constitution of Society*, Polity Press, Cambridge.

Giddens, A. (1990), *The Consequences of Modernity*, Polity Press, Cambridge.

Giddens, A. (1991) *Modernity and Self-Identity: Self and Society in the Late Modern Age*, Polity Press, Cambridge.

Gill, O. (1977), *Luke Street, Housing Policy: Conflict and the Creation of the Delinquent Area*, Macmillan Press, London.

Goffman, E. (1961), *Asylums*, Anchor, New York.

Golding, P. (1986), "Power in the Information Society", in Muskens, G.

and Hamelink, C. (eds.), *Global Networks and European Communities: Applied Social and Comparative Approaches*, IVA, Tilburg, pp. 73-84.

Golding, P. (1990), "Political Communication and Citizenship: The Media and Democracy in an Inegalitarian Social Order" in Ferguson, M. (ed.), *Public Communication: The New Imperatives*, Sage, London.

Golding, P. (1992), "Communicating Capitalism: Resisting and Restructuring State Ideology - The Case of 'Thatcherism'", *Media, Culture and Society*, Vol. 14, pp. 503-21.

Golding, P. and Billig, M. (1992), "Did the Race Card Tip the Balance?" *New Community*, Vol. 19, pp. 161-63.

Golding, P. et. al. (1992), "The Election Campaign: Two Shows for the Price of One", *British Journalism Review*, Vol. 3, pp. 6-10.

Gough, I. (1979), *The Political Economy of the Welfare State*, Macmillan Press, London.

Gough, I. (1994) "Economic Institutions and the Satisfaction of Human Needs", *Journal of Economic Affairs*, Vol. 28, pp. 25-61.

Gouldner, A.W. (1980), "Civil Society in Capitalism and Socialism', in his *The Two Marxisms: Contradictions and Anomalies in the Development of Theory*, Macmillan, London, pp. 355-73.

Gray, J. (1990), *The Moral Foundations of Market Institutions*, Institute of Economic Affairs, London.

Gray, J. (1992), *Beyond the New Right: Markets, Government and the Common Environment*, Routledge, London.

Gray, J. (1994a), "Against the World", *The Guardian*, 4 Janaury.

Gray, J. (1994b), "Looting the Leviathan", *The Guardian*, 2 February.

Green, D.G. (1993), *Reinventing Civil Society: The Rediscovery of Welfare without Politics*, Institute of Economic Affairs, London.

Greenberg, D. (1991), "The Cost-Benefit Analysis of Imprisonment", *Social Justice*, Vol. 17, pp. 49-75.

Gregory, C.A. and Altman, J.C. (1989), *Observing the Economy*, Routledge, London.

Gregory, D. and Urry, J. (eds.), (1985), *Social Relations and Spatial Structures*, Macmillan, London.

Grove-White, R. (1991), *The UK's Environmental Movement and UK Political Culture*, Report to EURES, Centre for the Study of Environmental Change, Lancaster University.

Gruber, J.E. (1989), "How Women Handle Sexual Harassment: A Literature Review", *Sociology and Social Research*, Vol. 74, pp. 3-9.

Gruber, J.E. and Bjorn, L. (1990), "Women's Responses to Sexual Harassment: An analysis of Sociocultural, Organizational, and Personal Resource Models", *Social Science Quarterly*, Vol. 67, pp. 814-26.

278

Guillaumin, C. (1980), "The Practice and Power of Belief in Nature, Part I: The Appropriation of Women", *Feminist Issues*, Vol. 1, pp. 3-28.

Gurvitch, G. (1964), *The Spectrum of Social Time*, Dordrecht, Netherlands.

Habermas, J. (1984), *The Theory of Communicative Action, Vol. 1, Reason and the Rationalization of Society*, trans. T. McCarthy, Beacon, Boston.

Habermas, J. (1987), *The Theory of Communicative Action, Vol. II, Lifeworld and System: A Critique of Functionalist Reason*, trans. T. McCarthy, Beacon, Boston.

Habermas, J. (1989), *The Structural Transformation of the Public Sphere*, Polity Press, Cambridge.

Habermas, J. (1992), "Further Reflections on the Public Sphere", in Calhoun (ed.) (1992), pp. 421-61.

Hagerstrand, T. (1970), "What About People in Regional Science?", *Papers of the Regional Science Association*, Vol. 24.

Hagerstrand, T. (1975), "Survival and Arena: On the Life History of Individuals In Relation to their Geographical Environment", in Carlstein, T. Parkers, D. and Thrift, M. (ed.), *Human Activity and Time Geography*, Edward Arnold, London.

Hall, P. (1986), *Governing The Economy*, Polity Press, Cambridge.

Halsey, A.H. and Dennis, N. (1988), *English Ethical Socialism*, Clarendon, Oxford.

Hapgood, H. (1965), *The Spirit of the Ghetto: Studies of the Jewish Quarter of New York*, Funk and Wagnall, New York.

Harris, K.M. (1993), "Work and Welfare Among Single Mothers in Poverty", *American Journal of Sociology*, Vol. 99.

Harry, J. (1982), "Derivative Deviance: The Cases of Extortion, Fag Bashing, and Shakedown of Gay Men". *Criminology*, Vol. 19, pp. 546-64.

Hartmann, H. (1979), "The Unhappy Marriage of Marxism and Feminism: Towards A More Progressive Union", *Capital and Class*, Vol. 8, pp. 1-33.

Harvey, D. (1985), *The Urban Experience*, Basil Blackwell, Oxford.

Harvey, D. (1989), *The Condition of Postmodernity*, Basil Blackwell, Oxford.

Hearn, J. (1983), *Birth and Afterbirth: A Materialist Account*, Achilles Heel, London.

Hearn, J. (1987), *The Gender of Oppression: Men, Masculinity and the Critique of Marxism*, Wheatsheaf, Brighton.

Hearn, J. (1992), *Men in the Public Eye: The Construction and*

279

Deconstruction of Public Men and Public Patriarchies, Routledge, London and New York.

Hearn, J. (1993), "Emotive Subjects: Organizational Men, Organizational Masculinities and the (De)construction of 'Emotions'", in Fineman, S. (ed.), *Emotion in Organizations*, Sage, London, pp. 142-46.

Hearn, J. (1994), "The Organization(s) Of Violence: Men, Gender Relations, Organizations and Violences", *Human Relations*, Vol. 47, forthcoming.

Hearn, J. and Collinson, D.L. (1990), "Unities and Differences Between Men and Masculinities". (1) The Categories of Men and the Case ofSociology: Paper at British Sociological Association Annual Conference, *Social Divisions and Social Change*, University of Surrey, April, University of Bradford, Mimeo.

Hearn, J. and Collinson, D.L. (1994), "Theorizing Unities and Differences Between Men and Between Masculinities", in Brod, H. and Kaufman, M. (eds.), *Theorizing Masculinities*, Sage, Newbury Park, Ca.

Hearn, J. and Parkin, P.W. (1987), *"Sex" at "Work": The Power and Paradox of Organisation Sexuality*, Wheatsheaf, Brighton.

Hearn, J. and Parkin, P.W. "Organizations, Multiple Oppressions and Post Modernism", in Hassard, J. and Parker, M. (eds.) *Post Modernism and Organization*, Sage, London, pp. 148-62.

Heelas, P. and Morris, P. (eds.), (1992), *The Values of the Enterprise Culture: The Moral Debate*, Routledge, London.

Hernes, H.M. (1984), "Women and the Welfare State: The Transition from Private to Public Dependence", in Holter, H. (ed.), *Patriarchy in a Welfare Society*, Universitetsforlaget, Oslo, pp. 26-45.

Hernes, H.M. (1987a), *Welfare State and Women Power*, Norwegian University Press, Oslo.

Hernes, H.M. (1987b), "Women and the Welfare State: The Transition From Private To Public Dependence", in Sassoon, A.S. (eds.), *Women and the State: The Shifting Boundaries of Public and Private*, Hutchinson, London, pp. 72-99.

Hernes, H.M. (1988a), "Scandinavian Citizenship", *Acta Sociologica*, Vol. 31, pp. 199-215.

Hernes, H.M. (1988b), "The Welfare State Citizenship of Scandinavian Women", in Jones, K.B. and Jonasdottir, A.G. (eds.), *The Political Interests of Gender: Developing Theory and Research with a Feminist Face*, Sage, London, pp. 187-213.

Hicks, A. (1988), "Social Democratic Corporatism and Economic Growth", *Journal of Politics*, Vol. 50.

280

Hilbert, R. (1986), "Anomie and the Moral Regulation of Reality: The Durkheimian Tradition in Modern Relief", *Sociological Theory*, Vol. 4, pp. 1-19.

Hirschmann, N. (1989), "Freedom, Recognition and Obligation: A Feminist Approach to Political Theory", *American Political Science Review*, Vol. 83, pp. 1227-1244.

Hirschmann, N. (1992a), *Rethinking Obligation: A Feminist Method for Political Theory*, Ithaca, Cornell University Press.

Hirschmann, N. (1992b), "Political Obligation Freedom and Feminism" *American Political Science Review*, Vol. 86, pp. 182-188.

Hirsh, F. (1976), *Social Limits to Growth*, Routledge & Kegan Paul, London.

Hirst, P. (1994), *Associative Democracy,: New Forms of Economic and Social Governance*, Polity Press, Cambridge.

HM Government (1994), *Sustainable Development: The UK Strategy*, HMSO, London.

HMSO. (1992), *The Future of the BBC: A Consultation Document*, (Cmnd. 2098), HMSO, London.

Hochschild, A.R. (1983), *The Managed Heart: The Commercialization of Human Feeling*, University of California Press, Berkeley.

Holliman, J. (1971), *Consumers' Guide to the Protection of the Environment*, Friends of the Earth/Pan Ballantine, London.

Holt, P. (1986), "The Local Community: Aldershot - A Case Study", in Sweetman, J. (ed.), *Sword and Mace: Twentieth Century Civil-Military Relations in Britain*, Brassey's Defence Publishers, London.

Holter, H. (ed.), (1985), *Patriarchy in a Welfare Society*, Universitetsforlaget, Oslo.

Home Office. (1988), *Private Sector Involvement in the Remand System*, HMSO, London.

Home Office. (1992), *The Future of the BBC: A Consultation Document*, Cmnd.2098, HMSO, London.

Hoogenboom, A.B. (1989), "The Privatization of Social Control", in Hood, R (ed.), *Crime and Criminal Policy in Europe: Proceedings of a European Colloquium*, 3-6 July 1988, University of Oxford Centre for Criminological Research, Oxford.

Hoogenboom, B. (1991), "Grey Policing: A Theoretical Framework", *Policing and Society*, Vol. 2, pp. 17-30.

House of Commons. (1987), *Fourth Report from the Home Affairs Committee: Contract Provision of Prisons*, HMSO, London.

Huizinga, J. (1971), *Homo Ludens*, Routledge, London.

Humpherys, A. (1977), *Travels in the Poor Man's Country: The Work of*

Henry Mayhew, Caliban Books, Sussex.

Indianapolis Star,(1990), "Judge Clears Two Men Of 'Illegal Hand Holding'", October 26, p. A12.

Irvine, S. (1989), "Consuming Fashions? The Limits of Green Consumerism" *The Ecologist*, vol. 19, pp. 88-93.

Jack Roller, and Snodgrass, J. et al. (1982), *The Jack Roller at Seventy*, Lexington Books, Chicago.

Jacobs, J. (1960), *Death and Life of Great American Cities*, Cape, London.

Jacobs, J.B. (1983), *New Perspectives on Prisons and Imprisonment*, Ithaca, Cornell University Press.

Jahoda, M. (1984), *Employment and Unemployment*, Cambridge University Press.

Janowitz, M. (1981), "Observations on the Sociology of Citizenship", *Social Forces*, Vol. 59, pp. 1-24.

Jessop, B, Bonnet, K., Bromley, S. & Ling, T. (1988) *Thatcherism: A Tale of Two Nations*, Polity Press, Cambridge.

Jessop, B. et al. (1990), "The Thatcher Balance Sheet", *New Left Review*, No. 179.

Johnston, L. (1992), *The Rebirth of Private Policing*, Routledge, London.

Johnston, L. (1993), "Vigilantism and Informal Justice in the United Kingdom", a paper presented to the *British Criminology Conference*, University of Cardiff, 28-31 July.

Jowell, R. and Airey, C. (ed.), (1984), *British Social Attitudes: The 1984 Report*, SCPR, Gower, Aldershot.

Jowell, R. and Witherspoon, S. (1985), *British Social Attitudes: The 1985 Report*, SCPR, Gower, Aldershot.

Jowell, R. et al. (1986), *British Social Attitudes: The 1986 Report*, SCPR, Gower, Aldershot.

Kant, I. (1963), *On History*, (original 1784/6), Bobbs Merrill, New York.

Kant, I. (1964), *The Metaphysical Principles of Virtue*, Bobbs Merrill, New York.

Kant, I. (1965), *The Moral Law: The Groundwork of the Metaphysic of Morals*, Hutchinson, London.

Karmen, A. (1983), "Deviants As Victims", in Donal, et al. (ed.), *Deviants: Victims or Victimizers?*, Sage, Beverley Hills, pp.237-54.

Kaufman, G. (1992), "Privatizing The Ministers", *The Guardian*, 7 December p. 7.

Kaus, M. (1992), *The End of Equality*, Basic Books, New York.

Kaye, H.J. (1988), *Selected Essays of George Rudé: The Face of the Crowd*, Humanities Press Int. Inc., New Jersey.

Keane, J. (1984), *Public Life and Late Capitalism*, Cambridge University Press.

Keat, R. and Abercrombie, N. (eds.), (1991), *Enterprise Culture*, Routledge, London.

Keat, R. et al. (eds.), (1994), *The Authority of the Consumer*, Routledge, London.

Kelly, J. (1979), "The Doubled Vision of Feminist Theory: A Postscript To The 'Women and Power' Conference", *Feminist Studies*, Vol. 5, Spring, pp. 216-27.

Kerr, M. (1958), *The People of Ship Street*, Routledge & Kegan Paul, London.

Kimmel, M.S. (1987), "The Contemporary 'Crisis' of Masculinity In Historical Perspective", in Brod, H. (ed.), *The Making of Masculinities: The New Men's Studies*, Allen & Unwin, Boston and London, pp. 121-53.

King, R. (1991), "Maximimum Security Custody in Britain and the United States: A Study of Gartree and Oak Park Heights", *British Journal of Criminology*, Vol. 31, pp. 126-52.

Kostof, S. (1993), *The City Shaped: Urban Patterns and Meanings Through History*, Bullfinch Press, London, Little Brown, Boston.

Kozar, C. (1992), "Three Years Spent Reclaiming Lost Ground", in *Public Transport: Security and Environment*, Proceedings of International Conference, La Defence, Paris. Brussels, Union Internationale des Transports Publics.

Krieger, E. (1984), *Bygone Manchester*, Phillimore and Co, Chichester, Sussex.

Kubey, R. and Csikszentmihalyi, M. (1990), *Television and the Quality of Life: How Viewing Shapes Everday Experience*, Hillsdale, NJ.

Lacey, N. (1988), *State Punishment*, Routledge, London.

Lange, P. and Garrett, G. (1986), "Performance in a Hostile World: Economic Growth in Western Market Economies", *American Sociological Review*, Vol. 50.

Lash, S. and Urry, J. (1987), *The End of Organised Capitalism*, Polity Press, Cambridge.

Laurin-Frenette, N. (1982), "The Women's Movement: Anarchism And The State", *Our Generation*, Vol. 15, pp. 27-39.

Law, C.M. (1986), "The Uncertain Future for the City Centre: The Case of Manchester", *Manchester Geographer*, pp. 26-43.

Lawton, D. (1992), *Education and Politics in the 1990s: Conflict of Consensus?*, Falmer Press, Brighton, Sussex.

Le Bon, G. (1920), *The Crowd in the Study of the Popular Mind*, Fisher

Unwin, London.

Lefebvre, H. (1974), *La Production de l'Espace*, Paris: Basil Blackwell Oxford, 1991. (English edition).

Liebow, E. (1967), *Tally's Corner: A Study of Negro Street Corner Man*, Little Brown, Boston.

Lifton, R. J. (1993), *The Protean Self: Human Resiliance in an Age of Fragmentation*, Basic Books, New York.

Lilley, R. and Knepper, P. (1992a), "An International Perspective On The Privatization of Corrections", *The Howard Journal*, Vol. 31, pp. 174-91.

Lilley, R. and Knepper, P. (1992b), "The Corrections-Commercial Complex" *Prison Service Journal*, No. 87, pp. 43-52.

Lister, R. (1990a), "Women, Economic Dependency and Citizenship", *Journal of Social Policy*, Vol. 19, pp. 445-67.

Lister R. (1990b), *The Exclusive Society: Citizenship and the Poor*, Child Poverty Action Group, London.

Littler-Bishop, S. et al. (1982), "Sexual Harassment In The Workplace As A Function Of Initiator's Status: The Case Of Airline Personnel", *Journal of Social Issues*, Vol. 38, pp. 137-48.

Locke, J. (1966), *Second Treatise of Government and A Letter Concerning Toleration*, 3rd ed. Basil Blackwell, Oxford.

Logan, C. (1990), *Private Prisons: Cons and Pros*, Oxford University Press.

Lukes, S. (1981), *Emile Durkheim: His Life and Work*, Penguin Books, London.

Lynch, K. (1964), *The Image of the City*, MIT Press, Cambridge, Mass.

Lynch, K. (1972), *What Time Is This Place?*, MIT Press, Cambridge, Mass.

Lynch, K. (1989), "Solidary Labour: Its Nature and Marginalisation", *Sociological Review*, Vol. 37, pp. 1-14.

McCarthy, T. (1978), *The Critical Theory of Jürgen Habermas*, Hutchinson, London.

McConville, S. (1990), "The Privatization of Penal Services", in Council of Europe, *Privatization of Crime Control*, Council of Europe, Strasbourg.

McDermott, K. and King, R. (1988), "Mindgames: Where The Action Is In Prisons", *British Journal of Criminology*, Vol. 28, pp. 357-77.

McKenzie, J. (1993), *Education as a Political Issue*, Avebury, Aldershot.

McLaughlin, L. (1993), "Feminism, The Public Sphere, Media and Democracy", *Media, Culture, and Society*, Vol. 15, pp. 599-620.

Macdonald, I. (1989), *The Burnage Report, Murder in the Playground:*

The Report of the Macdonald Inquiry into Racism and Racial Violence in Manchester Schools, Longsight Press, Manchester.

MacKinnon, C.A. (1982), "Feminism, Marxism, Method and the State: An Agenda for Theory", *Signs*, Vol. 7, pp. 515-44.

Maguire, M. et al. (1985), *Accountability and Prisons*, Tavistock, London.

Malinowski, B. and De La Fuente, J. (1982), *Malinowski in Mexico: The Economics of a Mexican Market System*, Routledge & Kegan Paul, London.

Marcus, S. (1973), "Reading the Illegible", in Dyos, H.J. and Wolff, M. (eds.), *The Victorian City: Images and Realities*, Routledge & Kegan Paul, London.

Marshall, R. and Tucker, M. (1993), *Thinking for a Living*, Haper Collins, London.

Marshall, T.H. (1963), "Citizenship and Social Class" (original 1950) in *Sociology and the Crossroads*, Heinemann, London.

Marshall, T.H. (1964), *Class, Citizenship and Social Development*, University of Chicago Press.

Maruyama, S. (1991), "Seikatsu: Japanese Housewives Organize", in Plant, C. and Plant, J. (eds.), *Green Business: Hope or Hoax?*, Green Books, Bideford.

Marx, G. (1987), "The Interweaving of Public and Private Police in Undercover Work", in Shearing, C.D. and Stenning, P.C. (eds.), *Private Policing*, Sage, California.

Mathiesen, T. (1990), *Prison on Trial*, Sage, London.

Mathiesen, T. (1991), "The Argument Against Building More Prisons", in Muncie, J. and Sparks, R. (eds.), *Imprisonment: European Perspectives*, Harvester Wheatsheaf, Hemel Hempstead.

Mawby, R.I, (1979), *Policing The City*, Saxon House, Westmead.

Mays, J.B. (1954), *Growing Up In A City*, Liverpool University Press.

Mays, J.B. (1959), *On The Threshold Of Delinquency*, Liverpool University Press.

Merton, R. (1968), *Social Theory And Social Structure*, Free Press, New York.

Mestrovic, S. and Brown, H. (1985), "Durkheim's Concept Of Anomie As 'Dereglement'", *Social Problems*, Vol. 33, pp. 81-99.

Meyrowitz, J. (1986), *No Sense of Place: The Impact of Electronic Media on Social Behaviour*, Oxford University Press.

Middleton, M. (1991), *Cities in Transition*, Michael Joseph, London.

Miller, B. and Humphreys, S.L H. (1980), "Lifestyles and Violence: Homosexual Victims of Assault and Murder", *Qualitative Sociology*,

Vol. 3. pp. 169-85.

Miller, J.P. and Luke, D.E. (1977), *Law Enforcement By Public Officials And Special Police Forces*, 4 Vols, Home Office, London.

Mills, C.W. (1970), *The Sociological Imagination*, Penguin Books, Harmondsworth.

Minarik, J.J. and Goldfarb, R.S. (1976), "AFDC Income, Recipient Rates And Family Dissolutiuon: A Comment", *Journal of Human Resources*, Vol. 11, pp. 243-50.

Mitchell, J. (1991), "Police Brutality Cases Stir Outcry", *Heartland*, (Indianpolis), May 1991, pp. 3 and 15.

MOD. (1986), *The Report of the Ministry of Defence Police Review Committee*, Cmnd. 9853, HMSO, London.

Mogey, J. (1956), *Family and Neighbourhood*, Oxford University Press.

Molotch, H. and Logan, J.E. (1985), "Urban Dependencies: New Forms of Use and Exchange in U.S. Cities", *Urban Affairs Quarterly*, Vol. 21, pp. 143-169.

Moore, H. (1987), *Feminism and Anthropology*, Cambridge University Press.

MORI. (1992), *Public Attitudes Towards Ecolabelling*, Research study conducted for the Department of the Environment, June-July 1992, Market and Opinion Research International (MORI), London.

Morton, A.L. (ed.), (1973), *Political Writings of William Morris*, International Publishers, New York.

Mouffe, C. (ed.), (1992), *Dimensions of Radical Democracy: Pluralism, Citizenship, Community*, Verso, London.

Mumford, L. (1961), *The City in History*, Harcourt Brace, New York.

Muncie, J. and Sparks, R. (1991), "Expansion and Contraction In European Penal Systems" in Muncie, J. and Sparks, R, (eds.), *Imprisonment: European Perspectives*, Harvester Wheatsheaf, Hemel Hempstead.

Munsterberg, H. (1970), *The Film: A Psychological Study*, Dover Publications, New York.

Murray, C. (1984), *Losing Ground: American Social Policy, 1959-80*, Basic Books, New York.

National Audit Office. (1989), *Publicity Services for Government Departments*, HMSO, London.

National Commission On Education. (1993), *Learning To Succeed*, Heinemann, London

National Gay and Lesbian Task Force. (1986), *Anti-Gay Violence: Causes, Consequences, Responses,* National Gay and Lesbian Task Force, Washington, DC.

Nasar, J.L. (1984), "Visual Preferences In Urban Street Scenes: A Cross Cultural Comparison Between Japan and the United States", *Journal of Cross Cultural Psychology*, Vol. 15, pp. 79-93.

Nelken, D. (1989), "Discipline and Punish: Some Notes on the Margin", *The Howard Journal*, Vol. 28, pp. 245-54.

New Scotland Yard. (1990-91), *The Constitutional Position of Bodies Such As "Wandsworth Parks Constabulary"*, New Scotland Yard, London [unpublished].

Norberg-Schulz, C. (1980), *Genius Loci: Towards a Phenomenology of Architecture*, Rizzoli, New York.

Normandeau, A. and Leighton, B. (1990), *A Vision of the Future of Policing in Canada: Police Challenge 2000: Background Document*, Solicitor General Canada.

Northam, G. (1988), *Shooting in the Dark: Riot Police in Britain*, Faber and Faber, London.

O'Brien, M. (1981), *The Politics of Reproduction*, Routledge & Kegan Paul, London.

O'Connor, J. (1973), *The Fiscal Crisis of the State*, St. Martin's Press, New York.

O'Donovan, K. (1985), *Sexual Divisions in Law*, Weidenfeld and Nicholson, London.

Oakley, A. (1974), *The Sociology of Housework*, Martin Robertson, London.

Offe, C. (1985), *Disorganized Capitalism: Contemprary Transformations of Work and Politics* (translation from German of essays published between 1974 and 1984), Cambridge: Polity.

Opie, I. and Opie, P. (1987), *The Lore and Language of School Children*, Oxford University Press.

Orru, M. (1987), *Anomie: History and Meanings*, Routledge, London.

Ortner, S. (1974), "Is Female to Male as Nature is to Culture?", in Rosaldo, M.Z. and Lamphere, L. (eds.), *Woman, Culture and Society*, Stanford University Press, pp. 67-87.

Pahl, R. (1984), *Divisions of Labour*, Blackwell, Oxford.

Palmer, S.H. (1988), *Police and Protest in England and Ireland 1780-1850*, Cambridge University Press.

Paneth, M. (1944), *Branch Street*, Allen and Unwin, London.

Parry, G. et al. (1992), *Political Participation and Democracy in Britain*, Cambridge University Press.

Pateman, C. (1983), "Feminist Critiques of the Public/Private Dichotomy", in Benn, S.I. and Gaus, G.F. (eds.), *Public and Private in Social Life*, pp. 281-303, Croom Helm, Beckenham, Kent.

Pateman, C. (1985), *The Problem of Political Obligation*, John Wiley, New York.

Pateman, C. (1988), *The Sexual Contract*, Stanford University Press.

Pateman, C. (1992), "Political Obligation, Freedom and Feminism", *American Political Science Review*, Vol. 86, pp. 179-182.

Paul, E. et al. (eds), (1984), *Human Rights*, Blackwell, Oxford.

Pead, D. (1986), "The Ministry of Defence Police", *Police Review*, 6 June.

Pease, K and Taylor, M. (1989), "Private Prisons and Penal Purpose" in Matthews, (ed.), (op. cit.).

Peck, J.A. and Emmerich, M. (1992), *Recession, Restructuring and the Greater Manchester Labour Market*, University of Manchester, School of Geography, SPA Working Paper No. 17.

Pepinsky, H.E. (1987), "Explaining the Police-Recorded Crime Trends in Sheffield", *Contemporary Crises*, Vol. 11, No. 1.

Perkin, H. (1981), *The Structured Crowd: Essays in English Social History*, Harvester Press, Brighton.

Peters, A. (1986), "Main Currents in Criminal Law Theory" in van Dijk, J. et al. (eds.), *Criminal Law in Action*, Gouda Quint, Arnham.

Peters, J.D. (1993), "Distrust of Representation: Habermas on the Public Sphere", *Media, Culture, and Society*, Vol. 15, pp. 541-571.

Philips, D. (1980), "A New Engine of Power and Authority: The Institutionalization of Law Enforcement in England 1780-1830", in Gattrell, V.A. et al. (eds.), *Crime and the Law: The Social History of Crime in Europe Since 1500*, Europa, London.

Phillips, A. (1991), *Engendering Democracy*, Polity Press, Cambridge.

Pierson, C. (1991), *Beyond the Welfare State*, Polity Press, Cambridge.

Piven, F.F. and Cloward, R.A. (1971 and 1993), *Regulating the Poor: The Functions of Public Welfare*, Pantheon and Vintage Books, New York.

Piven, F.F. (1982), *The New Class War*, Pantheon Books, New York.

Piven, F.F. and Cloward, R.A. (1987), "The Contemporary Relief Debate", in Block,F. Cloward,R. Ehrenreich,B. and Piven,F. (eds) *The Mean Season: The Attack on the Welfare State*, Pantheon Books, New York.

Plant, R. et al. (1980), *Political Philosophy and Social Welfare*, Routledge, London.

Polanyi, K. (1957), *The Great Transformation*, Beacon Press, Boston.

Police Review. (1992), "Private Mounties Will Not Be Vetted", *Police Review*, 7 February.

Pollner, M. (1987), *Mundane Reason: Reality in Everyday and*

Sociological Discourse, Cambridge, New York.

Popper, K. (1966), *The Open Society and its Enemies*, Vol. 2 (5th ed), Routledge, London.

Porrit, J. (1984), *Seeing Green*, Blackwell, Oxford.

Punch, M. (1985), *Conduct Unbecoming*, Tavistock, London.

Purnell, S. (1993), "Group 4 Seeks Contract To Patrol The Streets", *Daily Telegraph*, 25 October.

Ramazanoglu, C. (1988), *Feminism and the Contradictions of Oppression*, Routledge, London.

Reich, R. (1992), *The Work of Nations*, Random House, New York.

Reicher, S.D. (1984), "The Saint Pauls' Riot: An Explanation of the Limits of Crowd Action in Terms of a Social Identity Model", *European Journal of Social Psychology*, Vol. 14, pp. 1-21.

Roberts, R. (1978), *A Ragged Schooling*, Fontana, London.

Roche, M. (1973), *Phenomenology, Language and the Social Sciences*, Routledge, London.

Roche, M. (1987), "Citizenship, Social Theory and Social Change", *Theory and Society*, Vol. 16, pp. 363-399.

Roche, M. (1988a), "Feminism and Citizenship", *Policy Studies Centre*, PSC Working Paper, University of Sheffield.

Roche, M. (1988b), "Ecology and Citizenship", *Policy Studies Centre*, PSC Working Paper, University of Sheffield

Roche, M. (1990), "Time and Unemployment", *Human Studies*, Vol. 13 pp. 1-25.

Roche, M. (1992), *Rethinking Citizenship: Welfare, Ideology and Social Change in Modern Society*, Polity Press, Cambridge.

Roche, M. (1994a), "Rethinking Social Citizenship and Social Movements", in Maheu, L. (ed.), *New Classes and Social Movements* Sage, London (forthcoming).

Roche, M. (1994b), "Citizenship and Social Change: Beyond the Dominant Paradigm", in Lustiger-Thaler, H. and Salee, D. (eds.), *Artful Practices: The Political Economy of Everyday Life*, Black Rose Books, Montreal (forthcoming).

Roche, M. (1994c), "Radical Democracy" in Mouffe, C. et al, *British Journal of Sociology* (forthcoming).

Roche, M. (1994d), "Citizenship and Nationhood in France and Germany: Brubaker's analysis", *Theory and Society*, (forthcoming).

Rosaldo, M.Z. (1974), "Women, Culture and Society: A Theoretical Overview" in Rosaldo, M and Lamphere, L. (eds.), *Women, Culture and Society*, Stanford University Press, pp. 17-42.

Rose, C. (1990), *Perception and Deception: The Collapse of the Green*

Consumer, paper presented to the Wildlife Link conference, London, November 1990.

Rosenbaum, H.J. and Sedeberg, P. (eds.), (1976), *Vigilante Politics*, University of Pennsylvania Press.

Ross, H.L. and Sawhill, I. (1975), *Time of Transition: The Growth of Families Headed by Women*, Urban Institute Press, Washington D.C.

Routledge, P. (1993), "Citizens' Army Will Fight Crime", *Independent on Sunday*, 5 December.

Rowbotham, S. (1986), "Feminism and Democracy" in Held, D and Pollitt, C. (eds.), *New Forms of Democracy*, Polity Press, Cambridge.

Rowe, M. (1981), "Dealing With Sexual Harassment", *Harvard Business Review*, No. 59, May/June, pp. 42-6.

Royal Commission on the Press. (1977), *Final Report Cmnd. 6810*, HMSO, London.

Royal Statistical Society. (1990), *Official Statistics: Counting With Confidence*, RSS, London.

Rubinstein, J. (1973), *City Police*, Farrar, Straus and Giroux, New York.

Rudofsky, B. (1969), *Streets for People: A Primer for Americans*, Doubleday, New York.

Ryan, M and Ward, T. (1989), *Privatization and the Penal System*, Open University Press, Milton Keynes.

Ryan, M. and Ward, T. (1990), "The State and the Prison System: Is There a Role for the Private Sector?", in Light, R. (ed.), *Public and Private Provisions in Criminal Justice*, (British Criminology Conference, 1989, Vol. 3), Bristol and Bath Centre for Criminal Justice.

Sagoff, M. (1988), *The Economy of the Earth: Philosophy, Law and the Environment*, Cambridge University Press.

Saunders, P. (1981), *Social Theory and the Urban Question*, Unwin and Hyman, London.

Saunders-Wilson, D. (1986), "Privatisation and the Future of Imprisonment", *Prison Service Journal*, April, pp. 7-9.

Scannell, P. (1989), "Public Service Broadcasting and Modern Political Life", *Media, Culture, and Society*, Vol. 11, pp.135-66.

Scarry, E. (1985), *The Body in Pain: The Making and Unmaking of the World*, Oxford University Press.

Schiller, H. (1989), *Culture Inc.*, Oxford University Press.

Schlay, A.B. and Rossi, P.H. (1992), "Social Science Research and Contemporary Studies of Homelessness", *Annual Review of Sociology*, Vol. 18, pp. 129-60.

Schmitter, P. (1985), "Neo-Corporatism and the State", in Grant, W.

(ed.), *The Political Economy of Corporatism*, MacMillan, London.

Schochet, G.J. (1975), *Patriarchalism and Political Thoughts*, Basil Blackwell, Oxford.

Scott, A. (1990), *Ideology and the New Social Movements*, Unwin Hyman, London.

Seligman, A. (1992), *The Idea of Civil Society*, Free Press, New York.

Sennett, R. (1977), *The Fall of Public Man*, Knopf, New York.

Sennett, R. (1990), *The Conscience of the Eye; The Design and Social Life of Cities*, Faber and Faber, London and Boston.

Shaver, S. (1987), "Gender, Class and the Welfare State: The Case of Income Security", Sociology Programme, Graduate Centre, City University of New York, unpublished.

Shaw, S. (1989), "Penal Sanctions: Private Affluence or Public Squalour?" in Farrell, M. (ed.), *Punishment for Profit?* ISTD, London.

Shearing, C.D. and Stenning, P.C. (1983), "Private Security: Implications for Social Control", *Social Problems*, Vol. 30, pp. 493-506.

Shearing, C.D. (1992), "The Relation Between Public and Private Policing", in Tonry, M. and Morris, N. (eds.), *Modern Policing: Crime and Justice: A Review of Research, Vol 15.* University of Chicago.

Shichor, D. (1993), "The Corporate Context of Private Prisons", *Crime, Law and Social Change*, Vol. 20, pp. 113-138.

Showstack Sassoon, A. (1980), *Gramsci's Politics*, Croom Helm, London.

Siim, B. (1987), "The Scandinavian Welfare State: Towards Sexual Equality or a New Kind of Male Domination", *Acta Sociologica*, Vol. 30, pp. 255-70.

Siim, B. (1988), "Towards a Feminist Rethinking of the Welfare State", in Jones, K.B. and Jonasdottir, A.G. (ed.), *The Political Interests of Gender: Developing Theory and Research with a Feminist Face*, Newbury Park, London: Sage, California, pp. 160-86.

Sim, J. (1992), "'When you ain't got nothing you got nothing to lose': The Peterhead Rebellion, the State and the Case for Prison Abolition" in Bottomley, K. et al. (eds.), *Criminal Justice: Theory and Practice*, British Society of Criminology, London.

Simmons, P. (1993a), "Myths of Green Consumer Power? The Switch From CFCs by the British Aerosol Industry", *Working Paper, Centre for the Study of Environmental Change*, Lancaster University, Lancs.

Simmons, P. (1993b) "The Social Construction of Green Consumerism, *Interdisciplinary Research Network on Environment and Society Conference*, University of Sheffield, September 1993.

Simmons, P. (forthcoming), "EC Eco-labelling Policy and the Social

Construction of Environmental Risks", in Holmwood, J. et al. (eds.), *Constructing the New Consumer Society*.

Skogan, W. (1987), "The Impact of Victimisation on Fear of Crime", *Crime and Delinquency*, No. 33, pp. 135-54.

Skolimowski, H. (1981), *Eco-Philosophy*, Marion Boyars, London.

Smeeding, T.M. and Rainwater, L. "Cross-National Trends in Income Poverty and Dependency: The Evidence for Young Adults in the Eighties", Joint Center of Political Studies Conference on Poverty and Social Marginality, September, 20, 21, 1991, Washington D.C.

Smith, N.C. (1990), *Morality and the Market: Consumer Pressure for Corporate Accountability*, Routledge, London.

Smith, W.A. and Cutright, P. (1985), "Components of Change in the Number of Female Family Heads Ages 15-44, An Update and Re-Analysis: United States 1940-1983", *Social Science Research,* Vol.14, pp. 226-50.

Snow, D.A. and Anderson, L. (1993), *Down on their Luck: A Study of Homeless Street People*, University of California Press, Berkeley.

Sparks, J.R. (1994), "Can Prisons Be Legitimate?", *British Journal of Criminology*, Vol. 34, pp. 14-28.

Sparks, J.R. and Bottoms, A.E. (forthcoming), "Legitimacy and Order in Prisons", *British Journal of Sociology*.

Spinley, B. (1954), *The Deprived and Privileged*, Routledge & Kegan Paul, London.

Stacey, M. (1981), "The Division of Labour Revisited: Or Overcoming the Two Adams", in *Practice and Progress: British Sociology 1950-1980*, Allen & Unwin, London.

Stacey, M. (1982), "Masculine or Feminine Powers? Action in the Public Domain", *Paper at International Sociological Association Annual Conference*, Mexico, August, University of Warwick, Mimeo.

Stacey, M. and Davies, C. (1983), *Division of Labour in Child Health Care: Final Report to the S.S.R.C.*, University of Warwick, Coventry.

Stanko, E. (1985), *Intimate Intrusions: Women's Experience of Male Violence*, Routledge & Keegan Paul, Boston.

Stenning, P.C. and Shearing, C.D. (1980), "The Quiet Revolution: The Nature, Development and General Legal Implications of Private Security in Canada", *Criminal Law Quarterly*, No. 22.

Stevenson, Nicholas (1993) 'Habermas and the Future of the Public Sphere', paper presented to the International Conference on the Public Sphere, Manchester, Janurary 1992.

Sykes, G. (1958), *The Society of Captives*, Princeton University Press.

Taylor, I. (1990), "Sociology and the Condition of the English City",

Salford Working Papers in Sociology, No. 9.

Taylor, I. (1991a), *Not Places in Which You'd Linger: Public Transport and Public Well-Being in Manchester*, Report to the Greater Manchester Passenger Transport Executive.

Taylor, I. (1991b), "The Experience of Order and Disorder in Free Market Societies: New York Versus Manchester" in Turner, B.S. (ed) *Citizenship, Civil Society and Social Cohesion*, Colchester, University of Essex for the ESRC (mimeo) (November).

Taylor, I. (1992), "Public Sense of Well-Being and Transport Provision in Older Industrial Cities in the North of England", in *Public Transport: Security and Environment*, Proceedings of international conference, La Defence, Paris (May), Brussels, Union Internationale des Transports Publics.

Taylor, I. and Walton, P. (1971), "Hey Mister, This is what we Really Do: Some Comments on Vandalism in Play", *Social Work Today*, Vol. 2, pp. 8-9. Reprinted in Ward, C. (ed), *Vandalism*, Architectural Press, London, 1973, pp. 91-96.

Tessler, R.C. and Dennis, D.L. (1992) "Mental Illness Among Homeless Adults: A Synthesis of Recent NIMH-funded Research", *Research in Community and Mental Health*, Vol. 7, pp. 3-53.

Tester, K. (1992), *Civil Society*, Routledge, London.

Thompson, J.B. (1990), *Ideology and Modern Culture*, Polity Press, Cambridge.

Thompson, J, (1993), "The Theory of the Public Sphere", *Theory, Culture and Society*, Vol. 10, 1993, pp. 173-89.

Tuan, Y. (1979), *Landscapes of Fear*, Basil Blackwell, Oxford.

Turner, B. (1986), *Citizenship and Capitalism*, Allen and Unwin, London.

Turner, B. (1993), "Outline of a Theory of Human Rights" in Turner, B. (ed.), *Citizenship and Social Theory*, Sage, London.

US Congress House Committee of the Judiciary, Subcommittee on Criminal Justice. (1986), *Anti-Gay Violence*, US Government Printing Office, Washington, DC.

Ursel, J. (1986), "The State and the Maintenance of Patriarchy: A Case Study of Family, Labour and Welfare Legislation in Canada", in Dickinson, J. and Russell, B. (ed), *Family, Economy and State*, St. Martin's Press, New York; Croom Helm, London and Sydney, pp. 150-91.

US Bureau of the Census, Department of Commerce, *Workers With Low Earnings: 1964 to 1990*, US Government Printing Office, Washington D.C.

Vanderbilt, A. (1972), *Amy Vanderbilt's Etiquette*, Doubleday, Garden

City, New York.

Vickers, J.E. (1972), *Old Sheffield Town*, Applebaum Bookshop, Sheffield, (revised 1989).

Vickers, J.E. (1978), *A Popular History of Sheffield*, Applebaum Bookshop, Sheffield, (revised 1992).

Villa, D.R. (1992), "Postmodernism and the Public Sphere", *American Political Science Review*, Vol. 86, pp. 712-721.

Vogel, D. (1975), "The Corporation as Government: Challenges and Dilemmas", *Polity*, Vol. 8, No. 1.

Vogel, L. (1983), *Marxism and the Oppression of Women: Toward a Unitary Theory*, Pluto Press, London.

Waddington, D. (1992), *Contemporary Issues in Public Disorder*, Routledge, London.

Wainwright, H. (1994), *Arguments for a New Left: Answering the Free Market Right*, Blackwell, Oxford.

Walby, S. (1986), *Patriarchy at Work*, Polity Press, Cambridge.

Walby, S. (1989), "Theorizing Patriarchy", *Sociology*, Vol. 23, pp. 213-34.

Walby, S. (1990a) *Theorizing Patriarchy*, Basil Blackwell, Oxford.

Walby, S. (1990b), "Women's Employment and the Periodisation of Patriarchy", in Corr, H. and Jamieson, L. (eds.) *Politics of Everyday Life: Continuity and Change in Work and the Family*, Macmillan, London, pp. 141-61.

Walter, E.V. (1988), *Placeways: a Theory of the Human Environment*, University of North Carolina Press, Chapel Hill.

Walzer, M. (1985), *Spheres of Justice*, Basil Blackwell, Oxford.

Wandsworth Parks Constabulary. (n.d.), "What can they do for you?" *Wandsworth Borough Council*, London.

Wasik, M. and Taylor, R. (1991), *Blackstone's Guide to the Criminal Justice Act 1991*, Blackstone Press, London.

Webb, B. et al. (1992), *Preventing Car Crime in Car Parks*, Home Office Police Research Group Crime Prevention Unit Series, Paper 34

Weber, M. (1967), "Science as a Vocation" (orig. 1919), in Gerth, H. and Mills, C.W. (eds.), *From Max Weber*, Routledge, London.

Weinbaum, B. (1978), *The Curious Courtship of Women's Liberation and Socialism*, South End Press, Boston.

Werlen, B. (1993), *Society, Action and Space: an Alternative Human Geography*, Routledge, London.

Whyte, W.F. (1955), *Street Corner Society: The Social Structure of an Italian Slum*, University of Chicago Press.

Wilensky, H. (1975), *The Welfare State and Equality*, University of

California Press, Berkeley.

Wilensky, H. and Lebeaux, C.N. (1965), *Industrial Society and Social Welfare*, The Free Press, Glencoe.

Williams, T. et al. (1992) "Personal Safety in Dangerous Places", *Journal of Contemporary Ethnography*, Vol. 18, pp. 129-60.

Wilson, D. (1992) "Interview with Chief Executive of Group 4 Securitas", *Prison Service Journal*, Issue 87, pp. 13-16.

Wilson, E. (1991), *The Sphinx in the City: Urban Life, the Control of Disorder and Women*, Virago, London.

Wilson, J.Q. and Kelling, G. (1982), "Broken Windows", *Atlantic Monthly*, (March) pp. 29-37.

Winward, J. (1994), "The Organized Consumer and Consumer Information Co-operatives", in Keat, R. et al. (eds.), *The Authority of the Consumer*, Routledge, London.

Wirth, L. (1938) "Urbanism as a Way of Life", *American Journal of Sociology*, Vol. 44, pp. 1-24.

Wolfe, A. (1989), *Whose Keeper? Social Science and Moral Obligation*, University of California Press, Berkley.

Woolf, L.J. (1991), *Prison Disturbances: April 1990*, HMSO, London.

Worcester, R.M. (1993), "Business and the Environment: The Weight of Public Opinion", *Admap*, No. 325 (January), pp. 1-5.

Worpole, K. et al. (1988), *City Centres, City Cultures: The Role of the Arts in the Revitalisation of Towns and Cities*, Centre for Local Economic Strategies, Manchester. (second edition 1991).

Worpole, K. (1992), *Towns for People: Transforming Urban Life*, Open University Press for Comedia/Gulbenkian Foundation, Buckingham.

WWUI. (1978), *Sexual Harassment on the Job: Questions and Answers*, WWUI, New York.

Young, M. and Willmott, P. (1957), *Family and Kinship in East London*, Routledge & Kegan Paul, London.

Young, M. (1988), *The Metronomic Society: Natural Rhythms and Human Timetables*, Harvard University Press, Cambridge, Mass.

Young, P. (1987), *The Prison Cell*, ASI Research, London.

Young, W. (1986) "Influences on the Use of Imprisonment", *The Howard Journal*, Vol. 25, pp. 125-136.

Zerubavel, E. (1979), *Pattern of Time in Hospital Life*, University of Chicago Press.